BANK TO THE FUTURE
PROTECT YOUR FUTURE BEFORE
GOVERNMENTS GO BUST

Simon Dixon

First published 2012 by Searching Finance Ltd, 8 Whitehall Road, London W7 2JE, UK

ISBN: 978-1-907720-37-6

Typeset by: Deirdré Gyenes

BANK TO THE FUTURE
PROTECT YOUR FUTURE BEFORE GOVERNMENTS GO BUST

Simon Dixon

About Simon Dixon

Simon Dixon is an ex-investment banker and economist who now dedicates his time to changing the rules of money and banking through entrepreneurship, education and politics.

As the co-founder of BankToTheFuture.com, Simon and his wife Bliss Dixon created an alternative way for people, businesses and investors to fund, borrow, raise funds and invest in each other without banks.

As a financial political reformer he works with not-for-profits campaigning to reform our financial system.

As the founder of BankTalkShow.com and the worlds leading training and consultancy company for students and graduates seeking careers in banking, he educates the next generation of bankers on the need for change from the inside. He also published the book 'Student to CEO: 97 Ways To Influence Your Way To The Top In Banking & Finance'

For more information or to contact Simon visit www.SimonDixon.org

About Searching Finance

Searching Finance Ltd is a dynamic new voice in knowledge provision for the financial services and related professional sectors. Our mission is to provide expert, highly relevant and actionable information and analysis. For more information, please visit www.searchingfinance.com

Contents

Acknowledgements

THIS BOOK would not have happened without the loving support of the love of my life, my wife, Bliss Dixon. She gave up holidays that we had booked and instead turned them into book retreats to make sure I wrote the book I had wanted to write for years.

I would also like to thank my brother-in-law and host of BankTalkShow.com Jal Islam who helped put together many of the QR graphics in this book and I would also like to thank the team at ExLabs for their technical help with the book design.

Ben Dyson and the Positive Money team alongside the New Economics Foundation have been most helpful with their research on the banking system.

Thomas Power has been a great social media mentor to me throughout this book, helping me to become more open, random and supportive in my approach to sharing with others through social media.

I would also like to thank Ashwin Rattan of Searching Finance for his guidance and advice throughout the process of publishing this book.

Special thanks to all the Ecademy Blackstar community, the managing director of Ecademy Daniel Priestley and the Key Person of Influence community for continued encouragement throughout this process.

Thank you to all clients, customers, friends and team at BankToTheFuture.com, Bank Talk Show, Metal Monkey Enterprise and Metal Monkey Private Equity.

Using this book

THIS IS MORE than just a book. It has been created to be as interactive as possible so that you share a journey with the author as you read. Thanks to QR codes, if you have a QR scanner, you will be able to access videos throughout this book and remain in contact with the author through social networking sites. We are restricted to some extent by the limitations of print format. For a fully interactive experience, I would direct you to the e-book-format where all links are directly accessible. and which also contains further illustrations which we are unable to reproduce in print format. The e-book is available at http://www.searching-finance.com; a version for Kindle is also available from Amazon.

Here is how it works

If you choose, you can simply read the book as normal, but to get extra content, videos and interaction with the author, you will need to have a smart phone with a QR scanner app installed.

If you don't have a smart phone and can't scan, you can manually type the URLs into your browser. Please note that you must use the browser bar, not a search engine.

What is a QR Scanner and how do I get one?

A QR (Quick Response) code is a type of barcode as seen on the front cover of this book. It contains information, and once scanned with a QR scanner from your smart phone, it will redirect you to pre-set information.

To access the information, all you need to do is download one of the many QR scanner apps available in all major smart phone app stores. Simply search 'QR scanner' in your app store and you will be given many options, both free and paid. We recommend you choose one that displays the redirect URL and asks you to confirm the link before it directs you to the video, webpage or social network.

An example QR code is displayed below. Once you have downloaded your QR scanner, open the app and scan the QR code below. Depending on your scanner it will either redirect you straight to a video about this book or ask you to confirm that you want to watch the video. For best results make sure you use a wi-fi connection with your smart phone. Try it now:

QR1 Introductory video from Simon Dixon

NOTE: If you are manually typing the above URL, the first 'l' is a lower case 'L' and the second 'I' is an upper case 'i'. I know, confusing. It caught us out too, but we recommend you use the QR scanner!

What will the QR codes in this book do?

The QR codes will either redirect you to a special video recorded for that particular section of the book, or take you to a specific webpage, or ask you to send a tweet on a particular subject covered in the book for the author to read.

If you do not have a Twitter account, you can sign up for one very easily and for free at www.twitter.com so you are able to interact with the author throughout the book. We also recommend that you use hash tags (#) in your Twitter messages.

Hash tags allow your message to appear alongside all other messages with the same hash tag so Twitter users can search for all comments on that particular topic. Your message will then be displayed alongside all the other messages with the same hash tag.

We hope you enjoy this experience.

Introduction

YOU'RE BUSY, right? If you are anything like me, you cannot afford the time to read a book that does not deliver on its promise.

Well, I thought I would save you some time and summarise this book in the introduction, so you can decide early on if this book is a waste of time for you or something that is going to change the way you do things.

What this book will do for you

Here is what this book will do for you.

You will know how to thrive whilst most of the people around you will be struggling. I will also lay the case for the most important investment you will ever make now for the future of you and your loved ones.

I'll go a step further. I can give you the beginning, middle and end of this book, so if you never get past the introduction, at least you will know why we are where we are and what your future will look like if you do not prepare.

So here it is ...

If we continue doing what we are doing today, and do not reform our financial system, we're in trouble! Our financial system is in fact a debt trap that is guaranteed to collapse.

Yet, we live in a time of freedom, like no other with near limitless possibilities, thanks to seven hugely disruptive technologies.

There is also another force at work. I call it the 'free' economy. In a nutshell, you will not be able to find a job in the future because more and more 'things' will be free. As more and more 'things' become free, companies will cut costs. and substitute jobs with technology and computers.

So in the future you are more likely to be working freelance, as a contractor, as part of an outsourced team or as an entrepreneur.

I call the time we live in today 'The debt trap of 'freedom'.

On one side, we have never lived in a time where so much freedom is possible thanks to technology. On the other, we are stuck in a debt trap that requires reform.

The free economy is also moving us towards record unemployment that will persist.

Life is not fair, and if you don't understand the rules that govern the game of finance, technology and money, you will suffer in the future.

Financial reform is inevitable, predictable and guaranteed, but it might require a 1930s-style crash of our economy and a deep depression before governments respond appropriately. My goal is to prepare you, as it will be a rough ride.

Technology has given us the tools to prepare for the crises ahead and to create a financial system that works for everyone. When financial reform happens, I believe that technology will allow us all to live in the greatest time of freedom in history.

In the future you will not be relying on the government or an employer for your money.

We may not need to wait for the government to reform our financial system as entrepreneurs, technology geeks and you may create an alternative system thanks to some clever people in Silicon Valley and the seven hugely disruptive technologies that I discuss in this book.

It is my belief that if you do not get to grips with these seven technologies, you will be one of the many that suffer during the upcoming crash, and I don't want that for you or the people you know.

You could be a part of a revolution ... all of us can. A financial entrepreneur-led revolution which truly brings power to the individual.

Although I discuss the unsustainable nature of our financial system, this book is NOT about hating bankers or conspiracy theories. That would be too easy and I don't want to be another person blame-shifting and riding the bank-haters wave we see on the internet and in the mainstream media.

I don't want to leave you filled with anger and with no clear idea of what you can do to make a difference. There are too many YouTube videos and books that do that already.

I am an ex-investment banker myself and so are many of my friends and colleagues.

This book is my perspective on why we are all faced with the perfect opportunity to live our life how we want to live it and why you should care about the times we live in today, the debt trap of 'freedom, how we got to where we are and what your future will look like if you get to grips with the seven technologies.

In this book I have cut out all the unnecessary complex financial jargon from many of the hundreds of books, documentaries and interviews I have read, watched and conducted on finance, technology and money.

There is no book on the topic of finance, technology and money written for those without a finance PhD, with practical guidelines on where we are and what we can do next, written from the experience of an ex-investment banker, an entrepreneur and a financial political reformer.

So I wrote it.

This book will not include boring descriptions of how collateralised debt obligations relate to credit default swaps and yield curves, subjects that make us all yawn.

You will find stories of great people, great innovation and some forecasts that may sound a little crazy right now.

I will also share with you why our economy as we know it is inevitably and predictably guaranteed to crash and how we can prevent it being a disaster for us all.

So I think that is pretty important, regardless of whether you normally take an interest in this type of thing or not, as it affects us all.

As I have said already and I say again, those who ignore these three subjects – finance, technology and money – will suffer in the future.

I will not use academic jargon and complex financial words aimed at making myself sound more intelligent.

Back to the Future ...

I want to take you on a journey in time travel too, inspired by a classic film.

I don't think I have ever met anybody who has not watched the 1985 American science-fiction film 'Back to the Future'. But just in case, here's a brief description of the story.

The film tells the story of Marty McFly, a teenager who is accidentally sent back in time from 1985 to 1955. He meets his future-parents in high school and accidentally attracts his future mother's romantic interest. Marty must repair the damage to history by causing his parents-to-be to fall in love, and with the help of scientist 'Doc', he must find a way to return to 1985.

Then, in Back to the Future II, continuing where Back to the Future finished, Marty and Doc use the DeLorean time machine to travel to 2015. While there, arch rival, Biff steals the DeLorean to travel back in time and give his teenage self a sports almanac, creating an alternative 1985. Marty and Doc are forced to travel to 1955 to repair the timeline.

Well, if it is good enough for Stephen Spielberg, then it is good enough for me. I am not sure if this book can win quite as many awards as Back to the Future, but I would still like to take you on an adventure in time travel.

Part 1 begins with the present and why we are in a debt trap of 'free'dom.

I discuss why we live in a time of unparalleled freedom and opportunity amidst a financial system in the worst shape of recent history. I also discuss the 'free' economy and how it impacts your future.

In Part 2 of this book we travel back in time to make a few financial reforms.

As we alter history and travel forward to a sustainable present and then to the future, we look at the seven key technologies that will create unparalleled freedom and opportunity.

I call these innovations the seven hugely disruptive technologies – the World Wide Web, digital money, the social networks, crowdfunding, person-to-person lending, microfinance and the mobile smart phone. We will explore them all and why you will need to get used to them now.

It is with these seven technologies in mind that I reveal the investment you will need to make. It won't cost you any money and you can start investing today.

In Part 3 we end our adventure in time travel, by taking a journey to the most prosperous future we will ever experience filled with freedom and boundless opportunity, as a result of those reforms in our financial system.

Unfortunately, it may not last for long as our time machine could be stolen by a powerful banker, who could go back in time and change our future again.

Comparing these two parallel universes, we are now faced with the choice to go back in time and repair the timeline or leave everything as it is and face the consequences.

This comparison gives us the opportunity to fully understand the present situation as we are left with a choice of going back to the future under financial reform again or leaving the world as is and waiting for the crash.

... and Bank to the Future

As this book accounts a journey across time in finance, technology, money and seven hugely disruptive technologies, I call this journey 'Bank to the Future'.

This name came to me in the middle of the night when I was searching for the name for my new social network, founded as a way for people to fund, borrow, raise funds and invest without banks. I bought the domain www.BankToTheFuture.com immediately to host this social network.

Throughout this book I have recorded videos and given you opportunities to connect with me and share your experience of this book as you read, so we can time-travel together. Feel free to connect with me on the social networks you use.

But, before we start 'Mission Bank to the Future', a few words of warning on my style...

I have tried to make this book as entertaining as I can while writing on what is a very serious subject.

I know this book is filled with controversy. I know some people will hate what I write. I know some will completely disagree. And that's OK, I did not write on this topic to win a popularity contest.

But now you know the story, you can choose to stop reading now as I have told you the beginning, middle and end of this book, or you can start to understand why you are where you are today, what your future will look like if you don't understand finance, technology and money, and how you can play the game to make a difference in many people's lives, especially those you care about.

I hope I have your attention, because I know how understanding these concepts will protect your economic future from the inevitable crash ahead.

I aim for the book to be readable by everyone.

If you read the whole book, my hope is that you will not regret it and that the ideas are original, unique and offer practical insight.

Hopefully, you will enjoy this book even if you have never previously read a book on finance, technology or money. What I write about affects us all, whether you know it or not.

This book is not written with economics professors and financial whizzkids in mind. Economics graduates and professors are advised not to read this book as you will probably be offended, but it is my belief that what is taught at university economics is the major contributor to our problems.

It is also worth noting that I write this book at a time of massive change.

Another danger is that you might be reading this book in the future and all the reforms and innovations I discuss seem archaic, obvious and history. If that is you, you will have a good laugh at how crazy we were at the time I wrote this book.

At the time of writing, these ideas are extreme and controversial, I believe those reading this book in the future will look at these ideas as obvious.

Oh, and a final disclaimer...

I own several businesses that I have created to align my financial future with my forecasts from this book. Full disclosure: if you believe what you read in this book, I do have several for-profit businesses that stand to benefit if you use them.

Before you accuse me of just saying these things to benefit my business, I would like to make a few things clear. I founded my businesses on the back of what I believe the future will look like, rather than creating a business then spinning the truth to benefit me financially.

I contribute to not-for-profits which are busy implementing the reforms discussed this book. I work with charities and social enterprises that are all making a difference through finance, too.

I work with social bankers and micro-financiers busy reforming banking.

After a career in stock-broking, trading and investment banking, I founded what later became the world's leading training and consultancy for students and graduates seeking careers in banking and finance – BankTalkShow.com.

I later founded a boutique private equity company called Metal Monkey Private Equity which partners with experts that need investors who understand technology to turn their expertise into a business.

And my baby of love is the social network I founded to help people fund, borrow, raise funds and invest without banks – www.BankToTheFuture.com.

So this is why I believe there is nothing more important than this topic for you, the people you care about and the prosperity of our world.

If you like my 'say-it-as-it-is' in 'plain English' style so far, then you will love the rest of this book and it will only get better; if not, then I have saved you some valuable time as you can stop reading now.

Just before we begin you can tweet me and let me know you are ready to start by tweeting me and the others reading this book by including #BankToTheFuture in your tweet.

QR 2 Tweet Simon Dixon about #BankToTheFuture

Part 01

THE DEBT TRAP
OF 'FREE' DOM

1 The economy of freedom

BEFORE we begin, take a look at the introductory video below.

QR 3 Introductory video on the economy of freedom

NOTE: If you are manually typing the above URL, the first 'l' is a lower case 'L' and the second 'I' is an upper case 'i'. I know, confusing. It caught us out too, but we recommend you use the QR scanner!

Figure 1 The barriers to entry in business have dropped

When you understand the rules that govern finance, technology and money you are free, whatever happens.

I do not understand anybody who reads this book, who opts for the government or an employer for their income over a life of freedom.

If you have a good internet connection, a laptop, a smart phone and the ability to use them, then you live in an age where you no longer need to rely on the government or an employer.

The best part is, most people reading this book will already have all of the above – so congratulations, you have already made your investment in freedom.

This is why I see today as an unparalleled time for freedom and opportunity

There is no doubt that there is a freedom that comes from money. Don't get me wrong, money will not bring you happiness, but it does offer some freedom and choice.

Freedom, passion and money – sounds attractive?

It is my belief that you can make money from whatever you are passionate about without government or an employer, and today is the first time in history when anybody with an internet connection can do it.

The passion part is the part that only you can decide upon, but once you know your passion, your job is to be great at what you do. When you are great at what you do, technology has taken down every barrier that may have stopped you in the past.

Money is no longer a barrier to getting started. Finance is available for those who understand how to get it.

Never in history has there been a time where you can live your life on your terms like today.

Over the last few years there have been seven innovations that have completely changed the rules. I call these innovations the seven hugely disruptive technologies. Each technology gets its own chapter in Part 2 of this book, because of the profound effects they have on our lives.

These seven technologies help create millions of fresh new opportunities every day. They give you complete freedom to live your life on your terms as long as you have an internet connection.

The government has no more jobs ... no problem. Your employer lays off en-masse ... great. You can't find a job in a recession ... who needs one?

For this reason I call today 'the economy of freedom'. You are so free today because everyone and everything is fully available to you right now provided you have an internet connection, a laptop and a smart phone.

How it can work

This may sound hard to believe, so here's an example of how it can work.

Perhaps you have just graduated from university with a degree in graphic design and media. You apply for endless graduate schemes, but nobody will give you a job.

Figure 2 Record levels of graduates and fewer graduate jobs have made it extremely hard for those who took student loans to study

After giving up on graduate schemes, you decide to put together a portfolio of design work.

It used to be the case that you would carry around your portfolio and search for graphic design employers or go freelance and pitch for clients while claiming unemployment benefits.

The World Wide Web

Well, thanks to hugely disruptive technology number #1, you don't even need to leave the house anymore. Instead you can thank your lucky stars that you never got a graduate job.

The first hugely disruptive technology is the World Wide Web.

With a quick search on the internet you discover that you can design for clients all day on www.99designs.com from wherever you are in the world without ever turning up for work or searching for clients.

You wonder why nobody ever told you about the concept of crowdsourcing in bringing together a pool of designers and small to medium-sized businesses which need design solutions.

In the past you would have spent thousands on marketing, advertising and PR to attract the number of prospects that are waiting to give you money for your designs on 99designs.com

I just checked on the site now and see 1,099 open projects, 85,335 projects to date, US$335,111 currently on offer to designers, and in one month alone they paid designers $997,545 for their work ... not bad.

And nobody judges you on your academic background or your grades, they simply judge you on your design work.

So, rather than having to go to a good college or university and go deep into debt after gaining top grades to get an offer, you realise your job is simply to be great at graphic design, no matter what your education, race, accent, how you look, what you wear, or where you live in the world. There is simply no discrimination: the design that the client likes the most, gets the money. Simple!

Clients even provide feedback on other designs, so you can adjust your designs for the client's taste.

After submitting a few designs and winning your first payment, you decide to have a change in scenery and head to the coast for inspiration.

In the past you would need to take time out to go on holiday, or if you were working freelance you would need to give up some paid work to get away, but now you can have your holiday resort as your office all the time if you wish, because your office is fully mobile.

From your pocket, you take out hugely disruptive technology #7 – your smart phone – and download all the apps you need to be completely mobile and still continue designing.

First, you buy a domain with your name in it for your website and set up a quick blog on WordPress, just in case any potential clients search for you on Google. Within a couple of hours you upload a WordPress theme and have a design blog under your domain name. In the past you would never have been able to do this unless you were a programmer who could code in HTML, PHP or Java.

Your alternative would have been to hire somebody to establish a blog for you. It would have cost you thousands plus the time searching for the right company to do it. But now you simply install WordPress, a free WordPress theme and create your own blog with the same skills that you use to type in a word processor. Your investment is zero.

You get a little stuck when installing your WordPress theme onto your domain, but a simple search on YouTube and within seconds you have your own private coach showing you how to install it step-by-step. In the past if you were stuck, either you knew a programmer who was willing to help you or paid them by the hour to help with your frustration. Perhaps you would have had to go to college to learn how to create websites, but now instructional videos are free on YouTube.

You scan your portfolio of work and upload it to your new blog so people can comment on your work.

In the past you would have to meet each prospect one at a time and pitch. Now they can see your work wherever they are in the world and you have testimonials.

You download the free WordPress app on your smart phone so you can manage the blog from your mobile.

Next, you setup a Google apps email account allowing you to send your emails from the same domain as your blog. This helps you appear more professional when contacting clients, while storing all your emails in Google's cloud for a tiny annual fee.

As a bonus you realise that you no longer need to save documents, spreadsheets and slideshows to your computer as Google Docs lets you save and share these in their cloud for no extra charge, making you fully mobile.

You download the Google app on your smart phone and set up your new email so you can manage everything on the move.

The smart phone

You want to be able to speak to anybody, anywhere in the world without having to pay huge bills. So you download your Skype app to your smart phone for free.

In the past your phone bill would have cost hundreds and this would have been a service only available to the richest companies in the world.

You want to travel light, so you also download the Kindle app to your smart phone, allowing you to access all the books you bought on the Kindle store on Amazon from your smart phone and your iTunes app so you can leave all your CDs at home.

You also download your mobile banking app just in case you have any problems with your bank while you travel.

Armed with your laptop, your smart phone and a dongle you look forward to arriving at the coast. You know that your best design work comes when you are in places that inspire your creativity.

You download your Google Maps app and it directs you all the way to the coast.

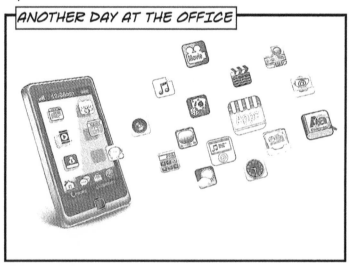

Figure 3 We live in a time where more and more can be done from your mobile smart phone

After producing your best work, inspired by the sound of the sea and the fresh air, your creativity flows and you start to win more and more contests on 99designs.

You now want to get paid. With people all around the world wanting to pay you in different currencies and not really knowing who they are, you are a little concerned about giving them your bank details.

Digital money

No worries ... hugely disruptive technology #2 – digital money – has solved that problem for you. All you need to do is give them your email address and they can pay you in your currency.

Prior to the rise of companies like PayPal you would either have had to beg your bank for merchant facilities in order to take card payments, which would require setting up as a company and visiting the bank to see if you can get a business bank account and all the hassles that go along with that, or giving the client your personal bank account details and trusting that they would not do anything fraudulent with them.

Instead, a few clicks on your laptop and you have your very own PayPal account. You download the free PayPal app to your smart phone so you can manage your finances on the move.

So now that you have a huge list of prospects waiting for your work on 99designs, your office is fully operational and completely mobile on your laptop and smart phone, you have the ability to get paid with just your email address, you decide that it is time to build your reputation and become a highly paid designer.

You realise that all the highest paid designers are established brands themselves, so you investigate what it takes to build your brand.

The top design companies are spending hundreds of thousands to advertise on TV, tens of thousands to get newspaper campaigns, thousands to get PR agents, hundreds to advertise with Google each month.

A few calculations later and you realise that even if you won every contest on 99designs, you would still be left with only a handful of change if you tried to compete with the top design companies.

Social networks

Using hugely disruptive technology #3 – the social networks – you decide to tap into a potential audience of over a billion by setting up your own channel on YouTube, your own broadcasting network on Twitter, your own fan page on Facebook and your own profile on LinkedIn and Google+ without spending a penny.

In the past you would have spent millions to get time on television and reach an audience the size of the number of registered users on the social networks – now you can set up your distribution channels for free.

You download your YouTube app, Twitter app, Facebook app, LinkedIn app, Google+ app and some other apps to your smart phone that allow you to manage your social networks on the move.

After winning multiple contracts and building valuable design experience, you want to improve things and register your own company and invest in some equipment to improve your design work.

A quick search on the internet and you calculate how much it will cost to get the latest MacBook Pro and the new Adobe suite to take your business to the next level.

You think about getting some business cards and brochures printed, but realise that after all the traffic you had been getting to your social network profiles and blog, that it would be better to guide clients to your profiles as there are loads of great comments and testimonials for your work on your WordPress blog and LinkedIn profile. You also search for your name in Google and are delighted to find out that your blog comes up number one followed by all your social network profiles underneath, so you think it's more friendly to the environment and just tell people to Google you rather than giving them a card.

You calculate your total start-up costs as only a few thousand pounds. You don't need a storage space or office as you have no paper or equipment outside of your laptop and smart phone.

Rather than filling in all the forms you keep receiving in the post with all the pre-approved credit card letters, you decide that you don't want to get caught up in the web of debt that all your friends seem trapped in after accepting their interest-free overdraft from their student days, that later stopped being interest-free once they finished, and so you decide it is time to tap your online social network.

You pull out your smart phone and record a video.

Pitching why you need a few thousand in funds to start your official mobile graphic design business, you upload the video to your own personal channel on YouTube and create a new project on www.BankToTheFuture.com

Crowdfunding

Hugely disruptive technology #4 – crowdfunding – allows you to raise funds for your projects, businesses and ideas by offering rewards to anybody that donates after watching your pitch. Your BankToTheFuture profile allows you to cut out the banks and stay in touch with all your donors as your project progresses. Donors can also find details on your social capital score, credit score and identity score to reassure them that you are a good investment.

You embed your YouTube video into your BankToTheFuture. com project and offer rewards to anybody that donates money to help you start your new business. Rewards include a personal logo design, a coaching session on how to design using the Adobe suite, a dinner with you after signing your first major contract. All allowing you to build your network.

You share your project from your smart phone to all your contacts in your social networks with the click of a few buttons and after 32 days you have 136 donations. Enough to get your business registered and started.

You now have a team of investors in your BankToTheFuture. com community.

In the past you would have had to borrow the money, pay interest and beg the bank to accept your loan request or have the pressure of borrowing all the money from one person, normally a friend or family member.

When the money arrives in your account after receiving your funds from BankToTheFuture.com, you download the eBay app to your smart phone to see who in the world is selling the equipment you want to purchase.

After a quick search you put in a bid to get a MacBook Pro for a few hundred cheaper than from the Apple store. A couple of days later you win the bid, pay with the money from your PayPal account and receive your MacBook Pro straight to wherever you want them to send it.

A few weeks later and you are all set up, you can take payments, you are building a reputation through social networking, you have invested in your start-up business, you have the equipment you need and a team of investors. So far, you have not borrowed a penny.

You check your smart phone and you get an email on your LinkedIn app from a big company that found some of your work on your blog and ask if you are available for a big project. They are going through a complete rebrand and want to take you on to do everything.

You chuckle to yourself as you remember applying to their graduate scheme and getting turned down. They are now offering you more for this project than an entire year's salary on their graduate scheme.

After a successful negotiation, you agree a very generous sum and they request a contract to get started. As this is for a lot of money, so you ring a couple of lawyers to get quotes on how much it would cost to construct your contract. They want thousands, costing a big chunk of your contract to write up your terms and conditions and contract.

In need of an alternative, you search on the internet and find that for a small annual fee you can download and adjust 1,950 legal documents for business in your country, in this example UK, from www.simply-docs.co.uk. You now have a full legal department for a small annual fee, something that would have been completely unaffordable in the past. You tell the lawyers where to go with their kind offer and sign up to simply-docs.

You get the signature on the design contract and nervously wonder how you are going to manage all the work you agreed to do. You knew it was a bigger job than you could handle and you start to panic. The job comes with more administration than design, and to your horror you remember that in the excitement of trying to seal the deal, you agreed to also build their website.

Calming your panic, you begin searching your Amazon Kindle store to find books on building websites after searching for YouTube videos on creating websites from scratch. The thought of learning how to do this horrifies you, so you decide you need to hire help. This contract is big enough for any company with a full team, let alone just you.

The good old internet comes to the rescue again and you set up an account with www.odesk.com. In the past you would have had to spend thousands of pounds and huge amounts of time getting an office, becoming or hiring an HR manager, developing contracts and passing health and safety inspections all before you have even done an interview. Now you simply post a job for free on odesk and receive more than 10 candidates for your job.

Each candidate has a profile with verified work history and feedback and you check them out. After reviewing profiles, covering letters, portfolios, and skill test scores, you contact the most qualified candidates. A few emails and online chats via Skype later and you're most impressed with Bognas and his team of developers in Russia, and Sven, an independent PHP developer in the Ukraine.

You click "hire" and start assigning work on a flexible hourly basis. Bognas and Sven log in when they are working. You can literally see the work in their work diaries – screenshots and memos are recorded as they work. You know your new hires are being productive and your project is on the right track for your client.

After a couple of months your client is delighted with your work and the referrals start piling in.

You reflect back and remember your early days when you first found a huge prospect list by searching the internet and stumbling across 99designs. A few months later and you now have the ability to take payments from anywhere in the world with your email address, you have developed a reputation through all your social network outlets, you have a great profile on Google, you have a team of backers that provided your start-up capital debt-free. You have a team that you can expand and shrink without hiring or firing and you still have the ability to be wherever you want in the world and only do the creative jobs that you love.

You are miles ahead of the big employers that turned you down from their graduate schemes who now have a huge headache trying to hire and fire graduates.

Armed with your competitive advantage, you decide that now is the time to expand.

Many of your clients have been asking whether you can make videos for their websites. You start to notice a trend from your clients – more and more are looking for marketing solutions rather than just great design work.

Most of your clients want websites at the same time as designing their logos, but not just any website – they want it ranking highly in Google, they want videos that explain to the customer what they do and they want their design work to tie in with the marketing goals of the company.

The very next day you get a notification on your smart phone from www.GroupOn.com offering you a course to learn from an ex-Hollywood videographer on how to create videos for business. With 75% off and a tiny fee, you enrol straight away.

You also notice that one of your Facebook friends is attending a Facebook event with the highest paid internet marketer in the United States. A bit of further investigation and you realise rather than having to fly across the world you can attend from the comfort of your laptop via www.GoToWebinar.com. The 'video for business' class begins next week and you register for your webinar starting tomorrow.

In a moment of quiet reflection, you remember how you spent tens of thousands and three years studying graphic design and media at university. You learnt from people with no experience in Hollywood or internet marketing and you left without knowing how to create design work that met companies' marketing needs, how to use a video camera when every business wants you to create video, how to create a beautifully designed website that is search engine optimised and designed to give your clients more leads and more sales.

You wonder why. Every client you have dealt with wants that, and they have never asked about your degree.

After attending the webinar you learn how to solve many of the problems that your clients need you to solve and enrol on a home study programme that the internet marketer was selling at the end of the webinar.

After your video course, you decide it is time to get serious and start investing in the video equipment you need to create Hollywood-quality videos for businesses.

So a few hours on Amazon and you estimate that you need to raise about £10,000 to expand and grow your business to meet your clients' needs. This time you decide that, as you have already funded your start-up by offering rewards on BankToTheFuture. com, you are going to borrow the money to finance your growth as you want to encourage investors to lend to you for more than just rewards and attract more money than before.

Person-to-person lending

Again, rather than using credit cards and paying the ridiculous interest rates, you login to your BankToTheFuture.com account and create a new loan request with hugely disruptive technology #5 – person-to-person lending.

BankToTheFuture.com allows you to submit your loan requirements and after passing a credit and identity check, you are matched with a pool of lenders willing to lend their money to you at a cheaper rate than most banks.

After submitting your loan request, you have all the funds you need and your monthly repayment to your investors is set. It is all managed through the platform and you have a community of investors to add to your team that all have an interest in your success.

In the past you would have had to complete a full business plan and pitch, turn up at the bank suited and booted and pitch to your business account manager; chances are, they would have said no, as the amount of money is too small and you are too high a risk.

When you created your profile, you already opted to get your identity checked and have a credit score assigned, so borrowers start to offer you money at agreed interest rates as they check your social capital score and are interested in lending to projects like yours.

Armed with your new-found training, equipment and knowledge, your client list starts to grow rapidly and finances seem like they will never be a problem again.

Grateful, you decide that now is the time to take some of your savings and make a difference in the world. Money has brought you the power to make a greater contribution.

Microfinance

You scroll through some of the causes that are looking to borrow money on BankToTheFuture.com and also find some inspiring stories of female entrepreneurs living in developing countries that need microloans on www.Kiva.com using hugely disruptive technology #6 – microfinance platforms.

As you realise what a difference you can make in developing countries with your savings and still receive a return on your investment, you wonder why anybody would leave their money at a bank or invest in any other way.

Figure 4 Microfinance has brought financial services to the developing world

You start to develop a real passion to make a difference in developing countries, as you realise that the only advantage you seem to have over those in poverty is an internet connection, a laptop, a smart phone and the knowledge how to use them.

It amazes you that others with the exact same privileges struggle to make ends meet, in jobs they don't even like, constantly fearing unemployment as more and more jobs are replaced by computers, contractors and freelancers.

Did nobody tell them that today we live in the economy of freedom?

Stuck relying on government and conventional employment, many never get to save enough money to make any kind of a difference in the areas that matter to them. They are too busy surviving month to month.

As more of their wage goes to a government struggling to control its debt, they never use their money to help others through micro-loans or social banking.

You realise that your bank has never told you what happens with your money and who it is loaned to, so you move all your deposits to a social bank where you get to allocate your deposits and savings to the type of businesses that matter to you.

You look back at your journey and feel completely humbled and grateful that today is the only time in history when you are able to live life on the exact terms you want.

You have complete freedom to be almost anywhere in the world with an internet connection and still be in business. You are able to allocate your money and savings to make a difference in the social matters that you care about and still get a return through a social bank. You know that you can get your funding needs met by real people without having to rely on your bank, just by the strength of your social network.

As you hear about companies around you that are going bankrupt during the financial crisis, you feel so grateful that your business overhead is virtually nothing and you have no staff to pay unless you are working on a paying project, unlike all the other big companies that are downsizing.

Out of curiosity, you research why businesses are going bankrupt and why the world seems to be in crisis simply because banks are not lending money any more. You are horrified as you learn exactly what the truth behind the financial crisis is and what the future of your new found freedom could be ....

Hold on! Before you start Chapter 2, tweet me your thoughts on the #EconomyOfFreedom.

Scan QR Code & Tweet Simon!

Can't scan? @SimonDixonTwitt

QR 4 Tweet Simon Dixon about #EconomyOfFreedom

2 The debt trap

BEFORE we start, take a look at the introductory video below.

QR 5 Introductory video on the debt trap

From Chapter 1, I hope that you can appreciate the opportunities of the time in which we live.

Quite frankly, there has never been a time like it and in the second part of this book we look at the rise of seven hugely disruptive technologies that I believe will be your life line when our financial system crashes and reforms.

It is my belief, as you are about to find out, that understanding and integrating these seven hugely disruptive technologies into your life will be the key to your future success.

In this chapter I turn our attention to why this financial collapse and reform is inevitable, predictable and guaranteed.

The time of limitless possibilities and the economy of freedom that I discussed in Chapter 1 could be taken away from you very quickly if you don't understand the flaws and rules that govern our current financial system.

Figure 5 The ticking time bomb called our financial system

While we have created seven hugely disruptive technologies that have led to the economy of freedom, our prosperity has come at great expense to many and is ultimately unsustainable.

In this chapter my goal is to explain to you why you need to be prepared. I want to help you get some answers to a lot of the financial mysteries that seem to confuse politicians, economists and even bankers themselves.

As promised in the introduction, I will not go all 'jargony' (if that is a word), just because it's finance. I still plan to write in real English, as I reveal the crazy debt trap that we call our financial system.

There is a reason for the craziness …

There is a reason why your country has taken on huge debt on your behalf for you or your children to repay. There is a reason why you pay so much tax. There is a reason why you have to borrow more to buy your house than your income may be able to support. There is a reason why everything feels expensive to you right now, even when more and more is becoming free.

There is a reason why people you know, companies started by your friends and family, countries you live in and your government are struggling to pay their debts.

There is a reason why they try to pay off debt by taking on more debt. There is a reason why the economy fluctuates and is never stable. There is a reason why our economy crashes when banks decide it is time to stop lending. There is a reason why banks are so called 'too big to fail'. There is a reason why your money is pooled with billions in taxpayers' money in order to bail out banks. There is a reason why banks make so much money. There is a reason why some bankers get paid such huge bonuses even after a bailout.

There is a reason why the developing world is stuck in poverty.

There is a reason why money is made available to create 'weapons of mass destruction' and to drill for more oil when alternatives exist.

There is reason why our financial system is inevitably and predictably guaranteed to crash.

And there is a reason why you should care.

The reason is more simple than economists and bankers would want you to think. It does not require that you understand complex theories on how to price exotic derivatives or interpret econometric models. In fact, it is these very complications and jargon that has blinded politicians into thinking that the problem is a lot more complicated than it needs to be. This jargon is why they scratch their heads searching for more complications when we present these ideas to politicians.

After reading this chapter you may wonder why nobody told you some simple truths about our financial system. They may want you to believe that it is complicated, but the truth is, there are simple reasons why we are where we are.

You may not know it, but there is a disease in our financial system that means you, your friends, your family, your business, your clients, your country and your government all have to go deep into debt, never to be repaid, at ever increasing amounts.

I call it 'the debt trap' and few people on the television, in the newspapers or from your government, is telling you about it at the time I write this book.

Well, actually, there are a few politicians campaigning for financial reforms as recommended in this book, but most would rather focus on patching up a broken system.

You may be reading this book after the inevitable big crash, when the financial reforms have already happened and people are talking about it like it was obvious.

"Here we go", I hear you say. "Is this one of those conspiracy theories that I watch on YouTube, reporting how a team of evil bankers from wealthy families like the Rothschilds, Morgans and Rockefellers, carved out an evil plan on how to rule the world and all its wealth?"

Well, no, quite the opposite. This is a simple account of why the amazing economy of freedom that you live in today is unsustainable when built on our current financial system.

In Chapter 4 you and I are going to travel back in time to fix the system, as there are some simple reforms required. I don't want to leave you thinking we have no solution.

We will discuss how we can make it sustainable, in simple language, but for now we focus on three fatal flaws in our current financial system.

Before I go into the three fatal flaws, I want to mention a non-profit organisation focused on researching our banking system – Positive Money. Most of the facts reported in this chapter have come directly from research that can be found at www. PositiveMoney.org.uk.

After spending years presenting on this topic at over 200 universities and colleges, banks and financial institutions, non-governmental organisations and charities (You can watch one of my presentations at www.SimonDixon.org by scanning the QR code below and registering on my blog), I found an organisation dedicated to researching and presenting on how to fix these three flaws.

QR 6 Simon Dixon's banking reform blog

This research was presented in 2011, after solutions were proposed to the Independent Commission on Banking (ICB), which was appointed by the UK government to investigate how to fix our broken financial system.

It is worth noting that similar research exists across the world on a global scale, but I focus on one country for simplicity, as most countries are in a similar situation, if not worse, operating a similar system and suffering similar consequences.

So while the facts and figures relate to the UK, you can bet that your country has similar problems.

One final point before we go into the three fatal flaws and rules that govern our financial system. My aim is to discuss the situation in plain English so that anybody can read it and understand it without falling asleep.

With that said, here is why your freedom will not last until we reform our financial system and why you should care.

The three fatal flaws of our current financial system

After interviewing the founder and director of Positive Money, Ben Dyson (which you can watch with all my other interviews on my YouTube Channel - simply hit the big yellow subscribe button at www.YouTube.com/user/bankingreform or scan the QR code below and subscribe), he concluded that there are three fatal flaws with our current financial system and I agree.

QR 7 Simon Dixon's banking reform YouTube Channel

Fatal flaw #1

Banks can lend your money whether you like it or not. You may think that the money in your bank account is yours, but the reality is, when you deposit your money with a bank, it becomes the legal property of the bank.

The true implications of this can only be appreciated when you understand what they actually do with the money you give them.

Fatal flaw #2

Banks can invest your money however they want. I call it your money, but as noted above, the bank actually becomes the legal owner of your money; but by 'your' money, I mean the numbers that appear on your internet banking screen.

You are given no choice as to what happens to that money. It could be used for trading the stock market, funding the creation of weapons of mass destruction, funding a war, drilling for oil in Canada, funding commodity speculation, gambling, creating a housing bubble – anything that the banks think will make a good return.

Some gambling goes wrong, and some very wrong, as we found out with the housing bubble.

To give you one example of how crazy this can be, when you invest your money with a bank in your pension, that money could actually be used to take a position on a stock that can decrease the value of your pension. You could be funding the bank to decrease your pension payout!

The point is, you have no idea what is happening with 'your' money. Have you ever had a phone call from your bank asking for your permission to use your money for what they consider to be an exciting new bet? Exactly.

But flaws one and two are nothing compared to flaw three...

Fatal flaw #3

Banks can create money. You heard me right. Almost all of the money that you think is yours when you login to your online banking, was, in fact, created by the bank itself. They literally have a licence to create money called a banking licence and in this chapter I will show you how it works.

So there you have it, three fatal flaws which might not upset you yet, but it is only when you investigate what this actually means that you really start to appreciate why we are where we are and what your future will look like.

Figure 6 When depositors' money is used to speculate through investment banking activities, the phrase 'casino banking' has arisen to describe investment banking

Do banks really create money and why should I care?

Whenever I present on this topic, I am normally confronted with disbelief, so to answer this question, you will need to understand a bit more about the rules that govern money and what money actually is.

I would like to tell you those rules and to illustrate the implications that the three fatal flaws have on us all. I am going to dig a little deeper into one particular case study.

I select the UK as a case study because the research that has been conducted by Positive Money highlights many of the important points. As mentioned earlier, I am certain that your country will operate of a similar framework and face a similar destiny, depending on where you live. While the figures will differ in your country, (they are actually a lot worse in countries like the US), the implications will be similar.

So what is money today?

In the UK, paper money is made by the Bank of England and in the case of coins, through the Royal Mint. Most people know that it is illegal and harmful to our economy if we create our own money. We all understand and appreciate that if we were able to create our own money, we are doing something wrong. If you get caught, you go to prison ... enough said.

We may not know why, but we all understand that if we all created our own money, then money would become worthless and the system would break down.

Most money is now electronic money. Over time, paper and coins have shrunk to 3% of the total money in the UK, with 97% in the form of electronic money appearing as numbers in a computer.

In the past, money consisted of metal coins of real value (most popularly gold) that you use and store in a vault called a bank. In exchange for storing your metal coins or gold, banks would have issued you a piece of paper that could be redeemed for the amount of metal coins or gold stated on the paper.

As people became more trusting of the banks, people started to use this paper to make payments to each other, rather than going to their bank to exchange their paper receipts for coins or gold every time they wanted to make a payment.

LEAVE YOUR GOLD WITH ME AND YOU CAN SEPND THIS RECEIPT INSTEAD...

Figure 7 Gold vaults were used to store depositors' gold in exchange for paper receipts

People gradually began to trust the paper as much as coins and gold, and paper started to function as money itself, even though paper had no real value, other than the belief that it could be exchanged for coins or gold.

However, banks slowly realised that if they created more paper than they had in coins or gold, not many people would notice. As long as they had enough money for those who wanted to exchange their paper for coins or gold each day, then they could make a lot more money.

The 1840s bubble

In the 1840s banks created more and more paper notes for profit and this started to push prices out of control. Eventually, this paper factory led to inflated prices and the complete destabilisation of the UK economy.

In 1844 the government recognised that there was a big problem with allowing banks to create paper money, so the then government, led by Sir Robert Peel, passed a law to prevent any other institution other than the Bank of England from creating paper money.

This took the power to create money away from the banks and gave a monopoly to the Bank of England.

Today, the nature of money has changed again and electronic money is the dominant form of money. The problem is that the law has never been updated and banks are allowed to create electronic money. All electronic money is created by normal high street retail banks.

The law was simply never updated as Sir Robert Peel could not forecast that money would be electronic in the future!

Don't believe me?

Because some of you might think I have eaten one too many bowls of coco pops and fruit loops, I have provided some sources confirming that, in fact, banks do create our countries' money.

A Bank of England Report states:

> "The money creating sector in the United Kingdom consists of resident banks, including the Bank of England and building societies."[1]

Did anybody tell you that there was a sector of private companies in the UK (called banks) that compete with each other called the 'money creating sector'? Anybody fancy setting up in the money creation business?

The report goes on ...

> "By far the largest role in creating broad (digital) money, is played by the banking sector; when banks make loans they create additional deposits for those that have borrowed the money."

To clear up the banking jargon, deposits are the numbers in your bank account.

How about a quote from the deputy governor at the Bank of England and member of the Monetary Policy Committee, Paul Tucker?.

> "Banks [make loans] by simply increasing the borrowing in customers' current account ... That is, banks [make loans] by creating money."[2]

The UK government appointed Martin Wolf, the Chief Economics Editor at the *Financial Times* to join the Independent Banking Commission (ICB), a team of independent researchers, to investigate the problems with banking after the 2007 financial crisis. Martin Wolf said:

> "The essence of the contemporary monetary system is the creation of money out of nothing by private banks' often foolish lending"[3]

Case in point.

So when you take out a mortgage, you are repaying your bank money that they never had in the first place and they are charging you interest on money they simply created. Meanwhile, until you pay off the money that they created, they hold the title deeds. So who owns the property?

And most economists think this is fine. Not a bad business to be in, eh?

There is no money in your bank account, it is not a safe deposit box, and the economists who deny this fact have definitely been eating too many bowls of coco pops and fruit loops.

When you put your money into a bank, you lend it to the bank and it becomes the legal property of the bank. Your bank balance becomes a record of what the bank owes you and you get digital numbers on your account in return.

The head-slapping part of this scenario is that the bank does not have the money to repay you. It is in fact borrowing way beyond its means, just like we have been accused of doing.

For those of you that are still thinking "so what?", wait until you hear what this means for you.

Today, if the entire UK population all decided to go to the bank and ask for their money, they could repay you £71 for every £1000 in your account. Before the 2007 financial crisis, they only had £12.50 to repay you.

Don't freak out if I show you a bank balance sheet, you don't need to be an accountant, but for those of you that like to see it to believe it, I have a copy of a balance sheet from Royal Bank of Scotland's annual report.

In case you don't know, a balance sheet is a summary of the company's financial position.

Feel free to believe me at this point, and forget about reading the balance sheet, but excuse me while I use a tiny bit of accountancy language (a language designed to make the people that speak it look more intelligent than everybody else, but if you speak to the right accountant, it is more simple than they would like you to believe).

Figure 8 Royal Bank of Scotland balance sheet 31st December 2007

A quick look at Royal Bank of Scotland's annual report and you notice under the liabilities section an item titled customer account, next to it you see the amount £680bn.

This is the money that they owe to the people that deposit their money with them (the total of all the numbers that all its customers see when they login to their online banking).

You also notice under the assets section of the balance sheet the item 'cash in balance at central bank', in this case the amount is £17bn. This is the amount of money that they have on deposit with the Bank of England.

For £680bn of money that they have taken in from customers, they only have £17bn.

So, your money is not available for you if everybody wants it back and the money you have when you log in to your internet banking is simply a record of what the bank promises to repay you if it can.

You promised you would not bore me with financial jargon ...

OK, let me try to quickly explain how our financial system works, and still keep my promise to you. Here we go ...

Almost everybody has a bank account with one of the major banks. Each bank operating in the UK has a bank account with the Bank of England. The Bank of England is a special bank just for banks. You and I cannot open an account with the Bank of England, as it is a very special bank at the centre of the whole system.

Prior to the 2007 financial crisis, there was only around £20bn in the Bank of England, deposited from all banks. The banks expanded this to around £1600bn of money on their deposits.

If you did not get that, prior to the crisis the average bank had 80 times more showing in their customers' account balances than the bank actually had itself. This means that if every customer wanted their money back at the same time, the banks would only be able to pay £12.50 for every £1000 in your account!

How do they do that?

In its simplest form, banks recycle money again and again by simply lending it out again and again. They do this because they can. Remember banks are allowed to create electronic money as the law has not been updated since making it illegal for banks to create paper money.

It is at this point that I could bore you with explanations of fractional reserve banking, reserve requirements, asset/liability ratios, gearing ratios, money multipliers, Basel rules and all sorts of terms that would violate my promise to you, but I refuse to go there.

If you really want to, go to www.neweconomics.org and download a free PDF version of the book 'Where Does Money Come From?' based on information from over 500 Bank of England documents, and the best description of how money is created.

There are three rules that you need to know about the creation of money.

Money creation rule #1

When a bank makes a loan to you, it increases the amount of money held by the public.

Money creation rule #2
When you repay your loan, it reduces the amount of money in the hands of the public.

Money creation rule #3
The only way that the public can get money into the economy is to borrow it. (With the exception of money banks create to pay their staff and suppliers etc.)

Figure 9 Almost all money deposited into your bank account is somebody else's debt

So that is as technical as we need to get ... in fact, pat yourself on the back, as that is as far as you need to go to get what your future will look like.

The debt trap paradox

If we want more money in our economy we need more debt. If we want less debt in our economy we have to have less money.

This is the debt trap paradox.

Say what? Either we go into debt or we have a recession – there is no third alternative.

This is why we are always either taking on debt or trying to save and pay down debt in a recession.

But it does not end there. There is one consequence from this problem that means our system is inevitably and predictably guaranteed to crash.

Let me explain ... Check out this graph from Positive Money.

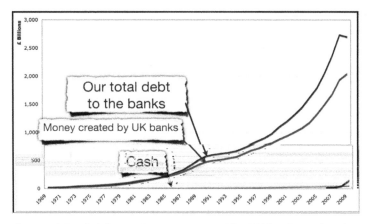

Figure 10 Total debt, and money created by UK banks and cash 1969-2009

It plots the total amount of debt we owe to the banks and the total amount of money we have on deposit at the banks, taken from the Bank of England's website.

The debt we owe to the banks far exceeds all the money we have in the banks. If we took all the money we have today and used it to repay our debts, we would be left with absolutely no money and we would still have owed the banks over £400bn in early 2011!

So how do we repay the money that does not exist?

Either you take on more debt, companies take on more debt, the government takes on more debt, or we raid another country's money supply, probably from a developing nation.

The money to pay the interest on the money that does not exist ... does not exist!

This is why debt has to increase forever as we try to pay down our debt with further debt, until the whole deck of cards tumbles. This is also why the combined intelligence of economists, bankers, professors and politicians will never prevent the next crisis. They come up with a million ways to fix and patch up our broken, guaranteed to fail, financial system ... instead of questioning the way money is created.

They have not questioned it seriously since last time we reformed our financial system way bank in 1844 and took the power to create paper money away from the banks.

Well ... many people submitted proposals for reform after the last great depression in the 1930s, but all were ignored.

So where exactly are we now?

We are completely dependent on banks to put money into our economy in order to make sure that we can function, but this money can only be accessed if we agree to go into debt.

I remember working as an investment banker, while my wife Bliss, worked as a retail banker. I would meet Bliss for lunch and discuss our day so far. When Bliss spoke to her customers she had two options. Lend or don't lend. If she lent, she got a commission, a potential bonus, she got to keep her job and the possibility of promotion. If she didn't lend she got nothing, and if she consistently didn't lend she would have got fired. What choice did she have?

Well, she chose a third option and quit to work with me at BankToTheFuture.com.

But the point is, the people who are deciding how much money we create are completely encouraged to lend.

Figure 11 The incentive for bankers is always to create more money as debt

They lend and they lend and they lend until we are so indebted that people can no longer repay their loans and we get a crisis as money disappears as it never existed in the first place.

This is what I call the debt trap – a trap because we have to borrow the money to keep the economy alive.

Remember, we have two options. To keep the economy growing, we need to take on ever increasing levels of debt. If we want less debt, then we have to have less money ... that is it. Boom or bust. Take your pick.

At the time of writing this book, the total amount of paper and coins in the UK is £57bn. Positive Money calculates that this is equal to the wealth of 19 Richard Bransons, or 251,851 houses.

The total electronic money is £2,200bn; that is 733 Richard Bransons, or 13,580,246 houses.

There are only 22 million houses in the entire UK, so effectively the UK banks have created enough money to buy up over half the houses in the UK.

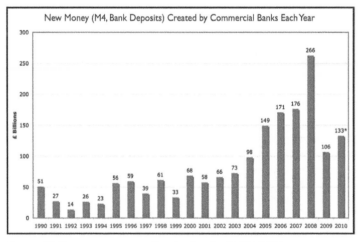

Figure 12 New money creation by banks 1990-2010

In Figure 12 you can see from the impact of the financial crisis that we have become completely dependent upon banks for the creation of money.

The £176 billion that banks created in 2007 is equivalent to everything that we spent on universities, schools, health, defence and police in the same year – approximately one-third of the spending power of the government.

And to top it all, the government is by far the largest borrower in the UK, with debts close to one trillion pounds.

So quite literally, the banks have more power than the government, which is why we are still patching up this system instead of reforming it.

That sounds pretty bad, but why should I care?

Here are 12 reasons why you should care, take your pick:

Reason 1

Either you will spend most of your lifetime in debt or somebody you care about will.

For every pound in the economy, there is more than a pound of debt. According to the Bank of England, at the time of writing, there is £2,200bn of deposits in the economy and £2,600bn of debt. This guarantees poverty and debt forever.

If we all repaid our debt, there would be zero money and we would still owe £400 billion to the banks.

The only way that you can pay your debt is if somebody else goes into debt. We can only grow the economy and avoid a recession by taking on further debt. So it's either you or the ones you care about.

You can imagine the effect that this has on our relationships with others and the chances of us all just getting on … let alone peace between countries.

Reason 2

You have to work for the banks for over a decade to buy a house.

In 1952, the average house price was £1,900; in 2010 it was £184,000! Over the last 60 years we have had housing inflation of 9,584%. This is because banks like the security of lending against houses.

If houses had kept in line with the average income over those years, then a house today would cost £88,000. By giving banks the ability to create money and pump it into housing speculation, they have effectively been able to double the price of property.

You now need to pay an extra £100,000 plus all the interest on your mortgage to buy a house. This translates into you paying the banks an extra quarter of a million on average as a result of the housing price bubble.

Figure 13 Banks' favourite tool for credit creation – housing

In 1952 it would have cost you 5 years and 3 months full-time average salary to buy a house. It now takes you 11 years and 8 months. This is assuming that you do not spend any of your wages on anything else, but paying off the banks. That means over a decade of your life will be spent working for the banks to buy a house.

Reason 3

Your money redistributes money from the poor to the bankers.

Money is redistributed from the real economy to the banking sector as almost all money is supplied through debt. The redistribution that occurs is a direct consequence of our current financial system, where:

→ Money is redistributed from the poor to the rich;
→ Money is redistributed from the rest of the UK to London; and

→   Money is redistributed from the developing world to the
    developed world.

Firstly, it tends to be the people on the lowest salaries that take on
the debt that creates the money for the rich who hold their money
in assets rather than on deposit in a bank.

Secondly, all cities across the UK depend on banks, but the
money created as debt tends to find its way to the investment
banks in London for speculation where the wages are disproportionately higher than the rest of the UK. Profits tend to get
distributed to the City of London to pay mega bonuses. Positive
Money estimates that this redistribution could be as much as £100
billion a year.

Thirdly, as the country is plagued by less money than debt, it
tries to find other countries to trade with so they can take some of
their money which they created as debt. This is one way they can
access debt-free money. As almost all countries are in the same
position, the world fights to trade and squeeze some debt created
money from each other. Developing countries always lose and
international relations are always under pressure.

IF ONLY THEY
KNEW HOW SIMPLE
IT IS TO CREATE
MONEY. SUCH A
SHAME!

**Figure 14 By allowing banks to create money as credit, inequal-
ity and redistribution from rich to poor can only get worse**

Reason 4

You will never live in stable times.

Creating money through banks as debt leads to a perpetual boom and bust economy. As banks start to lend more, you spend more. As you feel more confident, you borrow more, leading to more loans and money creation by banks.

You end up owing more and repaying more, but eventually somebody cannot repay. As people start going bankrupt, banks stop lending. You get scared and try to repay your debts, shrinking the amount of money in the economy.

Less money leads to less spending and a recession.

This cycle continues again and again and again, and with each recession the government ends up deeper in debt, adding to your tax bill.

Reason 5

You will always be surrounded by poverty, even if it doesn't happen to you.

You cannot tackle poverty without tackling this system. All who try are in for a losing battle.

Somebody must hold the debt, or there is no money. During a recession, the lowest paid tend to get laid off first and low to medium income families tend to hold proportionately large amounts of the debt. This indebtedness continues throughout their entire life as somebody has to hold the debt for the rest of us to survive.

This will never change under the current system as somebody has to lose.

Reason 6

The environmental crisis will not get solved in time.

When we allow banks to create money, they will always allocate money to the greatest short-term profitable funding needs. This can be oil, fossil fuels, housing bubbles, weapons development and other environmentally and socially unsustainable activities.

If you use a bank, you are funding these activities. The money needed to return the planet to one that we can live in will not reach the right people in time under our current financial system.

No planet, no economy!

Figure 15 Banks will not a locate the funding needed for the environmental crisis and government will not have the necessary budget under a system where banks create money as credit

Reason 7

You owe over £35,000 if you live in the UK, before you even borrow a penny...

As a UK resident in 1997 your share of the national debt was £8,900; today it's £20,577 and by 2015 it will be £35,600.

Your interest on your share of the national debt will be £81 per month. That is £120m a day spent on interest. This will continue to increase as long as politicians find it easier to borrow money over increasing taxes and risking losing votes.

When nobody else can afford to borrow, the government steps in.

Eventually the government will have to default on their debts and declare bankruptcy, even if they took all our money in tax.

As the government's credit rating is downgraded, pensioners will pay as their pension funds are the main lenders to the government and they will suffer as the government defaults.

Reason 8

You either lose all your money when the financial system collapses or face riots when the government declares bankruptcy.

With each recession, the government will have to bail out the banks, collect less taxes and borrow more to fund ordinary spending. This will continue until either the financial system collapses if the government no longer bails it out, or the government declares bankruptcy.

Either way it will not be pretty.

Reason 9

Your tax will always go up to pay bankers' bonuses.

The reason interest rates are so low as I write is because so many people have unaffordable mortgages where their monthly repayment moves in line with interest rates. When interest rates increase, many will go bankrupt. This means that a number of banking assets will disappear, leading them to ask the government for more bail-out money.

This leads to a redistribution of taxpayers' money to the banking system. The banks essentially have the power to rule policy.

Reason 10

You pay for the privilege to have guaranteed recessions and excessive government debt.

In the UK, banks have created 1.2 trillion pounds over the last 10 years, doubling the money supply in a space of only a decade.

The national debt currently stands at £925bn at the time I write. Rather than giving the banks a city champagne subsidy for the privilege of creating our nation's money supply, this money could have prevented the government taking on excessive debt or financed public services.

Year on year, businesses tend to make improvements on their product offering and service, but every seven years they have to deal with a recession due to money being created as debt that wipes out years of progress.

While many economists believe that recessions wipe out the inefficient, a point I agree with in most circumstances, in a debt-based economy, where debt increases forever, perfectly viable businesses fail as the banks trigger a debt-fuelled boom leading to a bust.

Reason 11

Your grandparents are in trouble, or you are. Your choice ...

We try to control our economy by attempting to manipulate the levels of debt by controlling interest rates. Lowering interest rates encourages people to borrow.

This is good for you if you have a mortgage where monthly repayment follows interest rates, as your monthly mortgage payment gets cheaper for you. This is not good for your grandma who has saved up all her life for her retirement and who receives less and less return on her savings.

As we gamble with interest rates and push them up and down, essentially we are bankrupting the people that borrowed the money when it was cheap to do so by making debt unaffordable. These are the very same people that saved the economy by increasing their debt when we were trying to get more people into debt by lowering interest rates.

If you were one of the people that saved the economy by going into debt when the Bank of England wanted you to, instead of receiving a thank-you, you are reduced to bankruptcy when the Bank of England tries to calm down the economy by increasing interest rates, eventually sending many into bankruptcy.

Thanks!

Reason 12

The things you want to buy will get more and more expensive.

Increases in prices are not caused by governments creating too much money, as some schools of economists would like you to believe; it is caused by banks creating too much money.

Increasing prices, known as inflation, transfer wealth from savers (those who have money) to those who have property, gold and other assets. The rich don't hold a large proportion of their wealth in money, so it does not affect them. It just affects those with moderate to small wealth. In this way their money is redistributed to those with huge wealth.

Do I need to say more?

In summary, banks are able to decide whether the money they are able to create goes on something useful or not.

Only 25% of the money created goes to small businesses that create employment.

There is no measure of social impact on the businesses they lend to.

75% of the money goes to creating housing bubbles and speculation.

Debt has to increase for our economy to prosper.

To decrease our debt, the money supply has to shrink.

Either you go into debt, your loved ones go into debt, your business goes into debt, your country goes into debt, or we cripple a developing nation with debt ... but somebody will lose. This is the debt trap paradox.

> "Of all the many ways of organising banking, the worst is the one we have today" *Mervyn King, Governor of the Bank of England, 25th October 2010*

So where will this all end?

I could go on and on explaining why this system has to be reformed, but fortunately it is inevitably and predictably guaranteed to implode when the government refuses to bail out the banks during the next financial crisis and the banking system tumbles, or when the government declares bankruptcy when they default on repaying their debt.

So we only have to play the game a little bit longer.

My hope is that financial reform gathers momentum before the next depression. My expectation is that we will wait for serious pain and destruction of our current system before we really reform finance.

Now you know the situation, there is a solution and there are things you can do to protect yourself.

We can escape the debt trap of 'free'dom; there is a financial entrepreneur-led revolution happening and thanks to the seven hugely disruptive technologies, you can get ready for the most prosperous time in history when we action some financial reforms.

A few changes, and we can enjoy the freedom that all our technical innovation allows for.

As entrepreneurs and entrepreneurs-to-be, we can do our part as you will find out in this book when we start our 'Bank To The Future' time travelling adventure in Part 2 of this book.

The fact is, we still need the co-operation of governments to fix the money creation problem. Only they can change the law. So before we change history, there is a final force that you have to be aware of that affects us all.

This is the subject of Chapter 3 – the 'free' part of the debt trap of 'free'dom has significant consequences on how we plan our future.

The main reason why you may be one of the people that cannot get a job right now is because the 'free' economy is here to stay, and it is only moving in one direction.

If you are not aware of what it is, you will not understand why you work so hard in your job and still get nowhere, and unemployment seems to increase each year.

We saw in Chapter 1 that today is a day of unparalleled freedom, where you no longer need to rely on the government or employers for your income. On the flip side, from this chapter, you now know that our financial system is the thing that will take away the freedom until reform.

Before we fix this and look at the seven hugely disruptive technologies and the one investment that that will allow you to prosper in any economy, it is time to understand why the final force – the 'free' economy, means that you will have no choice but to be an entrepreneur, a freelancer, a contractor or an outsourcer in the future.

The sooner you get started, the better prepared you will be.

As you now know the first two components of the debt trap of 'free'dom, let's turn our attention to the free economy.

Hold on! Before you start Chapter 3, tweet me your thoughts on the #DebtTrap.

QR 8 Tweet Simon Dixon about #DebtTrap

---

1   Available from http://www.bankofengland.co.uk/publications/quarterlybul-letin/ - Quarterly Bulletin 2007 Q3 p377
2   http://www.bankofengland.co.uk/publications/speeches/2007/speech331.pdf
3   *Financial Times*, 9th November 2010

3 The free economy

BEFORE WE BEGIN, take a look at the video that follows.

Scan QR Code and watch video!

Can't scan? http://bit.ly/qd89LN

QR 9 Introductory video on the free economy

It's 1895. King C. Gillette, a frustrated salesman, got inspired when his shaving razor got so blunt that he could no longer sharpen it. In that moment Gillette had the idea to invent a blade that could simply be thrown away once it became blunt.

A few years later and his first disposable shaver was born. It consisted of two parts – a disposable razor and a disposable blade.

Chris Anderson accounts the story of Gillette in his book 'Free: How Today's Smartest Businesses Profit By Giving Something For Nothing'.

Over the next couple of decades Gillette tried every marketing strategy he could think of, but the idea never took off. Through sheer frustration Gillette started pitching to large corporates in order to buy the disposable razors in bulk without the disposable blades.

His idea was that companies could give his razors away for free with their products as a bonus in order to sell more of the companies' products. When people received the free razor, it was useless on its own. You needed to purchase the disposable blades in order to make a complete disposable shaver that could actually be used to shave.

His break came when he started selling the razors in bulk to banks in the infamous "Shave and save" campaign. Depositors would get a free disposable razor when they made deposits with the bank. The goal was to get people curious to purchase blades.

This sparked a business breakthrough where Gillette sold disposable razors on their own in bulk, for companies to package up as free giveaways with coffee, tea, chewing gum, marshmallows and spices.

A few billion blades later and the 'free' economy had passed its first mainstream test.

Today, this model is used by some of the most successful businesses around. We have all seen it before. Give away the phone and sell the contract. Make the printer cheap and sell the ink cartridges expensive. Install the broadband wireless router for free and charge for the internet usage.

In this chapter we explore why this innovation in marketing has led to what I call the free economy. We also look at why this free economy could be the very reason why you find yourself without a job now or in the future.

It is the last of the three trends that make up the debt trap of 'free'dom, and one that has serious consequences for us all.

So what is the free economy and where did it come from?

The free economy is a trend that has evolved over the years, causing major shifts in our buying patterns and the way we work for income. It refers to an economy where more and more goods and services are free. The question then follows, in a world where everything is free, who pays your wages?

Contrary to many employees' understanding, if a company does not bring in enough money, they either take on more debt to pay you or they cannot pay you at all. Obvious I know, but a simple fact that many rarely think about in the complexities of large public companies and governments.

Traditionally your wages got paid through sales revenues. A model that is turning upside down as we speak. In fact, there is a trend as a direct consequence of the free economy that has caused employing you to be one of the least efficient ways of running their companies.

Before I explain why let's take a further look at the evolution of the free economy.

The rise of the free economy

The media industry really pioneered the free economy following the success of Gillette. Essentially they developed a whole industry where, by charging a third party, they paid for you to consume for free.

Media publishers provide free products for you, and advertisers pay. Radio is free, much television is free, even the newspaper and magazine publishers that charge for their newspapers and magazines don't charge readers anything like the cost of editing, producing, printing, and distributing their newspapers and magazines.

They're not in the business of selling newspapers and magazines to readers, they're in the business of selling readers to advertisers.

Today, the World Wide Web has become a globally viral version of the media business model for every industry. If any industry is not operating around a free model, they will be soon, or they will be gone.

What about huge companies like Apple? Give away the iTunes software for free. A few downloads later and you want to listen to your music on your newly purchased iPod, so you can listen when you're in the gym. You like the way the iPod works and notice an advert that comes through the post.

It lets you know about the new iPhone, which of course is free because your phone company buys it for you in exchange for agreeing to pay them a monthly guaranteed contract for 24 months. So you pop to your local phone store, sign a piece of paper and walk out with an iPhone.

You visit your local Apple store to purchase a case for your iPhone. You notice crowds of people surrounding Apple devices, and can't get to the area of the store displaying the iPhone cases, as it is swamped with free internet users seeking an alternative to paying for an internet cafe.

You notice the iPad, the iMac, the Mac Book Pro and wait in line to have a play. As you play, you imagine the possibilities of how you can organise your entire life around these products. After integrating your calendar, email, contacts, social networks, books, music, games and life around your iPhone, you can't imagine life without it.

Your trip to the Apple store left you thinking about having everything you own stored in Apple's iCloud, fully synced on every Apple device you own, anywhere in the world.

You don't want CDs, DVDs, books, notepads, diaries, address books or anything like that anymore. You want to save space and eliminate as many tangible products from your life as you can, leaving you fully mobile and free.

Suddenly your laptop and PC does not do it for you anymore, you are not in sync.

After your free play in the Apple store, you invest in a Mac Book Pro and become a fan of Apple for life. Forever you purchase the latest operating systems, the iPad of the year, the latest upgrades on the App Store, and you can't wait to pay them as your life gets more and more minimalist and in sync with each new release, to the point where you find yourself queuing outside the Apple store during their next launch and still having to add your name to a waiting list, in order to buy the latest innovation from Apple.

Figure 16 Queues outside the Apple Store in Regent Street, London for their latest product on launch day

Each year a new iPhone comes out, so you upgrade your contract for free in order to get the latest phone, never reaching the end of your 24-month contract. You are hooked for life, and it all began because you wanted to download some music and take it with you to the gym.

This is an example of the 'free bait' model of doing business. You are given something as free bait, to make further purchases. It is great for the consumers and producers, as you only buy things that truly deliver, and companies get to sell more than they could have without free bait.

But the media model discussed earlier is not just a free bait model like Apple, it actually is free to the end consumer.

You never really intend to pay to listen to your radio, and that is OK with them. It really is free for you, not just free bait. Your advertisers are paying the bill for you.

This is why Google, Yahoo and Bing offer you free search, Facebook, Google+, Twitter and LinkedIn offer you free social networking and why Firefox, Internet Explorer and Safari offer you free web browsing.

And that is just the beginning. The model of advertisers paying for everything has evolved even further.

Free website providers are able to give things away for free in order to sell information on you, add links to websites where they can receive commissions from products like Amazon's books, or Google's adverts, or simply sell links themselves for those looking to benefit from search engine optimisation. The list of free monetisation methods is endless, especially in the digital age.

The model has even gone a step further. Things are simply 'free' because they are. No catch at all, they simply rely on voluntary, no obligation, no pressure in-kind donations from fans.

Examples of this are Wikipedia, the free digital encyclopedia that we all rely on for information, created for us, by us.

How about the tremendous success of open source software like WordPress, which allows us all to create free blogs with no catch, and have complete flexibility to customise the blog with free plug-ins developed by millions of developers all around the world ... all for free.

In fact, I just used Wikipedia to instantly find out that Word-Press is in fact used by over 14% of the 1,000,000 biggest websites in the world. As of February 2011, version 3.0 had been down-loaded over 32.5 million times for free.

In the non-digital age the free bait model was very common. In the digital age, the model has evolved to the point where busi-nesses understand that most of their consumers will be free consumers forever. They know that they have no intention of ever paying, and that is OK with them.

Whereas, in the free bait business model, those who take the bait for free, without paying, eventually are made to feel like unwelcome guests. They are a company expense, a loss leader to be limited as far as possible. Today they are welcomed with open arms.

In many businesses, free users are welcomed en masse forever, paid for by a very small percentage of paying subscribers.

When *The Times* newspaper's website introduced a paywall in 2010, they lost 66% of their readers[1].

In fact, the tables have turned. I am a paying customer of Google. I pay an annual fee for my email, so I can access their Google Apps service. When Google released its answer to social networking, after failing to get mainstream usage of its social network, Orkut, by US and other English-speaking users, Google Buzz, Google Profiles and later Google+, I was actually unable to use them all. Google did not bother to make them compatible for paying Google Apps customers.

Google is actually penalising me for being a paying customer. The free customers are more important to them. They have even barred advertisers en masse from paying them to promote websites that they don't consider high quality content. I am not talking about offensive, illegal child pornography websites here, I am talking about sites that they don't consider to provide enough content.

The term 'Google Slap' was developed amongst internet marketers who were barred from giving Google their money.

NO PAYING CUSTOMERS PLEASE...

Figure 17 Google - pioneers of the free economy

Despite the fact that Google penalises you for being a paying customer and refuses to take your money if they don't like your website, they still turn over billions each year.

They are in the business of making sure that free web searchers are happy with their search results, so that high paying advertisers can get their message out to the right searchers.

In the same way that Google fights away money, the founder of Facebook, Mark Zuckerberg, resisted making money from Facebook for years, to the sheer frustration of board members and the venture capitalists.

Facebook now spends millions on servers every month to give us the tools to share our lives with others, paid for by advertisers who target us every time we hit the infamous 'like' button.

With Google, I actually needed to set up a separate free Google account and pretend to be a non-paying Google customer, in order to benefit from their advanced social networking features. Is this world crazy?

Outside the advertising industry, photo sharing sites like Flickr are paid for by Flickr Pro customers. Social networks like Ecademy operate with a large number of free users, paid for by a small number of power networkers and black star subscribers. LinkedIn allows millions to grow their professional networks and showcase their work experience to the world, paid for by companies and recruiters that use their advanced searching facilities to find staff.

The social network I founded, BankToTheFuture.com, provides an alternative way to fund, borrow, raise funds and invest without banks. It combines traditional credit scoring with input from free users who provide valuable information on other users to get an idea of their social capital score and likelihood to repay their loans. They get to build their social capital score and get feedback on their latest ideas for free, paid for by other users who want to fund, borrow, raise funds or invest in ideas, people, businesses, social enterprises and charities.

In all these models, the free users are equally as important as the paid ones, therefore we continually make the free experience great, to add value to both the free and paying customers.

Free consumers are a vital part of the business model for social networks like Facebook, search engines like Google, photo sharing sites like Flickr and alternative funding sites like BankToTheFuture.com, as they provide most of the network.

They are not 'loss leaders' or free bait that did not convert, as they are in the free bait world. This works because the cost to serving the free is low enough in the digital age.

Money isn't the only motivator

But the free economy has created a movement reaching further than just clever marketing and free business models. There is a whole economy for free with no agenda other than to disrupt industries or offer genuinely free services for the common good. Through WikiLeaks, which publishes submissions of private, secret, and classified media from anonymous news sources and whistleblowers, Freecycle, which gives away free secondhand goods for anyone who will take them away, to Wikipedia, where we are discovering that money isn't the only motivator.

Altruism has always existed, but the Web gives it a platform where the actions of individuals can have a global impact.

My whole awareness campaign to reform banking has been made possible because of free video sharing on my Banking Reform YouTube channel and my free WordPress blog at www.SimonDixon.org.

QR 10 Simon Dixon's banking reform YouTube Channel

QR 11 Simon Dixon's banking reform blog

In a sense, the digital age has turned sharing into an industry. We now enter an era where free will be seen as the norm.

But I thought there was no such thing as a free lunch...

Those of you, like me, who were consumers when free was something you were very sceptical about and still are, need to be aware that there is a new generation consuming right now, that knows no different.

In fact, they expect many things for free. In the UK there were riots when students realised they could no longer go to university without paying the price. The UK government, at the time of writing, now lends students the money for their tuition fees, which will be paid back when they graduate and begin working. They are not used to paying, hence the uproar.

The generation that are just about to become producers (as they start to enter the competitive market after finishing at school, college or university) are currently finding it hard to find employment.

Figure 18 Students protesting for free university education

We call them generation Y. Generation Y think differently. They continually seek the free way to do things. They don't understand paying for the things we pay for. Why would you pay, when you can get it for free?

On the contrary, those born before the birth of the digital era – generation X – are very sceptical of free and seek paid alternatives, because every time they have consumed for free in the past, it has always been substandard, free bait or a scam. They avoid free on purpose.

Two generations colliding...

Right now you have two generations colliding: those who are used to paying – generation X – and those who are used to getting everything for free – generation Y.

For generation X, it is a status symbol for them to pay top whack for everything; for generation Y, it is cool to brag about how you beat the system and got it for free. The two don't get each other. Generation X value paying their way and were brought up in the consumer economy. Generation Y think that those who charge are exploiting what should be for free.

So who is right? Isn't the free economy good for us all?

As the digital marketplace has become global, it has become common practice for businesses to give away some of their very best stuff for free (and lots of it), while ingeniously developing a way to compete with others who want to give away higher and higher value innovations for free and still have a business.

Give it away free, or somebody else will. This has brought industries crumbling down if they refuse to adjust.

The generational clash has also produced a major shift in behaviour and some serious consequences on employment.

Take a look at the newspaper industry. Free newspapers were given away with limited success since the first free newspaper launch in 1885 – *General-Anzeiger für Lübeck und Umgebung* in Germany. But it was not until a century later, in 1995, that the *Palo Alto Daily News* was launched in California, and within nine months it featured close to 100 adverts per day and was profitable within nine months of launch[2].

After its success, the free newspaper model was copied a number of times over the years. In 1995, the same year as the *Palo Alto Daily News*, the company that owns the *Daily Mail* newspaper, Associated Newspapers Ltd. launched *Metro* in Sweden[3]. After its success in Sweden, the newspaper was launched in the UK in 1999, and was given away completely free to anybody that would take it at selected spots in London (today, 14 different UK cities).

In less than 10 years, free newspapers were introduced to almost every European country and in several markets in the US, Canada, South America, Australia, and Asia[4]. Worldwide, there are now over 44 million free newspaper editions being distributed every day.

In 2007, through sheer pressure to compete, the *New York Times* went free, followed by much of the *Wall Street Journal*, and most major newspapers started giving away digital journalism for free online and through smart phone apps.

The consequences – more and more journalists and employees in the industry are losing their employment contracts and becoming freelance or finding their jobs become obsolete. Digital print is gradually replacing the need for thousands of jobs and the industry employs fewer people each year.

Today I watch people's reading habits as I travel from meeting to meeting, because I am sad like that. I split people up into four categories and do a quick mental survey every day.

I categorise people as: those who do not read news in the morning; those who buy magazines or newspapers in the morning; those who read free newspapers in the morning; and those who select their media inputs digitally through apps, websites and smart phone video channels. My results are as follows.

I generally notice generation X reading the newspaper that they have probably been purchasing every morning for years, or the magazine they have subscribed to for years, just like my dad does.

I more than often see those on the edge of generation X and generation Y reading their free *Metro, City AM*, or whatever the local free newspaper is.

I then see generation Y reading blogs and news apps on their smart phones and tablets and selecting the types of inputs they want to receive based on their interests.

This is a simplification, but observe for yourself next time you find yourself on a bus in the morning during rush hour.

The trend is clear though – there are fewer people reading both paid and free newspapers, instead choosing their smart phone and tablets to organise all the information that matters to them. Just take a look around you and you will see it for yourself.

Figure 19 The shrinking days of paid print newspapers

More and more media companies that create these smart phone apps, one by one, are giving more and more away for free, choosing digital media run by freelance journalists, contracting out their distribution and customer service to contractors and outsourcers. They are also producing much of their content from free guest bloggers, who every day give great content for free.

Activists are becoming a huge disruption to industry

What was once a marketing gimmick has become a huge disruption to industries.

Before the copyright law in the early 18th century, all music was free. Law later developed where copying a few words of music or a few seconds of a sound recording could be considered a crime. From then on, the music industry become a huge business.

In 1994, Ram Samudrala, a professor of computational biology, published 'The Free Music Philosophy', which predicted how the ease of copying digital information on the internet would lead to violations of copyright laws and new business models in the music industry.

Despite the efforts of the music industry, free music has become a reality. The question is no longer why and how music should be free, but rather how creativity would flourish while developing models to generate revenue when their music is free.

If you don't believe me, pick any song you like and enter the name of the song or artist into the YouTube search engines. You will find it there. If not try Google and there will be a way to listen for free.

Offering free music proved successful for Nine Inch Nails, Radiohead, and Trent Reznor, not forgetting the thousands of bands on MySpace and YouTube.

Unfortunately, most generation X artists do not know what you learned in Chapter 1 about how to make it standing on your own two feet, and are finding themselves in an economy they just don't get. They are used to the traditional music business model and the revenues are simply not there anymore. Unemployment has soared in the music industry as revenues have dropped year on year (more on this later).

The same is true for the movie industry, the television industry, the farming industry, the education industry, the legal industry, the accounting industry and many other industries, apart from the banking industry due to its special subsidy from their licence to create money and bail-outs.

Let's not forget the free software movement in 1983, to give the benefit of 'software freedom' to all computer users. This movement gave birth to 'open source software', free for all and innovations like WordPress.

I have not even really begun on the mega free businesses of today – Google, Yahoo, Facebook, Skype and all the other hugely disruptive free digital innovations and their future plans for the free economy.

While Skype has significantly reduced your phone bill and the way you communicate internationally, by offering free Skype to Skype calls, video conferences and screen sharing to anybody with an internet connection, what happens when phone providers realise that the data about who you call and what you talk about is more important than charging for phone calls?

At the time of writing, nobody has offered free phones and free phone calls from a phone without an internet connection as far as I know. I suspect this will have changed by the time this book has been published.

With the rise of cloud computing, the price of bandwidth and storage dropping fast, the 'free economy' has become a movement. But what is important for us all to understand are the consequences for every industry and your job.

So one of the reasons unemployment is so high is because I consume things for free?

In order for businesses to engage customers in a market where the whole world is competing for your attention, they must play in the free economy or they stand no chance today.

The interesting part is, because of the freedom we have today, as discussed in Chapter 1, more and more are turning to entrepreneurship rather than employment for their income.

As an entrepreneur, not only are you a consumer in the free economy, but you become your very own producer, where you need to give more and more away for free just to stand a chance of engaging a potential customer.

This means, if you are not already, that you are on the non-favourable side of the free economy. Even graduates seeking careers are finding that they need to work for free as 'free bait' to get employment.

There is a twin force that is also driving forced entrepreneurship today. In order to give all this stuff away for free, companies need to produce their free goods at minimal costs. This means increased digital activity.

Virtually every product or industry that touches digital networks, quickly feels the effect of falling costs, but more so when they figure out how to do it without the huge cost of staff. So one by one, companies are replacing staff with technology at a rapid rate as they automate their free offering.

All these forces mean that you, as a consumer in the free economy, are already a producer too, or will become producers shortly, through forced entrepreneurship.

Add to the mix a global recession caused by the debt trap, and many who have been laid off have had time to reflect about what they want to do in life. They have had no option of a job and therefore need to become producers, giving more and more away for free to compete and get started.

This is the very reason why working for a company in the free economy is the riskiest strategy for earning your income. It used to be that entrepreneurship was considered risky. This has now turned on its head – the riskiest strategy is employment!

The effect of turning products digital and reducing staff can be observed in many industries. Let's take a look at some of these companies.

Google and Facebook essentially turned advertising into software. Before Google and Facebook, advertising was a human business. Have you ever tried getting Facebook's or Google's customer support team on the phone? You probably don't even think of trying, instead searching forums to solve your problems. That is because companies like Facebook and Google do not need all the customer support team that a company of that scale would have needed in the past. The service is free, you don't even think that they would offer support for all those millions of free customers around the world.

You can even trace this effect in banking, where the branch is shrinking its human input by the day. The investments industry, where computers are trading computers on automatic trading platforms. In supermarkets, where we see more and more self-service checkout registers. In gambling, where croupiers are replaced with online platforms. In construction, where machines are doing the work that used to require hundreds of skilled workers. Even in the restaurant business, where we are seeing robots cook food served on a mini escalator!

Take a look at almost any industry and look at the trend.

> "The moment a company's primary expenses become things based in silicon, free becomes not just an option but the inevitable destination." *Chris Anderson*

Can advertisers afford to pay for everything to be free?

The quick answer is no.

Somebody has to pay for all this free stuff, and while the advertising industry is huge, it cannot afford to pay for the entire free economy, especially when companies are advertising free products.

That is why you would never see Wikipedia answers appear in the sponsored search results in Google, but always number one in the free search results. Wikipedia has no money to pay Google; it ranks it for free.

As more businesses become digital businesses, as more services become software, as more products become downloads, we move towards an economy where many things get cheaper every year.

So while debt increases in ever increasing amounts, caused by the debt trap described in Chapter 2, and the cost to becoming an entrepreneur, freelancer or contractor becomes cheaper and faster than preparing yourself for employment as described in Chapter 1, we have this battle between inflation caused by excessive levels of debt and deflation caused by the free economy.

A battle that the free economy will win, because consumers will use their wallets to vote for more free.

This is one reason why you see conflicting arguments between economists forecasting mass inflation (the general price level of goods and services increasing), and mass deflation (the general price level of goods and services decreasing) and nobody really knows what will happen as central banks pump more money into the economy and governments try to get banks to create more money by asking them to lend more, putting more people into debt, in an economy that has become uncontrollable.

Inflation or deflation: it is anybody's guess, because we live in strange times.

Figure 20 Did you hear about the economist, banker and politician that...

One thing is for sure: ever increasing debt combined with the free economy does not paint a rosy picture for the future of our monetary system or employment.

The inevitable destination seems to be free and unemployment.

So who is going to pay for all this free stuff?

The answer is, you do.

The implications of free are simple – we have mass unemployment, many will lose their job, if they haven't lost it already, and more and more end up entrepreneurs, freelancers, contractors or outsourcers competing with each other to give away goods and services for free, as the government certainly cannot afford to support us.

You probably already find yourself exchanging more and more goods and services with others with no monetary transfer right now.

The money from advertising simply does not stretch far enough to service the whole free economy.

So you will be taking on more and more debt, as you are unemployed for longer and longer, keeping the debt trap moving whilst millions of solo entrepreneurs spring up with new innovations. Eventually you will have to come out to play in the entrepreneurial economy.

As we fuel the debt trap further, we will all have to pay again when we get the inevitable collapse of our financial system. When we can no longer afford to repay our debts and the governments debts that you have to pay for in taxes, we have a complete breakdown of our monetary system.

But what would a world without money look like?

Well, you may not know about it, but there are actually radical movements and activists that have been aiming for a moneyless society for a while now. Hard to comprehend, but they could just get their wish.

The Venus Project advocates American futurists, Jacque Fresco's vision of the future, aiming to improve society by moving towards a global sustainable social design that they call a 'resource-based economy'.

The Venus Project was founded on the idea that all of society is fundamentally corrupt and that this corruption comes from the use of money. Fresco advocates an economy where resources are allocated by a computerised automated system.

Sounds crazy I know, but we live in crazy times.

In a resource-based economy, resources are allocated to the goods and services in demand, based on factors of availability, sustainability and technological advancement. In their vision, the role of money would be phased out and instead central computers serve a line-up of goods and services as we all work to contribute to the greater good of sustainable technological advancement.

It has already started...

In the 1980s while working in the London Stock Exchange, Dr Edgar Cahn, civil rights lawyer and activist, founded the 'time banking' system.

Time banking is a service exchange that uses units of time as currency. Essentially, the "time" one spends providing these types of community services earns "time" that one can spend to receive services.

Time banking today is primarily used to provide incentives and rewards for work such as mentoring children, caring for the elderly, being neighbourly – work usually done on a volunteer basis. Communities are already using time banking as a tool to forge stronger intra-community connections, a process known as building social capital. But what happens when time banking goes beyond voluntary work? Well, to allow that to happen, hugely disruptive technologies have evolved making an environment like this possible, as discussed in Part 2 of this book.

Have you been building your social capital score?

I think your social capital score will be your most valued asset in the future, and one of my goals is that by the time you finish reading this book you start immediately investing in your social capital and understand its importance.

Today, 26 countries have active Time Banks, just in the UK alone there are 108 Time Banks active and 53 officially recognised Time Banks in the US[5].

Do we really have to live without money?

Let's not do anything too radical: let's fix our debt trap and create a sustainable monetary system, giving people the choice to use a combination of money and non-monetary exchange, which will evolve naturally.

Let's see where the free economy goes and adjust as we need. One thing is for certain; wherever the free economy takes us, the sooner you get to grips with technology, the more prepared you will be.

Unemployment will be getting worse and worse. More and more companies will be choosing freelancing and contracting over employment contracts. More and more companies will be outsourcing functions of their companies. More and more people will engage in consultancy swaps and transactions that involve non-monetary transfers.

The more people you know and the stronger your network of people that you can collaborate and co-operate with, the stronger position you will be in. The higher your social capital score, the more prosperous your future.

Those who are actively using the seven hugely disruptive technologies outlined in Part 1 will be in a much stronger position to prosper when the banking system or the government goes bust.

Social capital is the greatest investment you will ever make.

So how do we fix the debt trap and how do we prepare?

In order to find out, in Part 2 of this book, we begin our journey in time travel by travelling back to 1844 to make changes in British history to fix the debt trap.

We then travel forward in time to compare the effects on our economy and watch the rise of the seven hugely disruptive technologies under a sustainable financial system.

But before we go back in time, let's recap Part 1.

We are currently living in a debt trap of 'free'dom. Due to seven hugely disruptive technologies, we have never lived in a time of freedom quite like today, as described in Chapter 1.

On the other hand we have built our seven hugely disruptive technologies and freedom on a debt trap that is inevitably and predictably guaranteed to crash, as discussed in Chapter 2.

To add more fire to the mix, we find ourselves in a free economy where unemployment is only going in one direction, as we replace humans with computers in order to give more and more away for free.

That is the complete 'debt trap of 'freedom'.

What will happen when the financial system collapses? Will we all become barbarians fighting for survival?

Will we all use the Time Banks to operate off a barter economy, where we trade goods and services for other goods and services using technology in a worldwide marketplace? Will we all live in a non-monetary resource based economy?

Or could we make a few reforms and continue life as we know it, minus all the booms and busts?

Maybe we don't need to be radical

Perhaps we can fix a few financial problems that make things a lot more sustainable for us all, without having to consider a moneyless world, or a world with a bankrupt government and collapsing financial system.

What if our financial system was not guaranteed to crash? Could we live in a time where most are entrepreneurs, freelancers or contractors? Could we live in a time where all the technological innovation exists for us all to earn money out of the area that matters to us, that we are passionate about? Could we live in a world where everything and everyone is connected? Could we live in a world where financial services stretch the entire world, including those who have never had access to financial services in the past? Could we live in a world where we get more and more innovative in an entrepreneur-led economy? Could we reach sustainability?

Well, to answer these questions, let's travel back in time and make a few minor changes.

Hold on! Before you start Part 2, tweet me your thoughts on the #FreeEconomy

QR 12 Tweet Simon Dixon about #FreeEconomy

---

1   *The Observer*, Sunday 18 July 2010 http://www.guardian.co.uk/media/2010/jul/18/times-paywall-readership

2   The Daily News (Palo Alto) Wikipedia contributors //en.wikipedia.org/w/index.php?title=The_Daily_News_(Palo_Alto)&oldid=445101846

3   Metro International Annual Report 2006 http://hugin.info/132142/R/1125327/208539.pdf

4   Newspaper Innovation, 'About Free Dailies, http://www.newspaperinnovation.com/index.php/about-free-dailies/

5   About Time Banking UK Accessed August 14, 2009. http://www.timebanking.org/about

Part 02

AN ADVENTURE IN TIME TRAVEL

4 Back to 1844

BEFORE WE START our journey, have a look at the introductory video.

QR 13 Introductory video on our adventure in time travel

NOTE: If you are manually typing the above URL, the first 'l' in the URL is a lower case 'L' and the second 'l' is also a lower case 'L' not an upper case 'i'.

Some inconvenient truths

There are three inconvenient truths that most economists, politicians and bankers have forgotten to tell you. Sounds unbelievable I know, but hardly any of them talk about the debt trap you read about in Chapter 2. They just don't think that it's important.

The battle over whether banks should or should not be allowed to create money used to be one the most furiously debated topics amongst politicians, economists and bankers.

Reformers like Abraham Lincoln, Thomas Jefferson, Andrew Jackson, economist Irving Fisher, British Prime Minister Sir Robert Peel, and countless others, all felt so strongly that banks should not be able to create money, that they spent most of their careers making sure of it.

While they all had major victories in their battles, one by one they all lost. Modern economists, politicians and bankers think it is perfectly fine for banks to create our money.

So before we fasten our seat-belts for our adventure in time travel, let's take a quick look at the inconvenient truths that time has forgotten.

Inconvenient truth #1
Economists have forgotten to debate whether banks should or should not be allowed to create money.

Inconvenient truth #2
Politicians are too busy adding to our national debt to understand that banks are creating money and indirectly lending it to them.

Inconvenient truth #3
Banks are happy to continue creating more and more money until economists tell politicians that they cannot create money forever. And the funny thing is, economists think it is OK, so that won't be happening any time soon!

Most students of economics and politicians just don't care either. So we can either wait for the crash, or we can do something about it.

Figure 21 The triangle of trust – bankers, politicians and economists

To risk destroying years of innovation seems crazy to me, so I have decided to do something with you.

I got bored of speaking with today's politicians who scratch their heads when I say there is a problem with banks creating money, so I thought it would be a better idea to travel back in time and speak to the politicians that actually used to talk about it.

Luckily, scientists have been busy at work inventing time machines. It is now time to take the future into our own hands and travel back to 1844.

Remember the Spielberg film 'Back to the Future II'? Biff wanted to change his future, so he travels back in time to give his younger self a sports almanac that forecasts the results of all the major sports events of the future. With the sports almanac in the hands of the past Biff, history is altered forever.

Inspired by 'Back to the Future II', we bring with us to 1844 a banking almanac, outlining all the major crisis events in banking from past and present and legislation recommendations to prevent the disasters happening.

Sir Robert Peel was the UK's Prime Minister in 1844 and he was already reforming banking. Our mission is to give Sir Robert the banking almanac and travel back to the future to see if we have prevented future crashes and made our financial system sustainable.

Could anybody in 1844 believe concepts like digital money? Well, persuading a politician in 1844 how computers are going to work actually sounds easier to me than telling our current politicians that there is a problem with banks creating money!

Our journey in time travel begins...

Figure 22 The Houses of Parliament, London, UK

1844 ...

It's the 6th May 1844 and we arrive at the House of Commons in London, UK. Sir Robert Peel begins his presentation to the House and proposes the introduction of a Bank Charter Act. Peel had come to office during an economic recession, and topping his agenda was banking reform.

Leading up to this meeting, the number of banks in Britain had increased tremendously, and, of course, with it the amount of paper money that they had created.

Laws of the early 19th century had permitted banks the right to issue bank notes subject to legislative restrictions, similar to the present day where banks are able to create digital money.

As with the years leading up to the 2007 crisis, where excessive mortgages caused a housing bubble, leading up to 1844, banks were issuing vast quantities of bank note loans and speculating on new companies.

Fears were expressed to Sir Robert by economists at the time concerning the stability of business, and sure enough, businesses started defaulting on their debts, causing a financial crisis.

Confidence in banks and businesses hit a low, so Sir Robert proposed a redraft of banking law and banking reform. After a lengthy debate about gold and the nature of money, the House agreed that something needed to be done about banks' ability to issue bank notes (now paper money). The only problem was that they had no idea that bank notes would be a tiny percentage of the total money supply in the future.

By the end of the meeting it is agreed that more research on money needs to be conducted with the goal of drafting the Bank Charter Act and implementing strong banking reform.

As the meeting wraps up, we quietly sneak over to a pile of research papers given to him by his advisors and slip the banking almanac into the middle of his pile of research papers.

In the pile are papers from eminent thinkers on this subject, including Sir William Petty, John Locke, Robert Banks Jenkinson (Lord Liverpool) and now, as well, our banking almanac.

Later that week, Sir Robert and his team go through the research papers and they are hooked by the forecasts laid out in the banking almanac.

That year, Sir Robert successfully passes the Bank Charter Act 1844, as an Act of the Parliament of the United Kingdom, restricting the powers of British banks, giving exclusive note-issuing powers to the Bank of England only. The Act that Sir Robert drafted this time round, had a few updates as a result of reading our banking almanac.

Under the original Act, no bank other than the Bank of England could issue new banknotes. The Act served to restrict the supply of new notes in the UK, and give the Bank of England an effective monopoly on the printing of new notes.

However, this Act was slightly different. In this draft, no bank other than the Bank of England could issue new banknotes or demand deposits.

OK, it's getting a bit tricky to stick to my 'no jargon' promise when discussing banking law, but without going into all the boring details and still remaining factually correct to prevent the attack of the economists, here it is.

The original Act exempted demand deposits (money that appears when you login to your online banking) from the legal requirement of a 100% reserve (banks being able to create money as debt out of thin air), but it did demand this requirement on the issuance of paper money (It became illegal for banks to create paper money).

Phew! We got through it, I hope!

This new Act submitted by Sir Robert, as a result of our banking almanac, future proofed the true intention of the Bank Charter Act, so that it became illegal for banks to create money in the form of paper and digital inputs in a computer in the future.

Job well done. We return to our time machine and travel forward in time to assess the impact our law has on the history book.

... To 1866 ...

Until the events at Northern Rock in September 2007, 1866 was the last run on a British bank, so we figured it would be a pretty good time to test our Bank Charter Act update.

Overend, Gurney & Company was a London bank at the time, which under the original Bank Charter Act collapsed in 1866 owing about £11 million, equivalent to approximately £1 billion in 2011 prices[1].

While the bank originally specialised in the buying and selling of products known as 'bills of exchange', during the financial crisis of 1825, the bank was in a strong enough position to make short loans to many other bankers.

The firm started offering banking services, paying interest to depositors and using its money to buy and sell stocks and bonds. Prior to 1866, for 40 years it was the greatest discounting house in the world. The house became known as "the bankers' banker", and secured many of the previous clients of the Bank of England.

However, 1866 was a period of collapsing stock and bond prices. Even with our new Bank Charter Act, based on our our banking almanac, Overend Gurney & Company begins experiencing monetary difficulties as stocks and bonds collapsed.

It's the 10th May 1866, and the bank suspends payments and a bank run begins as before.

Just as it did in our current history books, panic spread across London, Liverpool, Manchester, Norwich, Derby and Bristol the following day, and there were large crowds queuing outside Overend Gurney & Company at 65 Lombard Street, London, desperately trying to withdraw their money.

The failure of Overend Gurney & Company turned out to be the most significant casualty of the 1866 credit crisis, and our reforms failed to save the financial crisis that followed. When the bank went into liquidation, more than 200 companies, including other banks, went down as a result, causing a bigger crash. Learning from our trip back to the future in 1866, we make a couple of changes to the banking almanac and bring a couple of things to Sir Robert's attention. The goal is to highlight the importance of adding extra stipulations to the Bank Charter Act that meant banks had to ask depositors' permission before they used their money for loans. So armed with our re-drafted banking almanac, we travel back to 1844 in order to replace the old banking almanac that we slipped into Sir Robert's pile of papers.

We successfully get the new banking almanac to Sir Robert, and sure enough, additional clauses are added to the Bank Charter Act that force banks to get their clients permission before lending their money.

To check the effect of our new Act, we travel back to the future in 1866 and find nobody queuing outside 65 Lombard Street. History had been altered again.

To see how the law had changed the future, that day we decide to open a bank account for ourselves to test the changes in banking practices as a result of the Act.

Since the law was passed, the bank now had to ask my permission to use my money, so when I opened my bank account I was given two options:

1 Keep my money safe and the bank can't touch it (known as my current account).

2 Invest my money for me in whatever the bank likes (known as my investment account).

Current Account - Bank Holds Your Money & It Is Not Invested	Investment Account - Bank Invests Money & You Share The Risk

Figure 23 The separation of current accounts and investment accounts to prevent bank bailouts and the problems of 'lender of last resort' by a country's central bank

The money that I held in my current account was never lent out due to our second round of recommendations to Sir Robert, and the bank was unable to use it to create money out of thin air due to the first round of recommendations in our updated Bank Charter Act.

This means in my current account I can handle all my ordinary payment services, but the bank pays me no interest on my money, as it is not invested.

In the future this account will be used to manage my cash point (ATM) withdrawals, direct debits, debit card transactions, mobile payments and to receive my monthly salary.

Remember in Chapter 2, when we looked at the balance sheet of RBS?

The effect of this law was that my current account money was no longer included in RBS's balance sheet, as it was no longer theirs.

Since our updated law changes, banks simply hold my current account money in a separate account with the Bank of England. The bank cannot do anything with this money as I have not given them permission to do so.

In 1866, they would have charged me a small monthly fee for my current account service as they don't make any money from it, but I knew the future, and as we moved into the upcoming free economy a century and a half later, current accounts become free as they are used as free bait to get my investment account business.

I then opened an investment account. The investment account that I set up paid me interest. Funds were used by the bank to make loans; in exchange, they paid me interest for the privilege of loaning my money for a return.

After going through the terms and conditions, it was made very clear to me that I was sharing the risk on these investments with the bank. I was made aware of the risk that I could lose all my investment account money if things go wrong.

If I was not happy, they gave me the option to either leave the money in my current account with zero risk and no return on my money, or to invest the money in a slightly different investment account where I was happy with the investment strategy and the level of risk they were taking.

Seems like a minor change, but the effect is big.

With the Act passed, there is no longer any liability for the Bank of England, the taxpayer or the government to take the risk of my investment account going wrong, as there is today.

As we shared the risk with no plan B, the banks are a lot more cautious with their investments and when a bank collapses they are no longer 'too big to fail'.

Figure 24 Preventing the chaos and cost of bank bailouts

So, curious as to what happened with Overend, Gurney & Company in this new future, we do a little investigation.

Overend, Gurney & Company was still investing in stocks and bonds, and much as before, their investment prices started to fall. This time though, instead of a bank run, many investors simply withdraw their money from their investment accounts and move it into their current accounts.

To meet the demands of depositors, the bank sold many of its investments, causing the market prices to fall even further. The investment accounts performed poorly, but there was no risk to my current account and no crisis. It was not a good year, but it was still business as usual rather than liquidation.

Under this new legislation, if banks go bust, which was a lot less common, all the people that had money in their current accounts were safe, without any dependence on government bailouts.

If it does collapse, the assets of the bank are sold and divided up, with the money being used to repay those who accepted the risk, just like shareholders when a company goes bankrupt.

Banks are now ordinary companies like any other.

As we stand outside Lombard Street on 10 May 1866, we pat ourselves on the back. The run never happened, the investment accounts at Overend, Gurney & Company take a huge slump and this time the bank re-evaluates its investment strategy, but current account holders do not panic and there is no run on the bank.

The 200 companies and banks do not fail as a result of dealings with Overend, Gurney & Company[2].

Happy with our work, we travel forward in time to make sure we are still on track with our alterations in history.

Our next stop – Jekyll Island, an island near the coast of the US State of Georgia.

... To 1910 ...

Curious to see what effect our Bank Charter Act changes have had on the rest of the world, we travel forward in time to 1910.

It's November 1910, Senator Nelson W Aldrich arranges a secret meeting in Jekyll Island Club to discuss the banking system in the United States – an event that led to the creation of the current Federal Reserve system, the central banking system of the United States.

Nobody knew about this meeting, but as we were coming from the future, we knew that disguised as a 'duck hunt' on Jekyll Island, Senator Nelson Aldrich, his personal secretary Arthur Shelton, former Harvard University professor of economics Dr A. Piatt Andrew, J P Morgan & Co partner Henry P. Davison, National City Bank president Frank A. Vanderlip and Kuhn, Loeb, and Co. partner Paul M. Warburg, were all meeting to discuss the formation of an American central bank.

Prior to the meeting Nelson W. Aldrich toured Europe and collected data on the various banking methods being used, most notably by the Bank of England.

The meeting resulted in draft legislation for the creation of a US central banking system. They used the British model of banking as a basis to begin drafting the plans for the 1913 Federal Reserve Act.

Now that history in Britain is altered forever, we travel to 1913 and notice that instead of just granting the federal reserve the legal authority to issue Federal Reserve Notes (now commonly known as the US dollar), it followed the model of the Bank Charter Act in the UK and gave the federal reserve the monopoly to create deposit money also (e.g. digital money – the money in your online banking today).

So now we have a private bank called the Bank of England that has the monopoly on the creation of money in the UK and a private bank called the Federal Reserve with a monopoly on the creation of money in the US.

As most economies around the world used the Northern European banking systems as a template (after being influenced by the UK model), our hope is that the changes that we made to the Bank Charter Act back in 1844 will alter the world forever.

As the Federal Reserve Act is passed according to plan, we pat ourselves on the back again, and travel forward in time again, to find out if the world follows the Bank Charter Act and if we have created a financial system that works.

... To 1929...

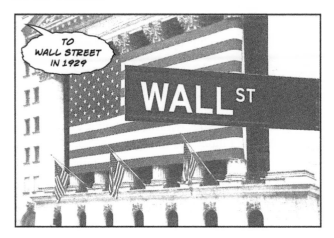

Figure 25 Wall Street, NY

Our hope is that owing to Sir Robert and the Federal Reserve removing banks' ability to create money out of nothing in the UK and US, the debt boom that led up to the infamous US stock market crash in 1929, followed by the worldwide great depression, is rewritten and eliminated from history.

Before we changed history, the Wall Street Crash of October 1929 was the most devastating stock market crash in the history of the US.

The crash signalled the beginning of a 12-year Great Depression that affected all Western industrialised countries, that did not begin to turn around in the US until 1933 when the government started to stimulate the economy by taking on huge levels of national debt.

We observe the time leading up to 1929 from the time machine, and are puzzled to see that throughout the 1920s, the Federal Reserve, following the revised Federal Reserve Act, had still created excessive sums of money leading to a stock market bubble.

Since we altered history, US banks were strictly prohibited from creating money and were only able to make loans with their clients' investment accounts.

As it turns out, instead of banks creating the bubble, as we remember from the roaring 20s, the Federal Reserve created the bubble this time round.

We soon realised that banks were simply creating money indirectly by influencing the Federal Reserve to create more and more money, which was pumped into the economy and people were speculating on stocks, driving up prices, and their investment accounts were booming.

The 1920s boom that we knew was coming before our adventure in time travel was happening again. Hundreds of thousands of Americans were investing heavily in the stock market and history was repeating itself, despite our reforms. A significant number of people were borrowing money to buy more stocks. Speculation fuelled further rises and created the same economic bubble that we know from the history books.

We knew what was coming next and sure enough, the market turned down, and panic selling started. The great crash of 1929 was happening all over again, right in front of our eyes.

We had failed to prevent it, so we jump back into the time machine to see if the Great Depression was still to follow.

We land in 1933 and many of the banks that went bust in the Great Depression, before we altered history, were still around, so we had prevented something.

As the banks were not able to create money and their clients' current and investment accounts were completely separate, rather than going bust, the banks only suffered bad losses, but nothing serious enough to threaten their solvency.

While this is a much better result than the Great Depression that occurred prior to our time travel, we still had more adjustments to make to the banking almanac.

To create our stable financial system, still more reforms were needed and 1844 was an inevitable destination for us once again.

Firstly, we learnt that it is not enough to stop banks from creating money and make banks inform their depositors that their money was going to be invested. They also had to disclose what they were actually going to do with that money. If they were going to use that money to fund loans for others to speculate on the stock markets, then we must be made aware.

Secondly, the Federal Reserve and the Bank of England were in fact private banks and were by no means independent of all the other private banks. So we needed to fix the collusion between the banks and the central banks to truly make the system stable.

As we are from the future, we know that the Bank of England is due for nationalisation in 1946, and in 1997 it will become an independent public organisation, wholly owned by the Treasury Solicitor on behalf of the government, with independence in money creation policies.

We also know that the Federal Reserve still to this day remains questionably private.

Perhaps if we update the banking almanac once again to emphasise the importance of an independent nationalised Bank of England and highlight the importance of making it compulsory for banks to disclose to customers what the money in their investment accounts will be used for, we can finally reach a stable financial system.

So rather than wait for the future change to the Bank of England's legal structure, we set about helping history and adjusting our banking almanac once again to influence Sir Robert Peel to make further reforms in the 1844 Bank Charter Act.

Our goal is to make the Bank of England independent of political and banking influence.

Again, we figured that if the Federal Reserve Act was drafted using the British financial system, we could prevent the Federal

Reserve from remaining private and exporting the UK's unsustainable financial system across the world.

We redraft our banking almanac with forecasts on the effects of transparency with customers' investment accounts and the importance of an independent Bank of England, free of political influence and banking influence.

Can we really trust the Bank of England to create money?

History shows we cannot trust the banks nor politicians with the responsibility of money creation.

Figure 26 The battle over who can be trusted with the power to create money

Most bankers have no idea that they are creating money when they issue loans, but they always have an incentive to make one decision – lend. It is for this very reason that we must take away their power to create money, so they can get on with the business of making loans, without the added responsibly of creating money. The conflict of interest is far too great.

On the flip side, if you are the president or prime minister and students are rioting, setting fire to your building outside your window because you have cut their student fee grants, it is too tempting to create more money to end the rioting. Or indeed, to create money to fund a war.

History has also proven that it is too tempting to create excessive money leading up to an election to make the economy appear healthier than it is. Politics should never be mixed with money creation. Again the history books have shown that politicians cannot be trusted with money creation.

The only solution is to separate the decision between how much new money is created and how that money is spent.

The only way we can reach stability in our financial system is to give the money creation power to an independent body, e.g. the Bank of England in the UK, run by an independent Monetary Policy Committee.

With our new Bank Charter Act, rather than trying to control how much money banks create by pushing interest rates up and down, the Bank of England now simply decides how much new money should be put into the economy.

It's that simple.

1. Monetary Policy Committee Creates Debt Free Money Based On Inflation / Deflation Targets Only

2. New Debt Free Money Is Gifted To The Treasury

3. Treasury Spends Debt Free Money Into The Economy To Pay Down The National Debt, Reduce Taxes & On Normal Public Expenditure

4. People Deposit Their Money In Their Risk Free Current Accounts

5. Banks Only Use Clients Investment Account To Invest In Products The Client Is Happy With, Sharing The Risk

Figure 27 The money creation process after our new Bank Charter Act reforms

There can be no political influence from government. There can be no connection between the board of the Monetary Policy Committee and elected politicians looking to get re-elected. The Committee is, however, to be made accountable to parliament.

This way we have complete transparency over how much money is created. To make everything transparent, decisions about money are announced publicly and meetings are published. For the first time in history information about the control of money will be out in the open.

So back in the time machine we go. Armed with another updated banking almanac, to 1844 again.

Slipping the new banking almanac into Sir Robert Peel's pile of research papers again, we prepare for our journey back to the future to see if Sir Robert adds our new recommendations into the Bank Charter Act.

To infinity and beyond ...

We watch our new timeline as we travel back to the future, noticing that our financial system for the first time in history is stable. I jot down in my notepad the 'three commandments' of banking reform:

1 Thou shalt make the banks ask depositors permission before they lend.

2 Thou shalt make the banks disclose to the depositors how they use their money.

3 Thou shalt give the licence to create money to a democratic power.

As I read through the Bank Charter Act after our third trip back to 1844, we notice that Sir Robert followed our three commandments and made it compulsory for banks to disclose what banks invest in using our investment accounts.

With these three commandments all written into the Bank Charter Act we travel beyond the present to see the future of our economy with a completely stable financial system.

I notice that as a direct result of banks having to disclose how they invest our money from our investment accounts, that the investment priorities of the bank now reflect the investment priorities of society as a whole, rather than simply the short-term interest of banks.

Under the three commandments and the new Bank Charter Act, I step into my bank of the future.

Before I agree to allocate my money to my investment account, I am given a list of possibilities that the money will be used for in the terms and conditions and investment account brochure.

I decide that I don't want to invest in the creation of weapons for war, the oil industry and some of the loans that involve buying up developing world assets.

I am happy for the banks to fund loans that invest in renewable energy, microfinance, organic farming and fair trade companies. Knowing that my investment is ethical makes me feel better about saving.

With every loan, banks share the risk with depositors and for each investment decision the banks need to find people that are willing to fund particular activities. We start to see considerably less money going to war and much more money moving to eco-friendly social enterprises.

Giving the licence to create money to the independent Bank of England opens up a whole new world of possibility.

The US copies our sustainable financial system and the rest of the world follows.

A whole new world ...

Before our adventure in time travel, the UK Treasury only profited from the creation of paper money and coins.

A £10 note was sold to banks for £10 and it only cost the Bank of England three pence to make the paper note. The £9.97 was profit and was handed over to the Treasury. This money was added to tax revenue, reducing the amount of tax we needed to pay.

Between 2000 and 2010 the UK profit from paper money creation was around £18 billion, which is £18 billion less UK taxpayers had to pay.

Since we gave our banking almanac to Sir Robert Peel, following our changes, the UK received an extra £2.1 trillion in revenue since 1844. This is the amount of money that banks created when they had their licence to create money.

So we now benefit from the creation of all money, rather than just paper notes.

By the way, that's £2.1 trillion that prior to the time travel, the UK taxpayers had to pay to the banks, simply because they had this privilege of creating money.

Now, for the first time in history, we are able to see who is creating money and how that money is being used.

As we travel to the future beyond 2050, we see a couple of scandals where excessive money was created, but it is quickly resolved as the controls over money are so much easier to manage. The Monetary Policy Committee is completely accountable to the public and parliament, it is very easy to point blame as the system is so much more transparent and easy to understand.

As profits from money creation are now added to tax revenue, we observe the future as the government uses the money that used to be spent on speculation and bankers' bonuses to reduce taxes, reduce down the national debt and use it for new spending projects.

Travelling further and further into the future, we observe falling debt and poverty, reduced inequality, significantly less power from banks, increased quality of living, a reduction in third world debt, funding for the environmental crisis and a stable environment for business.

One of the most exciting innovations we see is the growth of the non-banking sector where banking is fully democratised and ordinary people actually become millions of tiny banks, as we discuss in Chapters 8, 9 and 10, even serving the third world that financial institutions of the past would never touch.

This future where people become banks was made possible through seven hugely disruptive technologies that truly brought power to the people. These very same technologies will pay an all important role in your future too.

There are two reasons why I spend the rest of Part 2 accounting extraordinary events from entrepreneurs that have led to the abundance brought about by our future economy of freedom.

Firstly, I want you to understand that we live in a time like no other and that you can protect your future even as the government continues allowing banks to create money leading to the eventual collapse of our financial system.

Before the collapse, you can live in the economy of freedom if you use these seven technologies.

When the collapse happens, many will struggle as they are not prepared for the change ahead. If you understand how to use these seven hugely disruptive technologies from the next seven chapters, then as long as there is an internet connection, poverty does not have to be a part of your future and you will prosper during the collapse.

People will look to you for guidance and leadership as you are one of the few that will know how to adjust to the huge change a financial collapse will bring about.

You will not need to panic during the transition from the debt trap of 'free'dom to the economy of freedom. You understand that money is a human creation, invented to serve and that there is a way to bring money back to its original intention, to serve rather than us serving money, as many do today.

And now you know how to fix our broken system, if you buy the banking reforms that we implemented together in our adventure in time travel, you just need to prepare for both the debt trap of 'free'dom and the economy of freedom, as you may be alive for both.

Secondly, I want you to build your social capital.

Whether we continue in the debt trap of 'free'dom for many years to come, as we continue to patch up the Ponzi scheme for a bit longer with schemes like quantitative easing (the process by which the government goes into deeper debt to the central bank, rather than a central bank creating the money debt-free and adding it to tax revenues), or we transition into the economy of freedom quickly, it is my belief that these seven technologies will be the key to your prosperity in both the debt trap of 'free'dom and the economy of freedom.

I want you to feel the liberation that I feel every day knowing that no matter what happens, there are challenges ahead, but everything will work out for you if you are prepared and armed with the social capital that these seven technologies will allow you to own – forget gold, social capital will be your greatest asset.

Social capital is a concept that far too few understand and it is the asset of the future that will protect you and the ones you care about whatever happens in the future.

It is because I understand these seven technologies and I have integrated them into the DNA of my life and daily routine that I have no fear or worry for myself, my wife, my family, my friends and those who are connected with me through all my social networks.

Your network of connections will allow you to prepare for anything. The collective brainpower of your network will be your strength. By connecting we can both be a part of what I believe will be each other's most prized possession of the future – our social capital. More on what this is, how it became so important and how to build yours in the next seven chapters.

To fully understand what social capital is, and how you can build yours, it requires you to understand and start using the seven technologies to their full potential.

The biggest lie you have ever been told

After completing a Masters in economics, I was taught that we live in a world of scarce resources, where there is not enough and resources will run out.

Technological innovation (and that just means a process or innovation that improves our ability to get something done) changes scarcity.

We are told that oil will run out. Good: for the last decade we have been working on technological innovation that will replace the need for oil, work better and be more sustainable for our planet.

Figure 28 Technological innovation replacing scarcity

We are told that there is only so much land in the world, then somebody comes along and creates the skyscraper, allowing us to live further up in the sky.

History is full of examples where scarce resources are replaced by new technology removing the scarcity we were told to fear.

This is hard to take in when you think of those in poverty, those in starvation and those in financial crisis right now. The reason they live in a life of scarcity is because they do not have access to information and the speed at which they can process information is too slow.

For somebody to move out of an economy of scarcity to an economy of abundance where resources are limitless, they must have fast access to information that they can process faster than anybody else.

It is time to give that information to all and undo the belief that resources are fixed at a certain point in scarcity. And today we can thank seven hugely disruptive technologies for giving us this speed of information.

With these seven technologies and the introduction of our new Bank Charter Act, the debt trap of 'free'dom can be fully transformed into simply an economy of freedom.

Before we look at our future choices and how we can prepare for both worlds in Part 3, we now leave the financial system aside, and turn our attention to the seven hugely disruptive technologies which have given us such abundance.

In the chapters that follow we investigate how each of the seven technologies have come together to produce what could be the most abundant time in history. We look individually at the history of each technology that will contribute to the economy of freedom.

What led to the rise of the non-banking sector?

What is social capital and why should you care?

How did people become millions of little banks?

And what are the seven hugely disruptive technologies that are going to protect your future?

It is with these seven technologies that those with an internet connection can share that abundance with those who do not have access to the vast information made possible by the rise of hugely disruptive technology #1 – the World Wide Web.

Hold on! Before you start Chapter 5, tweet me your thoughts on our adventure in time travel – #BankToTheFuture.

QR 14 Tweet Simon Dixon about #BankToTheFuture

---

1   O'Donoghue, J.et al. (2004). 'Consumer Price Inflation since 1750'. Economic Trends 604: 38–46, March.

2   Weedon, A.Victorian Publishing: The Economics of Book Production for a Mass Market 1836-1916 (2003), Ashgate, pp. 47-48ISBN 0-7546-3527-9

5 Hugely disruptive technology #1 – the World Wide Web

BEFORE WE START, take a look at the introductory video.

Scan QR Code and watch video!

You Tube

Can't scan? http://bit.ly/r0NI7W

QR 15 Introductory video on the hugely disruptive technology #1

NOTE: If you are manually typing the above URL, the first 'l' in the URL is a lower case 'L' and the second 'I' is a capital 'i'. Also the first 'o' in the URL is the number zero rather than a capital 'o'.

It is now time to understand the roots of the only asset that will protect your future and allow you to live in abundance in both the debt trap of 'free'dom and the economy of freedom.

The ability to build your social capital began with the rise of the World Wide Web.

With our reforms complete, and our financial system stable, we now travel forward in time through to the 21st century. We watch the birth of disruptive technology after disruptive technology. Each technology brings us one step closer to a future of abundance and freedom.

Every innovation creates a new, unexpected market. One by one, each disruptive technology invades established markets, bringing with it new possibilities.

Due to our reforms, we are not plagued by boom and bust caused by the creation and destruction of money by banks. In this future, we have more say over where our money goes.

All future innovations are funded to reflect the appetite of society as a whole. In this future, as we start to feel the effects of innovations on our society and environment, brought about by disruptive technologies, less funding is made available when the public is made more aware of the social impact of such technologies.

While funding still goes to socially harmful companies and innovations, many invest with more than just profit in mind, or at the very least, are made aware of the social impact of their deposits in their investment accounts, to help them in deciding where funds are invested.

With a stable economy, we watch the birth of the industrial revolution, characterised by developments in textile manufacturing, mining, metals and transport, all driven by the development of the steam engine and cheap energy in the form of coal.

As we pass the 19th century, we see developments in transportation, construction, and communication technologies, with the birth of the steamboat and railway transportation.

We watch the second industrial revolution at the end of the 19th century with the rapid development of chemicals, electronics, petroleum, and steel technologies connected with highly structured technology and scientific research.

We watch radio and sound recording pave the way for the telephone, fax machine, and magnetic storage of data.

The list of disruptive technologies goes on and on.

As we progress and learn more about the social impact of each technology, people allocate their investment accounts to reflect their values and beliefs.

This causes new innovative disruptive technologies that reflect the values and beliefs of society to prevail over others.

Then the major catalyst for change under our new stable economy is born.

With it comes the complete democratisation of information and the media, it makes information available to all, allowing everybody to have access to anything or anybody. Everybody and everything becomes fully connected, bringing with it the opportunity to choose and the opportunity to learn about anything. It removes barriers to achieving financial freedom for anybody with an internet connection.

The rise of the World Wide Web is a story of remarkable change.

Figure 29 What would you do without the internet?

As we travel forward in time and broadband internet access becomes commonplace in developed countries, we see an exponential increase in the standard of living.

The major change we see this time, however, since our journey back in time to reform the Bank Charter Act, is in the developing world.

Due to our non-debt based monetary system, the emerging world is not forced into debt poverty and all countries worldwide are given equal opportunity to invest in infrastructure to make the World Wide Web available for all without going deeper and deeper into debt.

Rather than money redistributing to the banking sector, it is spent in the economy to fund many development projects, without the additional interest and debt, making its way through to the productive economy.

But most importantly, the funding needed for the ability of all to access the internet. An economy of abundance is characterised by the speed at which information can be accessed and processed. There is no greater gift you can give somebody than increasing their access to information and the speed at which they can process that information.

With the internet, the possibilities are endless.

It also paved the way for a non-banking financial sector revolution that brought financial opportunities to those who in the past were traditionally non-banked, who were cast aside by the old financial system.

Why did the World Wide Web have such a significant impact on opportunity, democracy and finance? Well, let's take a look at its creation.

The rise of the World Wide Web

It's 1980. Tim Berners-Lee, an independent contractor at the European Organization for Nuclear Research (CERN), Switzerland, is due to start on his latest innovative project.

CERN was set up to host the world's largest laboratory focused entirely on particle physics, an area of physics that deals with subatomic particles like electrons, protons, neurons and other 'physics things' that go over the head of most of us.

At that time approximately 10,000 people were working at CERN with different hardware, software and individual requirements[1]. The scientists working at CERN needed to keep track of their research as more and more projects within the laboratory became involved with each other.

Berners-Lee was appointed by CERN for six months on 23 June 1980 to develop a solution. He was appointed to set up a new system that allowed compatibility with different networks, disk formats, data formats, and character encoding schemes within the lab.

The system that evolved was never intended to be released to the general public, but six months later ENQUIRE was born as a network to connect all the scientists at CERN. The ENQUIRE system turned out to be the precursor to the World Wide Web.

After a successful launch of ENQUIRE, and having completed his six months, Berners-Lee later returned to CERN in 1984 and started on a more ambitious project to connect physicists that needed to share data all around the world.

The vision was to create a system with no common machines and no common presentation software that all physicians could access. He wrote a proposal in March 1989. His boss, Mike Sendall, encouraged Berners-Lee to begin building his system after suggesting some modifications. He considered several names for the creation that evolved, but later settled on the name 'World Wide Web'.

Six years later, by Christmas 1990, Berners-Lee had built all the tools necessary for a working web as we know today: the HyperText Transfer Protocal (HTTP), the HyperText Markup Language(HTML), the first Web Browser (named WorldWideWeb, which was also a web editor), the first HTTP server software, the first web server (http://info.cern.ch), and the first web pages that described the project itself[2].

The World Wide Web was born as a system to connect the work of scientists across the world.

It soon became clear that the idea was useful outside of the science laboratory and a series of innovations made it a system that could be used and adapted by all.

The vision for a World Wide Web of information for all was initially slow to take off, but the first tipping point came with the introduction of a web browser called Mosaic. Mosaic was backed by a funding program initiated by then-Senator Al Gore called the Gore Bill[3]. Mosaic went down in history as the world's first popular web browser. It made the World Wide Web system easy to use and more accessible to the average person.

Marc Andreesen, the founder of Mosaic, had sparked an internet boom in the 1990s due to the simplicity and usability of his Mosaic browser. Andreessen and James H. Clark, former CEO of Silicon Graphics, later founded Mosaic Communications

Corporation, with the goal of developing a Mosaic browser for popular commercial use by all. In 1994, the company changed its name to Netscape and its flagship product Netscape Navigator took off big.

The browser wars

Figure 30 The browser wars

Microsoft had stood on the side watching Netscape, as Bill Gates had dismissed personal use of the World Wide Web as a passing fad. But Microsoft finally entered the web browser market with Internet Explorer in August 1995, after seeing the global popularity and acceptance of Netscape.

This began what was known as the browser war – the fight for the web browser market between Microsoft and Netscape. This war put the web in the hands of millions of ordinary users, as both Microsoft and Netscape tried to gain an edge over each other by adding features and improving their browsers general usability.

By 1996, Netscape's share of the browser market had reached 86%, with Internet Explorer moving up to 10%[4]. But then Microsoft began a series of strategic moves, aimed at taking valuable market share in the web browser market.

The tables turned when Microsoft integrated internet Explorer with its Windows operating system, and within two years the balance had reversed. Internet Explorer for Mac was also the default browser prior to Mac entering the browser war with it's own offering - Safari, after launching operating system Mac OS X.

The browser war effectively ended once it was clear that Netscape's declining market share was not about to reverse. Unable to continue commercially funding Netscape's product development, they responded by open sourcing their product, creating Mozilla, for non-commercial use to be openly developed by all. The name came from the words "Mosaic killer", hinting that Netscape would be the end of the early browser, Mosaic.

Opening the browser to all developers helped it to maintain its technical edge over Internet Explorer, but did not slow Netscape's declining market share due to Microsoft's integration with Windows. Netscape was later purchased by America Online in late 1998.

By 1996 it had become obvious to most publicly traded companies that a public web presence was no longer optional as the web took off.

From 1998 to 1999, start-up capital going towards internet based companies boomed, giving birth to the company called a 'dot-com'.

The dot-com boom and bust

A dot-com company was the name given to a company that did most of its business on the internet using the popular domain, '.com' derived from the word 'commercial'. Investors were throwing money at dot-coms and investment bankers were bringing companies to public with nothing more than a dot-com idea.

This investment frenzy was also met by a period of low interest rates by central banks in order to stimulate debt created money by private banks, fueling mass money creation, translating into a stock market bubble.

Although a number of these new entrepreneurs had realistic plans and technical ability, most of them were only able to sell their ideas to investors because of the novelty of the dot-com concept.

Figure 31 The dot com boom

After huge price inflation of dot-com stocks, the bubble finally burst in 2001, as many dot-com startups went out of business after burning through their venture capital and failing to become profitable.

There were thousands of failed companies from the dot-com bubble, but a few that stand out included CyberRebate, which promised customers a 100% rebate after purchasing products priced at nearly ten times the retail cost, DigiScents, that tried to transmit smells over the internet with Whoopi Goldberg as their spokesperson and Flooz.com, who created an 'e-currency' that later crashed due to a basic lack of necessity.

Several companies and their executives were accused or convicted of fraud for misusing shareholders' money, and the Securities and Exchange Commission fined top investment firms like Citigroup and Merrill Lynch millions of dollars for misleading investors.

But from the aftermath of the crash, came a handful of dot-com companies that would change our lives forever – most notably Amazon.com's online department store (founded by Jeff Bezos in 1994), eBay.com's do-it-yourself auction site (founded by Pierre Omidyar in 1995), Paypal.com (resulting from a March 2000 merger between Confinity and X.com) and search engines Google.com (founded by Larry Page and Sergey Brin in 1998) and Yahoo.com (founded by Jerry Yang and David Filo in January 1994).

As the World Wide Web's usage reached record highs, sites such as Wikipedia proved revolutionary, bringing user edited content to the web and paving the way for the 'free' economy discussed in Chapter 3.

But the browser war was also running parallel to another battle for dominance over what would soon become a multi-billion turnover market – the 'search' market.

The search wars

During the early development of the web, there was a list of websites edited manually by Tim Berners-Lee himself. As more websites went online, the task became a huge administrative job and the central list could not keep up. To combat this, in 1990 Alan Emtage, Bill Heelan and J. Peter Deutsch founded the very first tool used for searching on the Internet, called Archie.

The tool downloaded the directory listings of all the files located on public anonymous sites, creating a searchable database of file names. This was shortly followed by a series of early search tools, each building on the last.

Despite many innovations, by the summer of 1993, no reliable search engine existed yet, beyond a database of files, though numerous specialised catalogues were maintained by hand. But later that year, the first search engines were launched. Due to the limited resources available on the platforms on which they ran, its searches were, however, limited.

In 1994, one of the first search engines was called WebCrawler. Unlike its predecessors, it let users search for any word in any webpage, which became the standard for all major search engines today. It was also the first search engine to become widely known by the public.

Soon after, many search engines appeared and battled for popularity. Yahoo! was one of the births and it soon became one of the most popular ways for people to find web pages, but it still had many search limitations.

In 1996, with the popularity of the Netscape web browser, Netscape sought a single search engine for an exclusive deal to be the featured search engine on their browser. There was so much interest that instead, a deal was struck with Netscape by five of the major search engines, where for $5 million per year each search engine would be in a rotation on the Netscape search engine page. The five engines were Yahoo!, Magellan, Lycos, Infoseek, and Excite.

Search engines were also some of the brightest stars in the Internet investing frenzy that occurred in the late 1990s leading up to the dot-com boom and bust.

Around 2000, a new player called Google was able to achieve better results for many searches with an innovation called PageRank. The Google team developed an algorithm that ranked web pages based on the number and PageRank of other web sites and pages that link back to them, on the premise that good or desirable pages are linked to more than others. Google also maintained a minimalist interface to its search engine.

Due to the superiority of the search results that Google's search engine produced, Yahoo! even switched to Google's search engine right up until 2004. It later launched its own search engine based on the combined technologies of its acquisition spree that it was going through at the time.

With the sheer scale of the World Wide Web, by 2004, Microsoft began to transition MSN search to its own search technology, eventually rebranding to Bing in 2009. On July 29, 2009, Yahoo! and Microsoft finalised a deal in which Yahoo! Search would be powered by Microsoft Bing technology.

But nothing could hold down the almighty power of Google's algorithm and the accuracy of its search results.

As of 2011, Google enjoys close to 83% of search traffic, followed by Yahoo! with approximately 6%[5].

The phrase "search the internet for it" has now been replaced by the words "Google it".

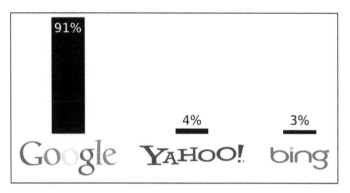

Figure 32 The three most widely used web search engines and their approximate share as of late 2010[6].

Great story, but what does this mean for me?

The economy of freedom, described in Chapter 1, was made possible thanks to those who played their role in the rise of the World Wide Web. It also gave rise to the free economy, discussed in Chapter 3, forcing many from employment into entrepreneurship.

If you are not living in the economy of freedom, preparing yourself for the major shift brought about by the free economy, then it is my belief that you will need to start looking into what your future will look like urgently.

Because of the World Wide Web, we now live in a time like no other as the next six hugely disruptive technologies were all built on its shoulders.

The web came just in time, as we start to see the end of our debt trap as we know it.

While it also brought with it money creation on steroids from banks when the ability to apply for loans on the web ballooned, it gave rise to the very same six innovations that will democratise finance for the world when we transition from the debt trap of 'free'dom to the economy of freedom as the banking system tumbles before reform.

For me, its most important creation was the ability it gave to all to build social capital. To understand more about social capital it is necessary to read the story of the rise the other hugely disruptive technologies in the next few chapters.

So before we go into how you can start investing in your social capital it is also worth pointing out the huge impact it had on financial services.

So how did the World Wide Web democratise finance?

The mainstreet adoption of personal home computers, the birth of the internet, the creation of the World Wide Web, the innovation of web browsers and the opportunities brought about by search engines has given birth to a wave of disruptive technologies that will make funding and investing available to all who have the ability to access the World Wide Web.

To understand how this chain of innovations built upon each other, leading to us all having the ability to act as bankers, venture capitalists and raise funds for our entrepreneurial ventures, secured through our social capital, we need to look deeper into the birth of the other six hugely disruptive technologies.

From the World Wide Web came the rise of: digital money (Chapter 6); the social networks (Chapter 7); crowdfunding (Chapter 8); person-to-person lending (Chapter 9); microfinance platforms (Chapter 10); and the smart phone (Chapter 11).

It is my belief that with a full appreciation of how you can integrate such technologies into your life, the banking crash ahead will be less painful for you and the ones that you care about, and after reform, will be the very technologies that allow you to flourish in the economy of freedom ahead.

Whatever happens to the debt trap, whatever happens in the free economy, building your social capital using these seven hugely disruptive technologies will allow you to live in an economy like never before.

So let's take a look at the rise of the next hugely disruptive technology – the rise of digital money.

Hold on! Before you start Chapter 6, tweet me your thoughts on the #WorldWideWeb.

QR 16 Tweet Simon Dixon about #WorldWideWeb

1 "Tim Berners-Lee: client". W3.org. Retrieved July 27, 2009.
2 "Tim Berners-Lee: client". W3.org. Retrieved July 27, 2009
3 "Vice President Al Gore's ENIAC Anniversary Speech". Cs.washington.edu. February 14, 1996. Retrieved July 27, 2009
4 History of the web browser, Wikipedia contributors, //en.wikipedia.org/w/index.php?title=History_of_the_web_browser&oldid=455042572
5 comScore Releases November 2009 U.S. Search Engine Rankings". December 16, 2006. Retrieved July 5, 2010 / 2011
6 StatCounter. Retrieved 17 January 2011.

6 Hugely disruptive technology #2 – digital money

YOU MIGHT LIKE to take a look at the introductory video before we start this exploration.

QR 17 Introductory video on hugely disruptive technology #2

NOTE: If you are manually typing the above URL, the first 'l' in the URL is a lower case 'L' and the second 'l' is also a lower case 'L', not a capital 'i'.

Travelling in time to observe the rise of digital money is an adventure that spans thousands of years, from its origins in trade, to the rise of gold, to plastic fantastic, to digital computer money, to Facebook credits and beyond.

But to understand our future, we have to first understand the rise of digital money.

Both the debt trap of 'free'dom and our new economy of freedom, following our Bank Charter Act reforms, in essence, are simply results of a debate about what the hell money is.

We can only understand how we have found ourselves in today's extraordinary times and how to handle tomorrow by travelling to the key monetary times in history.

Debate about the nature of money has raged for thousands of years; each form of money gave birth to another form.

Like the typewriter gave way to the word processor, which gave way to the personal computer, which gave way to the laptop, which is giving way to the smart phone, all leading to the inevitable destination where everyone and everything is available anytime, anywhere, money has evolved over thousands of years to reach an inevitable destination.

Humans gave birth to trade, trade gave birth to money, humans decided that precious metals like gold were good forms of money, gold as money gave birth to the safe storage of gold, the safe storage of gold gave birth to the bank, the bank gave birth to the creation of paper based on debt, the computer gave birth to digital money, the internet put digital money creation on steroids, the World Wide Web democratised money for those who could log on, the mobile phone allowed money to flow through developing countries, money gave birth to scientific research, science gave birth to biometric payments. Our adventure in time travel back to 1844 made money sustainable – but where does this journey end?

What is money's inevitable destination?

Well, to understand that, we need to understand how money got to where it is today and the rise of hugely disruptive technology #2 – digital money.

The mission...

First off, I set myself three rules in writing this chapter.

My first rule is to keep everything on money relevant to things we can all find interesting and that will actually matter to us all.

My second rule is to do this without you needing a PhD in economics and finance. After mastering in economics, spending years in banking, watching countless documentaries, interviewing hundreds of academics, bankers, economists and politicians, running training courses for future bankers, setting up businesses in the banking sector and reading hundreds of books on economics, money, finance and banking, unfortunately I have inevitably picked up a stupid amount of jargon that should never be used in the real world.

My third and final rule is to break through all the clutter and to do this in just one chapter.

It would be far too easy for me to spin off on tangents and write 57 chapters on this subject, but for those of you who are not as geeky as me when it comes to monetary history, it might bore you to tears.

This book was always meant to give you practical steps to prepare you for your future, rather than a history book alone.

My mission is to condense enough history on money into this one chapter, so you are armed with the tools to understand how to prepare for your future.

So with those rules in mind, feel free to connect with me on any of the social networks and tell me if I have succeeded or failed after you read this chapter.

In fact, to make it easy for you, you can connect with me here: On Twitter:

QR 18 Follow Simon Dixon on Twitter

On LinkedIn:

QR 19 Connect with Simon Dixon on LinkedIn

On Facebook:

QR 20 Add Simon Dixon as a friend on Facebook

On BankToTheFuture.com:

QR 21 Connect with Simon Dixon on BankToTheFuture.com

But just before we do that, let's look at the great debate.

The great debate – just what the hell is money?

If you pick up any text book or search Wikipedia, you will find money defined as something like this:

> "Any object or record that is generally accepted as payment for goods, services and repayment of debts. The main functions of money are distinguished as a medium of exchange, a unit of account and a store of value."[1]

This is the bit that bores me to death too, but there are literally hundreds of papers, books, blogs and journals that pull this definition apart.

But let's cast aside the boring bits, and look at the action part. The debates and consequences of these seemingly harmless definitions are actually stories of war, assassination, corruption, crisis and the very reason why you are fortunate if you are one of the few that is not maxed out on your credit cards right now.

There are really only three debates to settle:

1. Who controls money (or creates it)?

2. Does money need to be a store of value (like gold)? Or can money derive its value from law (like a dollar bill or the balance you see on your online banking computer screen)?

3. How is money created?

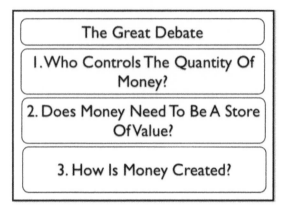

Figure 33 The three questions of the great debate about money

Our current system does not work, but currently money is almost entirely created by commercial banks; it derives its value from law and it is created almost entirely by people, companies and governments going deep into debt to the commercial banks.

So what does this debate actually mean to you, why it is important and how the hell did we get here?

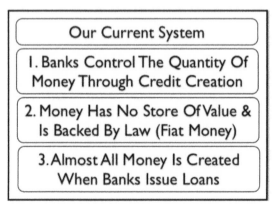

Figure 34 Money creation in most countries in 2011

Debate 1: Money rules the world, but who rules the money?

In Stephen Zarlenga's 'Lost Science of Money' he writes "Define money as wealth, and the 'wealthy' will be in control. Define it as credit, as is done today, and the 'lenders' will be in control. Define it as legal power and government will control it...".

Going with that, the debate is really one of 'control'.

Do we want the wealthy to control it, the banks to control it, the government to control it, or none of the above?

To settle this debate we turn to history.

Figure 35 The battle over who controls money

Debate 2 : Do I really need to hide gold bars under my mattress?

Many believe that money has to return to its roots as commodity money (like the gold standards of the past).

Today, nearly all money systems are based on what is called fiat money.

Fiat money is without intrinsic value like a physical commodity such as gold, but instead derives its value by being declared by a government to be legal tender; that is, it must be accepted as a form of payment within the boundaries of the country, for all debts, public and private and for the payment of taxes.

Stephen Zarlenga summarises this debate as the Adam Smith vs. Aristotle debate.

In Adam Smith's 'Wealth of Nations', Smith refers to money as follows:

> "By the money price of goods it is to be observed, I understand always, the quantity of our gold or silver for which they are sold, without any regard to denomination of the coin".

In other words, money is worth what it is made of and its weight.

On the other side of the debate Aristotle said that "Money exists not by nature but by law".

In other words, if our government tells us it has value and makes it valuable by law, it is money, and we do not need to find money by digging for commodities in mines and farms.

So to find out who was right, in this chapter we look at the history of money.

Debate 3: How is money created?

Well, unbelievably, almost all economists think that creating money as debt and controlling it indirectly by manipulating the cost of borrowing by sending people deeper into debt followed by bankruptcy, created by commercial banks, is the best way to create money.

I challenge anybody to design a money system from scratch and come up with that solution. Nobody would, but that is where we are today and it is not even debated by politicians any more.

It used to be a great debate between bankers and politicians.

So to settle the debates, in this chapter we take a quick look at money over time from shells to PayPal to implanted chips, and then we can get on with looking at our futures as more disruptive technologies evolve.

So fasten your seat belt, this is going to be a quick journey through monetary time.

We will then return and put an end to the great debate at the end of this chapter.

So what did we do before money?

Before money there was barter, where goods or services are directly exchanged for other goods or services without using a medium of exchange such as money.

If you wanted a sheep, you needed to find somebody that had a sheep and was willing to exchange their sheep for whatever you could offer.

If the two of you agreed, you had a deal.

Figure 36 A barter exchange

The use of barter-like methods dates back to at least 100,000 years ago, though there is no evidence of a society or economy that relied primarily on barter.

Instead, non-monetary societies operated largely along the principles of a gift economy, where goods or services are regularly given without any explicit agreement for immediate or future rewards.

And of course there was barbarianism, as there is today. "Give it to me, or I will kill you."

To make trade easier, many cultures around the world eventually developed the use of commodity money instead of relying on barter, gift and barbarian economies.

Early money included shekels (a specific weight of barley) and societies in the Americas, Asia, Africa and Australia used shell money.

People sold goods or services for shekels, shells or commodities, knowing that they could spend them on other goods or services later.

Money was born.

So when did we stop using shells and start using gold?

According to Heredotus, an ancient Greek historian, the inhabitants of Lydia were the first people to introduce the use of gold and silver coins.

It is thought by modern scholars that these first coins were minted around 650–600 BC[2].

From then on, commodity money, the value of which comes from the commodity out of which it is made, gradually became the global form of money.

The theory was that the objects had value in themselves as well as for use as money, so if anything went wrong they could still use the money for something else.

While today money has no value other than by law, during the time of hyperinflation in Germany, money was actually used to keep fireplaces burning and warm their homes when it became worthless.

But apart from fuel, commodity money had value other than simply being money as it is today.

Examples of commodities that have been used as mediums of exchange over the years include gold, silver, copper, peppercorns, large stones, decorated belts, shells, alcohol, cigarettes, cannabis, candy, barley – the list goes on.

But eventually we settled on gold and silver.

So how did gold become paper?

People wanted somewhere safe to store their gold.

Gold merchants (or banks) would offer a safe storage place for their gold and in exchange issue receipts to claim their gold deposits.

Eventually, these receipts became generally accepted as a means of payment and were used as money.

Private banknotes were first issued in Europe by Stockholms Banco, a Swedish bank, in 1661, and were used as money alongside coins[3].

Way before private banknotes, however, was government-issued paper money. This was born in China during the Song Dynasty, between 960 and 1279[4].

China was the first government in world history to issue its own paper money.

These banknotes, known as 'jiaozi', did not displace commodity money; they were used alongside coins and later privately created banknotes.

So what exactly happened to gold?

Out of the co-existence of banknotes and commodity money, came the 'gold standard'.

The gold standard was a monetary system where paper notes were made convertible into pre-set, fixed quantities of gold.

This standard replaced the use of gold coins as currency in the 17th-19th centuries in Europe. These gold standard notes were made legal tender, and redemption into gold coins was discouraged.

By the beginning of the 20th century almost all countries had adopted the gold standard, backing their legal tender notes with fixed amounts of gold.

So how can I exchange my money for a fixed quantity of gold?

Well, you can't any more.

After World War II, at the Bretton Woods conference, most countries adopted fiat currencies that were fixed to the US dollar.

While the convertibility of paper money into gold ended for most countries, the US dollar, however, remained fixed to gold.

In 1971 the US government was facing the fiscal consequences of an expensive war, so President Nixon suspended the convertibility of the US dollar into gold as its gold supplies were leaving their borders rapidly.

As a result, many countries de-pegged their currencies from the US dollar, and most of the world's currencies became unbacked by anything apart from the governments' fiat of legal tender and the ability to convert the money into goods via payment.

This was the birth of exchange rates as we know them today.

So, who creates all that money?

Well, out of this evolved two main forms of money – currency and commercial bank money.

Currency refers to physical objects generally accepted as a medium of exchange, like coins and banknotes of a particular government.

This makes up the physical aspect of a nation's money supply.

They are created by the government's central bank or mint. The profits from selling currency are added to tax revenues for the government to spend.

It is called 'seignorage'.

Still with me?

Since the end of the gold standard, the government declares this fiat currency to be legal tender, making it unlawful to not accept the currency as a means of repayment for all debts, public and private.

It is also illegal to counterfeit (i.e create your own) such currency.

The other part of a nation's money supply consists of bank deposits. This money can be created by anybody that has a commercial banking licence.

Bank deposits are what most of us use today, where withdrawals can be performed in person, via cheques or bank drafts, using ATMs to withdraw government created currency), or through online banking to access bank created money.

Commercial bank money, in legal jargon, is claims against financial institutions that can be used for the purchase of goods and services.

All commercial bank money consists of accounting entries on a computer system – it is digital.

So if commercial bank money is digital, how is that created?

Commercial bank money is created through a process called fractional-reserve banking.

This banking practice allows banks to promise all customers that they can get their money back whenever they want it, whilst actually only being able to pay back a fraction of their customers at the same time. This allows them to make loans even when they don't actually have the real money.

All these obligations are numbers in a computer that you see when you login to your online banking.

Commercial bank money differs from currency in three ways: firstly it is non-physical, as its existence is only reflected in the account ledgers of banks and other financial institutions; secondly, there is some element of risk that the claim will not be fulfilled if the financial institution becomes insolvent as they do not actually have the money; and thirdly, every bit of it is created through a loan and needs to be repaid plus interest.

The process of fractional-reserve banking has a cumulative effect of money creation by commercial banks, as it expands the money supply beyond what it would otherwise be with every new loan.

In a nutshell, it is created when you agree to take out a loan, and it makes up almost the entire money supply.

The money you borrow does not exist as somebody else's savings – it is simply created upon agreement of loan.

Because of this, the money supply of most countries is a huge multiple larger than the amount of currency created by the country's central bank.

In fact, currency is insignificant compared to the size of commercial bank money.

So how much money is created by the central bank and how much by commercial banks?

In modern economies, a tiny amount of the money supply is in physical currency.

For example, in December 2010 in the US, of the $8853.4 billion recorded money supply (known as M2 in the US), only $915.7 billion (about 10%) consisted of physical coins, paper money and central bank reserves. On their own, paper money and coins account for around 3 per cent[5].

As mentioned in Chapter 2, if the entire UK population all decided to go to the bank and ask for their money today, they could repay you only £71 for every £1000 in your account.

Before the 2007 financial crisis, they only had £12.50 to repay you.

So with commercial bank money becoming the dominant form of money, the banks started to rule the world by directing our nation's money supply.

Money was privatised.

In order for money to be created, somebody needed to go first into debt.

The banks created money by lending it to you and me, mainly secured by houses.

The banks created money by lending to businesses. The banks created tons of money by lending it to the government and everybody went deeper into debt to create the money the world needed to stimulate economic prosperity.

But there was one small problem: everybody was in debt, there was more debt than money, and with money being created as debt, the sheer weight of the debt meant that much of the interest could only be paid by people going even further into debt.

This is what is commonly known as a Ponzi scheme, named after Charles Ponzi, who became notorious in the early 1920s for running a fraudulent investment operation that paid returns to investors, not from any actual profit earned by the organisation, but from their own money or money paid by subsequent investors.

This Ponzi scheme model is the same scheme run by our government today, which pays interest on their debt, not from taxes, but by taking on more debt.

We needed a new way to make debt more accessible to all to keep our economic growth moving.

Remember, virtually all money is debt at this point, so we need to increase debt forever to prevent the collapse of the Ponzi scheme and sustain the illusion of economic growth.

So next, plastic came along to solve our problems.

Easy money for anything

With the vast majority of money now created as debt, the need to lend became essential for us to sustain our Ponzi scheme.

Up to this point, the easiest way for banks to create our money supply was to lend money secured by housing. Houses are not about to run away, so if the borrower could not repay their loan, at least the bank could take the house and sell it.

This became the banks' favourite method for increasing our money supply as it was very profitable and the politicians were happy as it created the illusion of economic prosperity.

This method of creating commercial bank money secured by housing was so popular that any country adopting this money creation process experienced soaring house prices.

This caused more people to want to speculate on the housing bubble and borrow more, making mortgages the dominant vehicle for money creation.

Figure 37 The housing bubble was a symptom of government policy and banks creating credit securing by housing

Couple this with the fact that this form of money creation was actively encouraged by the government which wanted everyone to own their own homes.

To encourage the process further, many governments formed banking partnerships to incentivise the adoption of mortgages, for example, in the US the biggest organisations were Freddie Mac and Fannie Mae.

But to continue the money creation process, as interest piled up, lending for housing was not enough.

Because money was debt, when people could not repay their debt, money would disappear from the economy as people defaulted on their mortgage repayments, causing boom and bust cycles where money was created through mortgages and disappearing through mortgage defaults.

Remember, money is now debt and we have to increase it to keep the Ponzi scheme alive.

So keep it alive we did, through plastic.

In 1958 Bank of America launched the BankAmericard that went on to become the first mainstream modern credit card.

In 1966, the ancestor of MasterCard was born when a group of California banks established Master Charge to compete with BankAmericard, which later became the Visa credit card issued by Visa Inc.

Also in 1966, Barclaycard launched the first credit card outside of the US in the UK.

Early credit cards in the US were mass-produced and mass-mailed unsolicited to bank customers who were thought to be good credit risks[6].

It turned out that these cards were also being mailed out to unemployables, drunks, and narcotics addicts as well as to good credit risk customers.

In 1970 due to the financial chaos that credit cards caused in the US, as people went on a spending spree they could not afford to repay, such mailings were outlawed, but not before 100 million credit cards had been issued into the US population[7].

Today, there are now countless variations on the basic credit card, including organisation-branded credit cards, corporate-user credit cards, store cards and so on.

To give you an idea of the number of credit card issuers, before floating on the stock market MasterCard Worldwide was a membership organisation owned by 25,000+ financial institutions that issued its card.

Credit card debt increased steadily ever since.

In 2011, the total US credit card debt stood at US$764.5 billion[8]; in the UK (March 2009); £64.7 billion[9], in Australia (2007) AUD$41 billion[10].

The money supply had risen significantly.

I love my plastic money, it is very convenient and currency smells …

As digital money became simply a function of debt, the combination of mortgagees and plastic credit cards issued by MasterCard and Visa became dominant vehicles for accessing money pools.

Freely available commercial bank money was not just used to speculate on property and fund retail therapy.

This easy credit also funded a wave of innovation – in fact, a wave of innovation that gave birth to alternative non-banks.

So before we put an end to the great debates on money, let's continue our journey in monetary history.

I don't want to deal with my bank anymore

The rise of digital debt money and plastic made exchanging goods and services easier than ever before, but with it came massive complications for banks.

Payments of commercial bank money and processing of currency needed to be safe and risk free.

As money became digital, great bank robberies gave way to banks having to fight with computer geeks and hackers.

As the first wave of internet only banks were born, the innovation headache for banks had just begun.

The conundrum … innovation in payments implies change.

Change implies risks.

So the banks' solution was – don't innovate.

So in come the non-banks to solve customers' headaches rather than worrying about the banks' headaches.

Digital payments systems came with literally hundreds of processes and systems behind the scenes of what seems to us like a simple process of transferring money electronically from one bank to another.

We were also fast changing the way we wanted to bank.

We now wanted speed, we wanted to pay anybody in the world, we wanted to pay in any currency and we wanted to do all this without having to queue up at a bank branch or having to call an outsourced call centre, and we wanted it all to work without risking any of our money, damn it!

I don't want to go to a branch anymore ...

With the rise of plastic money, Visa and MasterCard made it possible for most banks, citizens and corporates to hook up global systems and make payment to the other side of the world easily.

Then PayPal came along and after ten years, 164 million accounts were paying for things in 190 countries in 17 different currencies to the tune of around US$5 billion a month[11].

PayPal took the banking world by storm out of nowhere.

PayPal sat on top of hundreds of unconnected banking payment systems to make it easy to make payments with a simple email address, but it was not a bank.

PayPal gave birth to a whole new industry – person-to-person micro- payments which later gave rise to a whole non-banking sector, discussed in future chapters.

With the banks failing to innovate, PayPal – a system that made global person-to-person payments simple which was then acquired by dot-com success story eBay – sparked the most dramatic shift in payment processing since the rise of plastic. They also made paying almost anybody, anywhere easy.

As amazing as it was, however, PayPal did miss some countries out.

What about those who can't get a bank account or PayPal account?

In developed countries most people have a bank account and a mobile phone.

The need for convenience meant that customers demanded the ability for all payments and transactions to be made from the convenience of their mobile phones.

Since its early adoption in Sweden, Singapore, the Philippines and Hong Kong, mobile banking, where adoption rates reach 70-80% today, has become a phenomenon[12].

But the real phenomenon came in the unexpected opportunities and impact it had on the developing world.

In the developed world, the release of Apple's iPhone, Blackberry and Google Android enabled devices (discussed in later chapters on the rise of the smart phone) became less of a phone and more of a business tool, productivity device, fashion accessory, and frankly, a life-saver in today's rapidly changing world.

But very few forecast its impact on money.

It grew faster than most banks could handle. In August 2007, Bank of America finally released its banking iPhone app and had 500,000 customers by November 2007.

By 2010 this number rose to over 3.5 million[13].

In Brett King's book 'Bank 2.0', he mentions three areas in which smart phones and banking combined – mobile banking, mobile payments and a vehicle for assisting the giant unbanked market.

Now instead of paying with currency or plastic, we can use our mobile phone with a simple SMS text message or make a contactless payment through a technology called NFC (Near Field Communication).

This technology allows us to simply tap our phone over a retailer's payment system, enter a pin code and make payment.

In 2003 Sony implanted chips in their Japanese mobile phones to create the first 'wallet phone', where payments could be made by simply swiping our mobile phones.

Today, the majority of mobile phones in Japan are wallet phones.

According to the Bank of Japan, in 2009 mobile money accounted for more than 2.3% of all banknotes / currency in Japan[14].

Mobile banking became a huge convenience for us all in the developed countries, but in the developing countries, it provided the opportunity to help build the countries future and improve lives to those who were unable to access digital bank money, creating a mobile payments revolution.

I mentioned Kenya earlier.

In 2007 over 70% of Kenya households did not have bank accounts. Today millions of Kenyans make payments and store their funds for short periods without bank accounts at low risk and cost usting MPESA.

More on this in Chapter 11.

Meanwhile back in the US, PayPal's rivals Google Checkout and Amazon Payments and were busy entering the mobile payments market as they were sitting on two of the world's largest databases and most trusted brands.

Amazon Payments became a type of digital currency and payments platform that put Amazon into the online and mobile payments battle with their iPhone app.

But what brings this all together?

Our mobile wallet.

In 2011 Google launched its mobile payment system, Google Wallet, allowing its users to store credit cards, loyalty cards, and gift cards among other things, as well as redeeming sales promotions on their mobile phone.

Google Wallet uses near field communication (NFC) to make secure payments fast and convenient by simply tapping the phone on any PayPass-enabled terminal at checkout.

But my bank has only just got used to internet banking?

Interestingly enough, another hugely disruptive technology came out of nowhere, that we will go deep into in the next chapter, which began to play a role in the rise of digital money and deserves special mention here too.

This technology is now starting to play a significant role in the history of money.

The rise of hugely disruptive technology #3 – the social networks – gave birth to Facebook Credits, TwitPay, Linden dollars, Q coins, Bitcoins and many other phenomena.

This web 2.0 model of payments was focused on convenience and 'social' money.

HUGELY DISRUPTIVE TECHNOLOGY #2 – DIGITAL MONEY | 135

I don't know about my bank, but I can't keep up with it any more ...

In January 2011, Facebook announced that all Facebook game developers will be required to only process payments through Facebook Credits.

Facebook Credits are a virtual currency that enables people to purchase items on the Facebook platform.

One US dollar is currently the equivalent of 10 Facebook Credits.

Facebook Credits are today available in 15 currencies including US dollars, Pound Sterling, Euros, and Danish Krona.

With over 800 million users in 2011, what happens when Facebook expands credits into a micropayment system open to any Facebook applications?

Well Twipper and TwitPay already allow payments to be sent by tweeting a simple message to the service from your Twitter stream, but in March 2011, Facebook created an official subsidiary to handle payments: Facebook Payments Inc.

It was announced in April 2011 that Facebook users will be able to use credits to purchase vouchers that can be redeemed for real goods and services.

Could this be the next world bank?

Extreme?

You have not heard anything yet.

In June 2003 Linden Lab launched Second Life, the online virtual world.

Second Life residents interact with each other through avatars and can explore the world, get jobs, meet other residents, socialise, participate in individual and group activities, and create and trade virtual goods and services with one another in, literally, their second life.

What is interesting to me, is that as of 2011, Second Life has more than 20 million registered user accounts and the virtual world has its own currency referred to as Linden dollars (L$)[15].

In the Second Life economy, residents buy from and sell to one another directly, using the Linden, which is exchangeable for US dollars or other currencies on market-based currency exchanges.

Linden Lab reports that the Second Life economy generated US$3.5 million in economic activity during the month of September 2005, and by 2009 the total size of the Second Life economy grew to US$567 million. Currently US$1.5 million trades daily in Second Life[16].

In September 2005, Wells Fargo became the first real-world bank with a presence in Second Life.

In December 2006 ABN Amro followed to becomes the first European bank.

By 2007 BNP Paribas and Swiss bank BCV had opened their virtual doors, followed by Danish Saxo Bank announcing plans to create a virtual trading platform in Second Life.

Fortis Bank also began offering a virtual financial advisory service by purchasing its very own virtual space.

Interestingly, on the heels of banking scandals in the virtual world, Linden Lab announced that it is effectively banning all banks.

Linden Lab wanted to restore faith that some had lost in the stability of the virtual world's economy.

What does the virtual world know that we don't know?

What happens if the real world financial system is not reformed – do we look to our second life?

In 2009 James McKelvey was unable to complete a US$2,000 sale of his glass faucets and fittings because he could not accept credit cards. He explained his problem to his friend Jack Dorsey, one of the co-founders of Twitter, who immediately set to work and built a working prototype of Square.

Square now allows anybody with a smart phone in the US to accept credit cards through their mobile phones, either by swiping the card on the Square device or by manually entering the details on the phone.

Now you can be in business and take payments with a simple investment in a smart phone and a Square app.

Do you still fancy jumping through all those hoops to get merchant facilities from your bank to take card payments any more?

What if we could just make payments without any debit or credit card at all?

In September 1997 Octopus was launched in Hong Kong to collect fares for their transport system.

The Octopus smart card system became the first contactless smart-card system in the world and has since grown into a widely used payment system in Hong Kong.

This model gave birth to the Oyster card in London.

Interestingly the Octopus smart card is now also used for payment at convenience stores, supermarkets, restaurants, on-street parking meters, car parks, as well as service stations and vending machines.

There are more than 20 million cards in circulation, nearly three times the population of Hong Kong[17].

The cards are used by 95% of the population of Hong Kong aged 16 to 65, generating over 11 million daily transactions worth a total of over US$12.8 million every day[18].

When banks started complaining that Octopus was acting like a bank, the regulators responded by giving Octopus a banking licence for the purpose of deposit-taking.

So what happens when every country adopts a smart card payment system with the ability to hold deposits and make payments for goods and services?

Or what happens when people elect to receive their wages on their Oyster card?

Is that taxable?

With all this innovation, in theory, banks are used simply because we are used to them, we pay our wages into them and we rely on them for the creation of money.

But we changed the way money is created in the Bank Charter Act of 1844, when we went back in time, didn't we?

So what do we need banks for under banking reform?

Oh, of course, we need to get a return on our savings and borrow money from banks, don't we?

Well, in the next few chapters we'll find out that we can do that with much better results and returns without banks too.

So really, today, the main purpose of a bank is that we rely on them for the creation of commercial bank money.

What if we just created our own alternative currency instead?

You can.

In 1983 Michael Linton created a system called the 'Local Exchange Trading System' (LETS).

The system he designed gave localised communities the ability to run their own monetary system through a complimentary local currency.

It was designed to work alongside government currency and debt-based commercial bank money.

LETS networks use interest-free local credit to trade goods and services with its members. For instance, a member may earn credit by doing childcare for one person and spend it later on carpentry with another person in the same network.

LETS technology is now being used to stimulate the economies of depressed towns that have goods and services, but little official currency, as the LETS scheme does not require outside sources of income as a stimulus.

A quick search on the web site LETS-Linkup.com and you will find an international LETS directory featuring over 1,500 LETS and Community Currency groups from 39 countries on every continent in the world. And there are many more.

A LETS system is probably in full operation in your local community right now.

That's OK for the locals using it, but what about the rest of the world?

Could a currency exist on a global scale independent of government and banks?

Too late – we already have one.

In 2008 Satoshi Nakamoto published a white paper for a digital currency that enables rapid payments at a very low cost, and avoids the need for central authorities and issuers.

In 2009 Bitcoin was born.

As of July 2011, there are just over 6.8 million Bitcoins in existence.

Currency exchanges also exist now between Bitcoins and other virtual currencies, such as the Linden Dollar.

By May 2011, the price of a Bitcoin rose from just over $1 to almost $30, some exchanging all their dollars for Bitcoins and working in Second Life while speculating on the exchange rates between USD, Bitcoins and Linden dollars.

If you spoke to one of these people, they really are indifferent if you pay them in virtual currencies, Facebook Credits, or US dollars.

Today, many small businesses and not-for-profits have started to accept payments and donations in Bitcoins.

They have even developed a way for merchants to accept payments in stores using payment terminals and QR codes.

You can even order physical Bitcoins with holograms, moving beyond just a virtual currency.

What happens when a large publicly traded company decides to accept payments in Bitcoins? Or even Facebook starts accepting them?

What happens when our children brought up on Bitcoins and Facebook Credits as standard enter the workforce and demand their wages in more convenient forms?

Well, the Chinese government took virtual currencies seriously when Q coins disrupted their entire economy:

> "...did you know that perhaps the greatest risk to the yuan in terms of competing currency in the last two to three years actually came from a local online currency known as QQ coins?" *Brett King*

In February 1999 Ma Huateng launched an instant messaging service platform called Tencent QQ.

Tencent QQ, generally referred to as QQ, is now the most popular free instant messaging service in the world.

If you are not Chinese, this may be the first time you have heard of QQ.

As of July 2011, active QQ user accounts totaled 812.3 million, making it the world's largest online community at the time of writing[19].

But where this became interesting is when QQ launched a Q coin as a virtual currency used by QQ users to purchase QQ related items for their avatars and blogs.

Q coins are obtained either by purchase, one coin for one Renminbi, or for using their mobile phone service.

Due to the popularity of QQ among young Chinese, Q coins are now accepted by more and more online stores and gaming sites in exchange for real merchandise such as small gifts.

The People's Bank of China, China's central bank, says it is investigating the possibility of cracking down on Q coin, due to people using Q coins in exchange for real world goods.

They are becoming such a significant currency that the central bank is concerned about inflation.

In 'Bank 2.0', Brett King goes on to describe how Q coin speculators have opened up a Forex trade in the currency, as with Linden dollars in Second Life, which currently has a daily trading volume of US$6.6 million.

People are hiring professionals to play online games on their behalf, earning them Q coins as currency. Hackers are trying to steal Q coins and sell it below its official rate.

When the Chinese government tried to apply capital controls on the Q currency, the price was driven up by 70% in a matter of weeks.

In February 2011, QQ.com was ranked 10th overall in the Alexa Internet rankings, just behind Twitter, ranked 9th.

Think this only applies to China?

On 10th May 2011, Microsoft Corporation agreed to acquire Skype for US$8.5 billion.

What are their plans for returning on that investment?

Well, with over 700 million Skype users as of 2011, they could make a pretty decent virtual currency used to pay for your next version of Microsoft Windows.

Let's not forget, on Skype's first day of launching its iPhone app, it had over 1 million downloads.

Will banks be crying out to stop these virtual currencies? Remember what happened when they tried this with the Octopus smart card: the HKMA (Hong Kong Monetary Authority) gave Octopus a banking licence to regulate their deposit-taking.

Speaking of iPhone, what if Apple starts using iCurrency for downloads on their iTunes and App stores?

Like Paypal, Q coins, Second Life's Linden dollars and all these virtual currency players, they are all trying to export their currency to mobile platforms as a tool to allow transferring money or buying goods, services and gifts securely and easily, on the go.

But I don't trust all this online stuff – there is too much fraud and what if my mobile gets stolen?

You are right, online fraud is huge, but check out what is happening in Mexico.

In 2001, Grupo Elektra, a retail group with years of experience providing in-store credit, saw the need for a financial services unit.

In August of that year it applied for a banking licence to open Banco Azteca.

Banco Azteca launched in 2002 and what is interesting about this bank is their use of biometric science.

Biometric methods are used to uniquely recognise humans based upon one or more physical or behavioural traits.

In particular, biometrics is used as a form of identity access management and access control.

Humans can be identified by fingerprint, face recognition, DNA, palm print, hand geometry, iris recognition (which has largely replaced retina recognition), and scent.

These forms of identification enable secure and reliable authentication like never before.

This has been used to great success in countries with a high population of people without driving licences and passports as identification.

Hence the uptake by Banco Azteca in Mexico.

Banco Azteca now operates in Mexico, Panama, Guatemala, Honduras, Peru and Brazil and is already among the largest banks in Mexico with more than 6.8 million savings accounts holding 45,441 million pesos in deposits, and 9 million credit accounts, representing a credit portfolio of 25,000 million pesos[20].

They have over 8 million customers making over 200,000 biometric payments daily using their fingerprints as authentication.

Now it is a valid concern that biometrics might lead to the removal of eyeballs and hands in the name of fraud, but what happens when it is combined with implanted chips that monitor heart rates?

Is that a step too far?

Where is this all going, I hear you ask.

Well, just before we discuss the inevitable destination of money and put an end to the great debate, let's see how far we have come now.

Is it really possible now to do everything without a bank?

The honest answer is ... no, but we are close.

We still rely on banks for the creation of money out of debt.

Systems like PayPal, Visa, and MasterCard have built their systems on top of our banking systems. Square has built its systems on top of Visa and MasterCard's systems and services like Facebook Credits and TwitPay are built on PayPal.

Developing countries are finding a way through microfinance and m-payments to gain access to finance without banks, but what about the full service in developed countries?

WikiLeaks – operating outside the conventional financial system

In 2006 a website called WikiLeaks was launched.

WikiLeaks is an international non-profit organisation that publishes submissions of private, secret, and classified media from anonymous news sources, news leaks, and whistleblowers. It is funded through public donations.

Within its first year of launch, it had a database of more than 1.2 million documents[21].

In April 2010, WikiLeaks published gunsight footage from the 2007 Baghdad airstrike in which Iraqi journalists were among those killed by an Apache helicopter.

In July of the same year, WikiLeaks then released the Afghan War Diary, a compilation of more than 76,900 documents about the war in Afghanistan not previously available to the public[22].

In October 2010, the group released a package of almost 400,000 documents called the Iraq War Logs in coordination with major commercial media organisations. This allowed every death in Iraq, and across the border in Iran, to be mapped[23].

In November 2010, WikiLeaks began releasing US State department diplomatic cables.

In April 2011, WikiLeaks began publishing 779 secret files relating to prisoners detained in the Guantanamo Bay detention camp[24].

On December 2009, WikiLeaks announced that it was experiencing a shortage of funds and suspended all access to its website except for a form to submit new material.

Material that was previously published was no longer available.

WikiLeaks stated on its website that it would resume full operation once the operational costs were covered.

In 2010, WikiLeaks received almost €650,000 in PayPal donations and €700,000 in bank transfers[25].

In December 2010, PayPal, permanently cut off the account redirecting donations to WikiLeaks.

PayPal alleged that the account violated its "Acceptable Use Policy", specifically that the account was used for "activities that encourage, promote, facilitate or instruct others to engage in illegal activity."

Shortly after, MasterCard announced that it was "taking action to ensure that WikiLeaks can no longer accept MasterCard-branded products".

The next day, Visa Inc. announced it was suspending payments to WikiLeaks, pending "further investigations".

In fact, on 18th December 2010, Bank of America announced it would "not process transactions of any type that we have reason to believe are intended for Wikileaks".

So I think we can use WikiLeaks as the perfect case study of an entity that has been cast aside from the banking system.

So let's take a look at how they might get round this.

What WikiLeaks needs to be able to do is: receive payments, send payments, make card purchases, borrow money, raise funds, invest funds, make card payments and withdraw cash.

Receiving and sending payments

As PayPal is no longer an option, in a move to support WikiLeaks, XipWire established a way for people to donate to WikiLeaks, and waived its fees.

It developed a mobile payment system that allowed payments and money transfers to be made with mobile devices using simple text messages.

A XipWire account can be funded with an electronic debit from a bank account or by a credit card.

The mobile-to-mobile service allows consumers and merchants to send money to WikiLeaks through text messages, protected by a PIN.

WikiLeaks can use this mobile application to send payments to anybody in the same way.

Make card payments and cash withdrawals

If WikiLeaks was not cast aside by MasterCard and Visa, it could have used a prepaid card to top-up without ever using a bank. It can even use such a card to make cash withdrawals from ATMs, but as this is not an option, it has to stick to mobile money.

If it was in Hong Kong it could use its Octopus smart card at participating retailers.

Give it a little time and this will be a global option, in fact it probably is by the time you read this book.

Borrow money, raise funds and invest funds

Person-to-person payments and crowdfunding platforms would have been a perfect option if WikiLeaks was not barred from Paypal, but it is only a question of time before this platform can be used with a similar mobile payment system as WikiLeaks is using.

These online platforms allow you to raise funds, invest, lend and borrow without banks (covered in depth in upcoming chapters).

However, to use these platforms, if it cannot use PayPal, WikiLeaks would need to have a bank account that allowed standing orders or direct debits.

It has the option of pitching to a social bank if it could pitch that WikiLeaks was for social benefit.

Many of us do all our business through social banks, also known as ethical or sustainable banks.

They are banks concerned with the social and environmental impacts of its investments and loans.

Ethical banks are part of a larger movement towards more social and environmental responsibility in the financial sector and is also related to such movements as the fair trade movement, ethical consumerism and, importantly for WikiLeaks, boycotting.

I am not saying they would accept, but they might.

I would put my pitch to Charity Bank, Co-Operative Bank and Reliance Bank if based in the UK; Triodos Bank if based in the Netherlands, UK, Belgium, Germany or Spain; ShoreBank, RSF Social Finance and Wainwright if based in the US; Cultura Bank if based in Norway; GLS Bank and EthikBank if based in Germany; JAK members' bank if based in Sweden; Citizens Bank if based in Canada; Credit Cooperatif and NEF if based in France; The Alternative Bank Schweiz if based in Switzerland; or Banca Etica if based in Italy.

Armed with this it could borrow, raise funds and invest through people rather than banks through crowdfunding and person-to-person lending platforms like BankToTheFuture.com.

Or it could just go fully virtual.

On 15th June, 2011, WikiLeaks began accepting donations in Bitcoins.

They are yet to purchase their plot on the grid of Second Life, but despite boycotting from the financial world, funding still goes on and the website remains.

So what is the inevitable destination of money?

If you think this world is beyond your comprehension, try this one on for size.

Banking and payments commentator Chris Skinner forecast that beyond mobile, contactless and biometric payments, we will inevitably end up with invisible payments through chips implanted in our bodies.

Unthinkable, I know, but we are almost there already.

All of today's payments are based upon chips and the chip is getting more powerful each day.

In 'Money for Nothing and your Cheques for Free',[26] Chris Skinner explores what might happen if RFID chips were implanted into our bodies direct.

An implanted RFID chip could automatically track blood pressure, brain activity and heart rate 24 hours a day.

Should the chip be removed from your body, it becomes null and void. It will only work as long as its owner is implanted.

Using the same technology that American Express's Express Pay, MasterCard's PayPass and Visa Contactless, as well as most Japanese mobile phones, use today your implanted chip recognises the price of products in stores that operate of the implanted chip payment system.

Currently, contactless payments work by holding your phone over the payment station, and the payment is made from the balance on your mobile wallet. As the chip used in your mobile becomes more powerful it can sense your chip all over the store when implanted in your body.

When you pick up a product from the store that you want to purchase, the wireless sensors pick up your chip signal, activating the payment process.

If you walk out of the store, the payment is confirmed; if you leave the store without the product, the payment is never taken.

No authentication or identification is needed as the system is just looking for the chip to be live.

The chip will not work if removed from the body and furthermore, the chip is monitoring your heart, brain and blood and knows there is no change of situation. The system can tell that you are not being robbed, mugged, forced to make payment or that somebody else is making payment with your dead body.

The technology is not actually that far away.

Crazy?

Well, you would have called me crazy if I told you not too many years ago that there will be this thing called the internet that gives you access to anything you want any time, that money will become digital transacted through a mini-computer in your pocket, that you will be able to connect with most people in the world through something called a social network, that the strength of your contacts on your social network will be the likelihood of you raising funds for your future, that you will borrow and invest without banks and become a mini venture capitalist with as little as £10, that you can lend to women in developing countries to start their businesses and be more likely to get your money back than a bank lending to a man in the developed world, and that all this will be done from a small device in your pocket.

So gradually, one by one the 5,000 year-old coin, the 200 year-old cheque and the 50 year-old plastic card will disappear. But the question still remains, will we still need money in the free economy?

You can watch a video presentation I gave at a Positive Money conference on my future vision for banking and money here:

QR 22 Watch Simon Dixon present on alternative money at the Positive Money Conference 2011

Invisible money or moneyless?

I bet that whacky vision of a moneyless society put forward by the Venus Project, discussed in Chapter 3, does not seem so crazy right now.

Perhaps money will be invisible in the future or perhaps the free economy will wipe out money all together as we move into a technology-driven barter and gift economy – who knows?

With Time Banking, do we have everything we need to be moneyless?

Who knows, but the one thing that is for sure, banking reform has to happen as we cannot refinance our debt created commercial bank money supply forever.

The US already suffered a credit rating downgrade in 2011 as a result of the last round of government bailouts for banks following the 2007 financial crisis. What happens when the next one comes along and the government no longer has the credit rating to borrow the money to bail them out? What happens when all governments get downgraded?

It happened to the US, how about your country?

The double-edged sword of digital money

So we can see that digital money has become something of a double-edged sword for us all.

On one hand, it has democratised money and financial services in developing and developed countries around the world.

On the other hand, it allowed money creation to be privatised, fuelling a ticking time-bomb Ponzi scheme in a world where all countries are plagued with more debt than money.

But could we just take the good of digital money and lose the Ponzi scheme side of things?

That all depends on our opinion to the answers of the great debate.

So what about the great debate? Who was right?

I began this chapter by saying there are three great debates in the tale of monetary history.

1. Who controls money (or creates it)?

2. Does money need to be a store of value (like gold)? Or can money derive its value from law (like a dollar bill or the balance you see on your online banking computer screen)?

3. How is money created?

Before explaining how hugely disruptive technology #3 changed the world, I would like to end this chapter with my perspective on the three debates so that we can prevent the inevitable collapse ahead, and move from the debt trap of 'free'dom to simply the economy of freedom, driven by more choice, more innovation and more freedom than ever before.

Now that we know the history of money, whichever way money goes in the future, let's put an end to these great debates once and for all.

Debate 1: Who should control and create money?

History has proven that when the government is directly in charge of creating money, the political pressure to create ever growing quantities of currency is far too great and will always end in economic disaster.

History has also proven that by giving the power to create commercial bank debt money to banks, the profit pressure to create ever growing quantities of debt is far too great and will always end in economic disaster.

Inflation and destruction are the inevitable result of both forms of money creation, which in turn will always lead to economic disaster.

For me, the only option is to give the power to create money to an independent monetary policy committee that is independent of both government and private banks, but answers directly to parliament. These are the proposals put forward by monetary reformers like James Robertson and Positive Money, and I agree.

This prevents the political and profit pressure and conflict of interest that surrounds money creation today. The decision between how much money is created and how it is spent in my opinion must be separated.

Debate 2: Should money be commodity or fiat?

To say that money should be dependent upon the fluke of a country's gold supply is archaic.

What happens if your country has very little gold?

A gold standard is a better system than we have right now as it regulates the creation of money when money is created by banks; however, it will always be inevitably removed in light of the scarcity of money it will create. It does not solve the problem that banks create money as debt; it merely regulates it, leaving with it all the problems discussed in previous chapters.

Under an independent monetary policy committee, gold is no longer necessary – in fact, it is counterproductive.

I know I will get a huge backlash from the gold bugs that are reading this now, but gold has become a tool for speculation, not a monetary system for a stable economy. Don't make the mistake of judging a fiat currency by the current system. Gold bugs often mislead people into saying that too much money is printed by government if we do not have a gold standard, but as we know, almost all money is created by banks and not printed by governments. This is a big misunderstanding of how money is in fact created.

If we want to stick with our current system, I would agree gold is a better short-term option, but it will lead to further boom and bust and the eventual destruction of our economy. This is the same Gold Standard that was around during and before the Great Depression. It will not get us any closer to solving the problem that we are in a Ponzi scheme. It will inevitably be removed as a currency during the next crisis, as it has been in the past.

Fiat money is convenient, it is the future and we believe it will work when its power of creation is taken away from the banks and politicians who are trying to win elections.

Moving back to commodity money will be a hugely disruptive archaic movement back in time with the problem still persisting and inevitably leading to the suspension of money's convertibility into commodity money again as government wrestles with uncontrollable debt.

So fiat it is for me.

Debate 3: How is money created?
Money cannot be created as debt.

To charge interest on money created out of nothing is both unsustainable and unjust.

Do not get me wrong here, I am not saying that you cannot charge interest on money, I am saying you cannot *create* money out of thin air with interest on top.

Money should be created debt-free.

When the independent monetary policy committee creates money, it should be gifted to the Treasury to add to its tax revenues to be spent as the elected government wishes under our current democratic process.

This takes away the special subsidy that we currently pay banks by giving them the interest earned from having the ability to create money, and returns it to the taxpayer.

So how will we know how much to create?

It is simple: the independent monetary policy committee will have clear, transparent and simple goals.

They must control inflation and deflation.

I hear you say that they try to do this now and they don't succeed.

That is because they don't have control of the money supply; they try to indirectly control the supply of commercial bank money through interest rates, driving people from debt to bankruptcy and back again.

Money supply figures are then distorted through different definitions like M0, M1, M3, etc.

There will be simply one money supply – 'M' – and it can be directly controlled rather than indirectly as it is today.

For the first time in history, we will have a transparent, controlled and easy to understand money supply.

If we get excessive inflation and deflation, it is easy to point the finger of blame and sack the board of the independent monitory policy committee because they only have one goal – to control inflation and deflation.

It is my belief that an independent monitory policy committee that reports to parliament in the creation of debt-free fiat money is the most transparent and sustainable monetary system we can transition to with minimal disruption to the financial markets that underpin life as we know it today.

```
┌─────────────────────────────────────┐
│  ┌───────────────────────────────┐  │
│  │       Our Reformed System     │  │
│  └───────────────────────────────┘  │
│  ┌───────────────────────────────┐  │
│  │   1. Money Is Created By An    │  │
│  │       Independent MPC          │  │
│  └───────────────────────────────┘  │
│  ┌───────────────────────────────┐  │
│  │ 2. Money Has No Store Of Value & │
│  │  Is Backed By Law (Fiat Money) │  │
│  └───────────────────────────────┘  │
│  ┌───────────────────────────────┐  │
│  │ 3. Money Is Created Debt Free For│
│  │  Inflation / Deflation Targeting │
│  └───────────────────────────────┘  │
└─────────────────────────────────────┘
```

Figure 38 Money creation under our reformed system

Fix these three debates and digital money will be the greatest technology of all, democratising money and financial services around the world.

Couple this with our banking reforms from our adventure in time travel and digital money will allow for true innovation and human development in a sustainable way.

OK, there we have it: I know that I will be attacked by gold bugs, communists, capitalists, economists, politicians and bankers, but look at what you see in front of you today and in history.

Back to 1844 we go ...

Before we watch the birth of the next hugely disruptive technology, we travel back to 1844 and put an end to the great debates about the nature of money that Sir Robert Peel was proposing in parliament, by slipping in some additional research on the benefits of a fiat debt-free money supply and this time he forms an independent monetary policy committee who take full responsibility for the creation of money independent of banks and politicians.

As mentioned before, whether you live in the debt trap of 'free'dom, the economy of freedom, an economy with invisible money, or a moneyless economy ... social capital will be the greatest investment you will ever make. It is hugely disruptive technology #3 that made building and measuring your social capital so easy.

So now we have got that out of the way, it is now time to see how everything changed when hugely disruptive technology #3 was born – the rise of the social networks..

Hold on! Before you start Chapter 7, tweet me your thoughts on #DigitalMoney.

QR 23 Tweet Simon Dixon about #DigitalMoney

1 Money, Wikipedia contributors, http://en.wikipedia.org/w/index.php?title= Money&oldid=455780903
2 "Goldsborough, Reid. "World's First Coin"". Rg.ancients.info. 2003-10-02. Retrieved 2009-04-20
3 Stockholms Banc, Wikipedia, http://en.wikipedia.org/w/index.php?title= Stockholms_Banco&oldid=439647712
4 Money, Wikipedia, http://en.wikipedia.org/w/index.php?title=Money&oldid =455780903
5 US Federal Reserve historical statistics, October 13, 2011, http://www.feder- alreserve.gov/releases/h6/hist/h6hist1.htm
6 Paul O'Neill, "A Little Gift from Your Friendly Banker", Life Magazine, April 27, 1970
7 "History of Visa", Visa Latin America & Caribbean
8 "Q2 2011 Credit Card Debt Study". CardHub.com. Retrieved 2011-09-13
9 British Bankers' Association
10 Marc Moncrief; Nassim Khadem (September 21, 2007). "Credit card debt hits record high". Melbourne: The Age. Retrieved 2011-05-01
11 *It's Banking Jim, but Not As We Know It*, Chris Skinner, 2010
12 *Bank 2.0*, Brett King, 2010
13 NetBanker http://www.netbanker.com/bank_of_america/

14 *Money for Nothing and your Cheques for Free*, Chris Skinner, 2010

15 Singularity university (August 18, 2011). "Philip Rosedale, Creator of Second Life speaks at Singularity university". Retrieved 2011-08-19.

16 "Second Life Economic Data". Secondlife.com. Retrieved 2010-02-19

17 "Statistics". Octopus Cards Limited. Retrieved 2010-11-14.

18 Bank 2.0, Brett King, 2010

19 "About Tencent". Tencent.com. Retrieved 2011-01-23.

20 Banco Azteca Wikipedia contributors, http://en.wikipedia.org/w/index.php?title=Banco_Azteca&oldid=441586408

21 "Wikileaks has 1.2 million documents?".WikiLeaks. Archived from the original on 16 February 2008. Retrieved 28 February 2008

22 "WikiLeaks to publish new documents".MSNBC. Associated Press. 7 August 2010. Archived from the original on 5 December 2010. Retrieved 5 December 2010.

23 Rogers, Simon (23 October 2010). "Wikileaks Iraq war logs: every death mapped". *The Guardian* (London). Retrieved 11 January 2011

24 Leigh, David; Ball, James; Burke, Jason (25 April 2011). "Guantánamo files lift lid on world's most controversial prison". The Guardian (London). Retrieved 25 April 2011

25 "Project 04: Enduring freedom of information" Preliminary transparency report 2010". Wau-Holland-Stiftung (WHS) via Cryptome. 26 April 2011.

26 *Money for Nothing and your Cheques for Free*, Chris Skinner, 2010

7 Hugely disruptive technology #3 – social networks

YOU MIGHT WANT to take a look at the introductory video before we begin.

QR 24 Introductory video on hugely disruptive technology #3

As we move forward in time under our new financial system, our Bank Charter Act reforms ensure that the birth of the World Wide Web does not lead to the mass creation of digital debt money by banks as before; it instead leads to the birth of innovative sustainable digital money, democratising financial services around the world.

By moving to our new system for creating money, based on an independent monetary policy committee setting the fiat money supply debt-free to control inflation and deflation, our financial system becomes completely transparent and sustainable for the first time in history.

The rise of the World Wide Web gives birth to a new efficient form of digital money, focused on the socialism and convenience of money for all worldwide.

Money has never been more convenient and transactions never faster as we pay and send money for everything through our smart phones, leading to the worldwide adoption of mobile wallets.

Without the banks' licence to create money, non-banks also rise and are free and able to compete with banks, without the economic burden of a shrinking money supply that we would have experienced under our old debt-based monetary system when people stop borrowing from banks.

Then a new form of technology completely changes the way we communicate, opening a whole new world of possibility for us all.

This innovation later went on to have a serious impact on the way we finance our ideas, projects, businesses, social enterprises and charities worldwide, as we will find out in future chapters.

Social networks have changed the world

Social networks have changed the way business is done, the way relationships are formed, how we spend our day, how we share important messages with the world, the way politicians campaign, the way we fund, borrow, raise funds and invest and, quite frankly, everything.

The social networks have opened up a world of possibilities for us all that were never there before, unless you were a hugely connected celebrity billionaire, of course.

Maybe you use the social networks today to maintain contact with your friends and existing networks, in a time when it has become increasingly difficult to physically meet with those you care about.

Maybe you use the social networks to reach out to new people that share the same interests, political views, religious beliefs or shared visions as you.

Maybe it is purely a business tool for you to meet new customers, business partners, employees or find new freelance work, employment and contracts.

Maybe it is where you met your current wife, husband, partner or fling.

Whatever it is for you, my guess is that you probably have not sat back and truly contemplated how big an effect it has had and how much more it can have on your life. The social networks have completely changed the way we communicate. It has also democ-ratised the media for all.

Think about this ...

I am amazed that today we live in an age where we can have all the news that is important to us, fed straight through to our smart phones and within a couple of seconds, we can immediately share that news with all our friends on Facebook.

We can then select the exact people that we want to read the news by only sharing it on one of our Facebook pages or Facebook groups, where only the right people get it, who are all interested in this particular topic.

We can then take that very same news article and share our opinion on it with all our Twitter followers in seconds.

Maybe the article contains news about a key person we would like to do business with. A quick search for their name and company on LinkedIn and we can join their network and connect to congratulate them or propose a business deal that we may have for them.

We can then take those contacts and completely organise them into the right circles on our Google+ accounts, allowing us to categorise the people we know, so we can communicate with different people in the most appropriate form for that circle.

At this point we are still on our way to our first meeting of the day and have not sat in front of a computer yet.

After meeting another interesting person that we may have connected with on LinkedIn, we can propose to do a quick video interview with them after the meeting, as it turns out they have a very interesting perspective on a topic that would help our circles.

This unique perspective on a subject that interests our followers can be recorded into a video in seconds using an app on our smart phones that allows us to share that video with all our connections.

As the video is uploaded to our personal broadcasting chan-nel on YouTube, to be shared with the thousands of subscribers who have opted to be notified when our videos are released, we can select other groups of people that we would like to share our videos with.

As our followers share their opinions on the interview and leave comments under the video, we are notified immediately and can respond from our smart phones while we are in the taxi to our next meeting.

If we choose, with each comment we can notify all our Facebook friends and Twitter followers about a debate we may be having where they can join in and all their friends that may also share a common interest, can add their opinions.

We suddenly get notified of a series of new contact requests from interesting people because of the debate, allowing us to increase our connections and future social capital.

We get notified about a documentary that one of our connections is looking to make on a topic that interests us.

We find out that they are looking to raise finance using BankToTheFuture.com and we can contribute a small amount of money to the documentary production and get a behind-the-scenes look at the making of the documentary. This also increases our social capital for the future, when we might need funding.

We fancy this, as our partners or friends are interested in making a documentary, so quickly we leave a comment in the BankToTheFuture.com investors forum asking if we could bring our partners to the behind-the-scenes visit. Within seconds we get a positive response and invest.

After giving our contribution by logging into our PayPal account without ever having to pull out our credit card, we can now login to our BankToTheFuture.com account and share the journey of the creation of the documentary with all the other investors, as we share ideas to make the documentary a huge hit.

While in the community of investors for the documentary on BankToTheFuture.com, we have an online conversation with somebody from the other side of the world that is looking to expand their business in our country and is seeking investments.

After checking their social capital score on BankToTheFuture.com and seeing they have been identity checked, credit checked, have a high Klout influence score and a ton of connections and positive ratings, we search the major social networks for extra information on that person.

With a couple of clicks we can see that we share a couple of mutual friends on the business-to-business social network Ecademy, so we contact them to discuss how they know each other.

We arrange to have a video conference on Skype so we can see a live demonstration of their new plans as we flick between sharing our computer screens and video conferencing all from opposite sides of the world.

We decide to lend a few hundred pounds and increase our portfolio of loans that are automatically administered through our BankToTheFuture.com account.

These loans offer a much higher return than the money in our bank saving accounts, but we choose to leave some money in our social bank account anyway, as we are happy knowing that it is helping social entrepreneurs.

We move money automatically from our bank social current accounts that is used to help social entrepreneurs, but pays us low interest rate, as with all banks, through to our PayPal account, straight to our new investment where we have pooled our money across many people to protect ourself from default risk, all automatically administered in BankToTheFuture.com.

Turns out that we know others that would like to invest in that type of project too, as they are very passionate about this particular field and want a better return on their money than their banks offer, so we Ping an announcement to the hundreds of social networks connected to our FriendFeed accounts, where completely different people connect with us in the way that they like to connect most.

It makes no difference to us how or where we are connected as all our hundreds of social network accounts are all linked to our main accounts and pull all communications together straight to our phone.

With every bit of useful information we share with the right people, we are building our social capital for when we need it.

We jump in a taxi to our next meeting after a morning of venture capital investing and quickly 'check-in' on our FourSquare account and share an interesting picture with our community that lets them know where we are and if they are close, we can meet.

And by the way, we have not logged into any of our social network accounts, sat in front of our office computer or spent a penny beyond making our investment yet, and we have done more in a typical morning than we could have done in weeks at the office just a few years ago!

Already our social capital has increased significantly today without any major time investment as it has been done from our mobile on the move.

This is why I am able to run multiple businesses, publish multiple books, create documentaries, do public speaking engagements all over the world, engage in charity work and still have some time to spend with my wife.

When you get this right, what would you like to be doing?

Everybody and everything can be connected and fully mobile, which means that anybody with a decent internet connection has the same resources available to them as everybody else, if they educate themselves on how to use them. This used to be a privilege for the rich and elite, but those days are now over.

The most expensive mistake you could ever make

Some people are scared to use these freely available tools, others think they are only for kids, whilst others think it's only a game. Standing on the side while all this is going on around you could be the most expensive mistake you ever make.

This is how you build your social capital and this will be the most important investment you could ever make to protect yourself during the debt trap of 'free'dom and allow you to live in abundance in the upcoming economy of freedom.

OK I get it, but what exactly is a social network anyway?

First off, a geeky definition of a social network, for those of you that like to do things that way or have perhaps been hiding under a rock for the last few years.

A social network is a web-based service that allows you to create a public profile, create a list of other users that you share connection with, and view and connect with their list of connections and others within the system.

The nature of these connections may vary from site to site. For example, you may connect with your professional network on LinkedIn, your business colleagues on Ecademy, your friends on your Facebook profile, your customers on your Facebook page, the people behind your investments on BankToTheFuture. com, your idols and mentors on Twitter, your favorite bands on MySpace and your potential dates on Bebo.

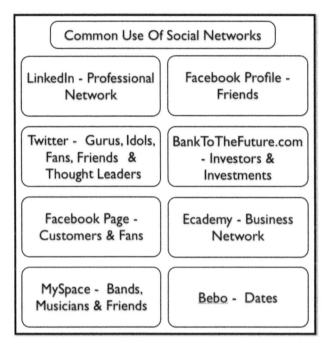

Figure 39 Common uses of different social networks

But what makes a social network a social network, is the fact that they allow you to meet people at the same time as making your connections visible to others. This often results in new connections that would not otherwise have been made.

The different social networks offer a wide variety of features, such as the ability to join groups of people with similar interests, live chat, photo sharing, video sharing, event sharing, blogging, poll facilities, music sharing and an endless list of features across all social networks, but their backbone consists of visible profiles displaying information about you and a list of friends/connections who are also members of your social network.

So now we all know what we are talking about, let's take a look at how we got here.

The rise of the social network

In 1979 students Tom Truscott and Jim Ellis came up with the idea of creating a bulletin board system for use on the internet. In 1980 they launched Usenet, the first worldwide discussion system that captured large numbers of non-technical users on the internet, which turned out to be the precursor to modern internet forums as we know them today.

Over a decade before the World Wide Web was developed, Usenet allowed users to post articles organised into categories called newsgroups. When a user subscribed to a newsgroup, the software kept track of which articles that user had read.

Usenet gave birth to the user-generated online content that we know and love today and paved the way for the next generation of innovation.

The early innovators

The next major online community success after Usenet came from France in 1982 when the Poste, Téléphone et Télécommunications (PTT) launched Minitel, which went on to become one of the world's most successful online services.

Users were able to make online purchases, make train reservations, check stock prices, search the telephone directory, have a mail box, and (the reason it gets mentioned in the history of social networking) chat in a similar way to modern social networks.

With the concept of online communities growing in popularity, though still tiny, in 1985 Stewart Brand and Larry Brand developed the Whole Earth 'Lectronic Link (WELL), a dial-up bulletin board system. It became best known for its internet forums where discussions and topics ranged from the deeply serious to the generally silly, depending on the nature and interests of its participants.

For example, it became a major online meeting place for fans of the band The Grateful Dead in the late 1980s and early 1990s. *Wired* Magazine at the time called WELL "the most influential online community in the world."

With the success of WELL, in 1985 a struggling computer gaming company on the verge of bankruptcy called Quantum Computer Services Inc. appointed Jim Kimsey as Chief Executive Officer to turn the company around. Kimsey changed the company's strategy, and in 1985 licensed a system that allowed them to launch a chat room.

This new form of communication gave us the ability to instantly send text messages to other users from our computers as long as we were both online and logged in. Chat rooms were very different to how we communicated before because they allowed a large group of people with similar interests to convene and hold conversations in real time without having to meet in person in one location.

In October 1991, Quantum Computer Services Inc. changed its name to America Online and at its peak had 27 million users chatting online.

Before the widespread use of AOL, 1988 brought together broadcasting network CBS, computer manufacturer IBM and retailer Sears, Roebuck and Company, which launched an online service named Prodigy. The online service later offered over a million subscribers access to a broad range of networked services.

Before Prodigy's success, CompuServe became known as the first online service to offer internet connectivity as early as 1989 when it opened its email service to allow incoming and outgoing messages to other internet email addresses.

Both CompuServe and Prodigy were paving the way for the biggest shift in human behaviour. We were all about to shift our habits to spending most of our days in front of a computer screen.

By the early 1990s, CompuServe was enormously popular, with hundreds of thousands of users visiting its thousands of moderated forums. Their forums were forerunners to the endless variety of discussion sites on the World Wide Web today.

Competing head to head, by 1990 Prodigy had become the second-largest online service provider, with 465,000 subscribers trailing CompuServe's 600,000[1].

Up to this point, America Online (AOL), Prodigy and CompuServe provided the main way for ordinary people to connect and communicate with each other online.

As more and more users started to use e-mail during the 1990s internet boom, the popularity of instant messenger services grew alongside.

Some early email systems required that the author and the recipient both be online at the same time, in common with instant messaging, but this soon became a thing of the past. With the World Wide Web, email became available with friendly web interfaces by providers such as Yahoo and Hotmail, without charge, leading to worldwide adoption. Email had become affordable, especially as pay-per-minute internet services declined, and everyone wanted at least one email address.

Instant messaging also exploded on the internet scene in 1996 when Mirabilis introduced ICQ, a free instant messaging utility that anyone could use.

In 1997, AOL, by that point the pioneer of the online community, gave its users the ability to talk in real time with each other through chat rooms and instant messages for free when AOL acquired Mirabilis and ICQ.

When you coupled the largest internet provider with such communication tools, email and instant messenger was adopted by not just millions, but hundreds of millions of people, changing the way we communicate forever.

Then the innovation flowed. More advanced instant messaging software clients started to offer enhanced modes of communication like video calling, Voice Over Internet Protocol (VOIP – as Skype uses), web conferencing integrating both video calling and instant messaging abilities, desktop sharing and IP radio.

This form of communication was becoming disruptive to the traditional media as we began to shift the way we access information.

theGlobe.com

In 1994, students Stephen Paternot and Todd Krizelman founded theGlobe.com. Paternot and Krizelman used a primitive chat room on their university's computer network and quickly saw the business potential. They raised US$15,000 over the 1994 Christmas break and purchased an Apple internet server, spending the next few months programming what would later become theGlobe.com[2].

The site was launched as an online community giving users the freedom to personalise their online experiences by publishing their own content and interacting with others with similar interests.

Demonstrating how people were looking to communicate in different ways, when they launched in 1995, they attracted over 44,000 visits within the first month. A year later they had a million users.

The pair used the popularity of the site in 1997 to secure US$20 million in financing through Dancing Bear Investments, showing that venture capitalists and investment banks were now interested in online communication tools[3].

As a result, Paternot and Krizelman received salaries in excess of US$100,000 and revenues from preferred shares sales of US$500,000 each.

On Friday, November 13th, 1998, theGlobe.com issued its IPO, and had nearly 20 million monthly users: that was 10% of the web universe at the time.

When it floated on the stock market, the stock's target share price was initially set at US$9, yet the first trade was at US$87 and the price climbed as high as US$97 before closing at US$63.50. At the end of the trading day, the company had set a record for IPOs with a 606% increase over the initial share price[4].

The possibilities for computer geeks had changed forever. Based on their holdings, the young founders were worth close to US$100 million each[5]. Unfortunately for them, during the dot-com bust, share prices began to decline rapidly and theGlobe.com saw its share price drop from a high of US$97 to less than 10 cents.

In 2000, Paternot and Krizelman were forced out of the company, but their innovation will go down in history as one of the first and largest social networks in history, alongside sites like Tripod.com and Geocities.com.

While a failure, a wave of followers were watching and launching.

These early communities were all focused on bringing people together to interact with each other through chat rooms, all encouraging users to share personal information and ideas via personal web pages. They provided easy-to-use publishing tools and free or inexpensive web space.

In 1993 Gary Kremen founded Match.com, which later became a hugely popular online dating company, reportedly attracting more than 20 million members at its peak[6].

In 1995 Randy Conrads launched Classmate.com, originally designed to assist members in finding friends and acquaintances. What was unique about Classmates.com is that they took a different approach, simply having people link to each other via email addresses. As of 2008, Classmates.com had more than 50 million members with 3.8 million paid subscribers[7].

Now people were willing to pay subscriptions for such services, demonstrating a new commercial viability.

Social networking had officially changed the way we communicate forever.

SixDegrees.com

But the first social network to operate the way we know social networks to operate today, was created by Andrew Weinreich – SixDegrees.com. The name came from the well known 'six degrees of separation' concept originally coined by Frigyes Karinthy.

Six degrees of separation refers to the idea that everyone is on average approximately six contacts away from any other person on earth through a network of friends-of-friends.

By creating an online platform where users could list friends, family members and invite contacts to join the site by email, in theory, you were able to connect with anybody. All you had to do was join and connect. Registered users could send messages and post bulletin board items to friends in their first, second, and third degrees, as well as see friends' connections.

People who confirmed a relationship with an existing user, but did not go on to register with the site, continued to receive email updates and solicitations until they joined.

This was a new and unique online combination.

Creating profiles already existed on many other community and dating sites prior to SixDegrees.com. Listing friends already existed on platforms like AOL Instant Messenger and ICQ called them 'buddy lists'. Classmates.com already allowed people to connect with their high school or college network and search for others who were also in the network. But, SixDegrees.com was the first to combine profiles with friend lists, the ability to display your friends and search your friends' connections.

At its height, SixDegrees had around 100 employees, and the site had around one million fully-registered members[8].

While they were the first social network that attempted to collect real names and connect people with real relationships, they were a victim of being too early. Dial-up internet was expensive, the cost of servers was restrictive and there were huge costs associated with hosting users' photos at the time. Without photos, the social network felt much less personal than today and at the time there were few digital cameras in existence.

Despite this challenge, by 1999 they had 3.5 million registered users. The site was later bought in 2000 for US$125 million and shut down in the dot-com bust of 2000 with very little revenue.

Founder Weinreich did, however, buy a patent on this innovation that would later play a role in the rise of modern social networks like LinkedIn.

A newer generation of social networking sites began to flourish after the popularity and format of SixDegrees.com. They had cracked the social networking code for others to follow.

Ecademy

In 1998, Ecademy, the first business-to-business social network was founded by Penny Power, Thomas Power and Glenn Watkins with the aim of helping business people achieve success through online tools, community and friendship.

What makes Ecademy unique today is how they combine online and offline networking for business owners; they have a boardroom service which allows entrepreneurs to use peer-to-peer mentoring to crowdsource their very own boardroom. I am an active member and Ecademy is the only social network I know where you can actually engage and connect with the founders, Penny and Thomas Power.

The Powers provide a working example of what can be achieved when you invest in your social capital. I recommend watching one of their videos on YouTube about their 'Open, Random and Supportive' philosophy and for a sample of Thomas Power's foresight, check out the YouTube video titled 'Bank Of Facebook'.

MakeOutClub followed in 1999 when Gibby Miller launched her site as a music social network, to provide a community for people with similar style and musical tastes.

These niche communities provided a place for those who shared interests in many different areas to aggregate and connect with each other sharing common interests and goals.

After investors in public companies got burnt during the dot-com bust, Silicon Valley stepped in as social networking started to get the attention of venture capitalists.

In 2000 Sean Parker, who later played a huge role in the success of Facebook, Minh Nguyen, Todd Masonis and Cameron Ring launched Plaxo as an online address book and social networking service.

Plaxo was launched with venture capital from Sequoia Capital, the most influential venture capital firm in the entire history of social networking. In May 2008, the website reported 20 million users[9].

Ryze.com was next, launched in late 2001 by Adrian Scott, following in Ecademy's footsteps as a free social networking website designed to link business professionals, particularly new entrepreneurs. The site now claims to have over 500,000 members in 200 countries, and is funded by charging employers to search for employees[10].

Ryze's founder, Adrian Scott, first introduced the site to his friends, primarily members of the Silicon Valley business and technology community, including the entrepreneurs and investors behind many future social networks.

While it did not take off big, Ryze.com was a heavy influence on the next major social network success, Friendster, founded by early Ryze member Jonathan Abrams in 2002.

The people behind Ryze, Tribe.net, LinkedIn, and Friendster were tightly entwined personally and professionally. They believed that they could support each other without competing.

College networks

Also, just before the launch of Friendster, a handful of social networks popped up just for college students, most notably Stanford University's Club Nexus.

This network gets special mention here, as one of its founders went on to create Google's first move into social networking.

Founded by Orkut Buyukkokten and Tyler Ziemann, Club Nexus was the first social network that required you to have a

Stanford email address to join, a concept that was later used by Facebook for Harvard University students.

Orkut left Club Nexus to work for Google where he was given the opportunity to launch Google's social network named after him – Orkut.

In 2003 social networks for colleges were being created everywhere, including Collegester.com, WesMatch, Yalestation, CUCommunity and many others. But the next major breakthrough in social networking came when Jonathan Abrams founded Friendster.

Friendster

Following on from SixDegree.com, Friendster insisted on users only submitting real names, kicking out those with fake names. The difference with Friendster, unlike SixDegrees.com, was not a unique social network, but rather the timing was right for pictures.

The addition of pictures, the lower cost of hosting pictures by Friendster and the mainstream use of digital cameras, gave that extra personal touch that would generate user participation like never before.

Friendster was an immediate hit. Within months they had several million users.

As of 2008 Friendster had a membership base of more than 115 million registered users[11]. In 2003, Friendster management received a US$30 million buyout offer from Google, which they declined[12].Unfortunately the success of Friendster was too big for them to handle. As millions joined, Friendster could not handle the growth and their servers slowed significantly. Pages were so slow to load that users started dropping out and giving up.

But Friendster goes down in history as the first to use the social networking code that SixDegrees.com had cracked, and couple it with pictures to break through over 100 million users.

After the success of Friendster, other large social networks started launching. Friendster was followed by MySpace, Linkedin and Bebo a year later.

Tickle.com, which was founded on the idea that personal insight and connections to others can be scientific, fun and profitable, focused on quizzes and tests and was an early example of viral marketing. By sharing tests such as 'What Breed of Dog Are You?',

Tickle started to show the viral nature of such user generated content, receiving heavy traffic from word-of-mouth and pass-along emails.

They demonstrated that by giving certain tools to users, these tools could be used to increase user sign-ups significantly, a concept that Facebook used a few years later with the popularity of photo tagging, where users would use Facebook just to see who was uploading photos of them on the social network.

In 2003 Paul Martino, Mark Pincus and Valerie Syme founded Tribe.net where users were able to create a tribe around a specific interest, getting mention here as they later played an interesting role in the success of the major social network – LinkedIn.

LinkedIn

2003 saw the launch of LinkedIn by founder Reid Hoffman, based on a very similar concept as Ryze.

LinkedIn was a professional social network funded by venture capital from Sequoia Capital and later became a hugely disruptive technology for the traditional recruitment industry as a tool for finding new employees.

As of 2011, LinkedIn reports more than 120 million registered users, spanning more than 200 countries worldwide[13] [14].

In the summer of 2003 SixDegrees.com put its patent up for auction, which threatened the business models of these major social networks if it found its way into the wrong hands.

It had patented the process that most of the social networks were already using like maintaining a database, enabling members to create an account, then encouraging members to invite others to connect via email.

LinkedIn and Tribe.net were concerned that with Friendster receiving millions in venture capital, Friendster could afford to buy the patent and threaten legal action against them. Hoffman, Tribe.net's founder and Pincus, LinkedIn's founder, decided to pool their own money to buy the patent.

Yahoo wanted to join in and entered the auction, but Pincus and Hoffman won the auction for US$700,000, putting an end to their nerves[15]. The patent was never used to threaten any of the social networks.

MySpace

Alongside LinkedIn, 2003 gave birth to MySpace. In sheer frustration of how slow Friendster had become for its users, Tom Anderson and Chris DeWolfe founded MySpace and launched within days. According to co-founder Tom Anderson, the founders wanted to attract estranged Friendster users.

The timing could not have been better, as its launch was timed perfectly with the broadband internet boom and the popularity and affordability of digital cameras, making uploading photos easier and cheaper than ever before.

MySpace was an instant success, choosing to market in clubs, which shortly became an essential promotional tool for bands and nightclubs. The bands-and-fans side of MySpace was mutually beneficial. Bands wanted to contact fans, while fans desired attention from their favourite bands.

The 100 millionth account was created in 2006 and by late 2007 into 2008, MySpace was considered the leading social networking site in the world[16].

MySpace got so large, that it actually got the attention of media mogul giant Rupert Murdoch and in July 2005, News Corporation purchased MySpace for US$580 million, attracting massive media attention.

Around the same time, Attorney General Richard Blumenthal launched an investigation into minors' exposure to pornography on MySpace. This resulted in a media frenzy and MySpace's inability to build an effective spam filter gave the site a reputation as a "vortex of perversion".

As MySpace was launched and built so quickly, it was built using inflexible technology that made changes and updates very difficult. They could not keep up with the spammers and the site soon became very messy for its users.

Around that time, specialised social media companies such as Twitter formed and began targeting MySpace users, while Facebook launched a safe social network, in comparison to MySpace. The perception of MySpace eventually drove advertisers away and users flocked to the new startup, Facebook.

Orkut

Just before the launch of Facebook, the founder of Club Nexus, Orkut Buyukkokten, who had left Nexus to work for Google, approached a product executive at Google and told them he had built a social network and he owned the domain Orkut.com.

Google responded by naming their answer to social networking after him and in January 2004 launched Orkut, but with the wave of venture-backed startups launching in Silicon Valley, few people paid attention to social networks that gained popularity elsewhere, even those built by major corporations like Google.

By the end of 2004 Orkut, strangely, became dominated by Brazilians and Americans dropped away as more and more were networking in Portuguese. By 2008 Google moved Orkut's headquarters to Brazil as 50% of its members were Brazilian and 20% Indian[17].

Orkut had shown that language was a huge factor in the success of a social network, a lesson that Facebook noted, as they later invested significant time in making sure that it could operate in multiple languages worldwide. Facebook uses the collective power of its significant user base in order to translate its social network into multiple languages.

While MySpace attracted the majority of media attention in the US and abroad, social networks were growing in popularity worldwide.

Friendster gained users in the Pacific Islands, Orkut became the number one social network in Brazil before gaining users in India, Mixi become a major social network in Japan, LunarStorm took off in Sweden, Dutch users embraced Hyves, Grono captured Poland, Hi5 was adopted in smaller countries in Latin America, South America, and Europe, and Bebo became very popular in the United Kingdom, New Zealand, and Australia.

The Chinese QQ instant messaging service instantly became the largest social network worldwide when it added profiles to its instant messenger service and made friends visible, while the forum tool Cyworld cornered the Korean market by introducing homepages and buddies.

Facebook

In February 2004 TheFacebook.com was founded by Mark Zuckerberg with his college room mates and fellow computer science students Eduardo Saverin, Dustin Moskovitz and Chris Hughes.

Before TheFacebook.com, Mark Zuckerberg, a programmer, wrote a website called Facemash in 2003, while attending Harvard University. According to The Harvard Crimson, the site was comparable to 'Hot or Not', and "used photos compiled from the online facebooks of nine houses, placing two next to each other at a time and asking users to choose the 'hotter' person".

Facemash attracted 450 visitors and 22,000 photo views in its first four hours online, showing Zuckerberg how quickly he could attract attention to a website[18].

On February 2004, Zuckerberg launched "Thefacebook", originally located at thefacebook.com.

Users flocked to the social network as they spent hours running their online social lives through the site. Colleges were literally lining up and begging Zuckerberg to open TheFacebook.com up to other colleges.

Facebook incorporated in the summer of 2004, and the founder of Plaxo and Napster, Sean Parker, who had been informally advising Zuckerberg, became the company's president. It received its first venture capital investment later that month from PayPal co-founder Peter Thiel.

The social networks membership was initially limited by the founders to Harvard students, but later it gradually added membership for students at various other colleges, before opening to high school students, and, finally, to anyone aged 13 and over.

Users were able to create a personal profile, connect with other users as friends to exchange messages with automatic notifications when they update their profile. Later, users were able to join common-interest user groups, organised by workplace, school or college and other characteristics, allowing tribes to form.

The company dropped 'The' from its name after purchasing the domain name facebook.com in 2005 for US$200,000[19].

The success of Facebook became a worldwide phenomenon, surpassing all that launched before, connecting most of the world with the exception of China.

In November 2010, based on SecondMarket Inc., an exchange for shares of privately held companies, Facebook's value was US$41 billion (slightly surpassing eBay's) and it became the third largest US web company after Google and Amazon with over 500 million active users.

Traffic to Facebook increased steadily after 2009 and eventually more people visited Facebook than Google for the week ending 13th March, 2010. By 2011, Facebook had more than 800 million active users.

As the social media and user-generated content phenomena grew, websites focused on media sharing began implementing social networking features and becoming social networks themselves. Examples include Flickr (photo sharing), Last.FM (music listening habits), and YouTube (video sharing).

YouTube

During the early adoption of Facebook, in 2005 Chad Hurley, Steve Chen, and Jawed Karim, a team of employees from PayPal founded YouTube where users could upload, share and view videos.

YouTube began as a venture-funded technology startup, primarily from a USUS$11.5 million investment by Sequoia Capital. YouTube socialised online videos, allowing users to leave comments, like, favourites and rate videos, making them an integral part of the social networking story.

Twitter

In July 2006 Jack Dorsey launched Twitter, an online microblogging service that enabled its users to send and read text-based posts of up to 140 characters, known as "tweets."

Twitter rapidly gained worldwide popularity, with 200 million users as of 2011, generating over 200 million tweets and handling over 1.6 billion search queries per day[20]. It was described as the SMS of the Internet.

Google+

Then in 2011 Google finally got the social networking thing right, after numerous failed attempts. Their service launched on 28th June, 2011 in an invitation-only 'field testing' phase.

The following day, existing users were allowed to invite friends to the service to create their own accounts. This was suspended the next day due to an "insane demand" for accounts.

On 14th July, 2011, Google announced that Google+ had reached 10 million users just two weeks after it was launched. After four weeks in operation, it had reached 25 million users[21].

In under a day, the Google+ iPhone app was the most popular free application in the Apple app store.

To put that into perspective – Facebook took three years to reach 25 million users, Twitter took two and a half years, MySpace took 1 year and 8 months, whereas Google+ took one month!

So where are we now?

First disclaimer: this will be out of date by the time you read it, but technology moves too fast for any book and you will get the point.

At the time of writing, it is estimated that there are now over 200 active sites using a wide variety of social networking models.

Based on TNS research, 46% of people online globally access a social network every day[22]. Every minute, 24 hours of video is uploaded to YouTube. There are more than 2bn video views on YouTube every 24 hours[23]. Every minute, 66,667 tweets are made on Twitter. 95 million tweets are written each day[24]. Every hour, approximately 10.5 million songs are illegally downloaded[25]. Every day 2,300 new Wikipedia articles are created, adding to the 17 million articles with contributions from 91,000 active contributors[26]. Every day, more than 175 million Facebook user log on to Facebook[27]. 50% of Facebook's users login every day, 200 million login everyday from a mobile device[28]. People spend over 700 billion minutes each month on Facebook[29]. More than 30 billion pieces of content (web links, news stories, blog posts, etc.) is shared each month, which is an average of 7 billion pieces a week[30].

More than a million companies have LinkedIn company pages. There were nearly 2 billion people searches on LinkedIn during 2010[31]. The average profile age on LinkedIn is 40 years, Twitter

35 years. Facebook's biggest age group of followers is now in the 35-54 range.

Don't fall into the trap of thinking that those on these sites are just for kids. The rise of the social network is a mind-boggling story that involved us all.

The world will never be the same again

The rise of the social network made it possible for us all to connect and build relationships with people who share interests and activities across political, economic, and geographic borders around the world.

If you are not actively engaging in the social networks then you currently have a social capital score of zero. It is my belief that this will cost you big in the future and if you get one thing out of this book, it is to start investing in your social capital.

Online communities are now formed everywhere, allowing systems like gift economies to work through cooperation, giving people alternatives that were never available before.

Scholars in many fields have investigated the impact of social networking sites, researching how such sites may play a role both negatively and positively in issues of identity, privacy, social capital, youth culture and education, to mention a few.

Millions of websites, businesses, causes, social enterprises and charities are beginning to tap into the power of the social networking model for philanthropy and fundraising.

Such models provide a means for connecting otherwise fragmented industries and small organisations without the resources to reach a broader audience.

Social networks are providing a different way for individuals to communicate digitally. These communities allow for the sharing of information and ideas, an old concept placed in a digital environment.

The debates will continue, the online arguments continue, the bullying is horrific, more problems will arise, but the world will never be the same again as long as everyone and everything remains connected.

Before discussing the profound impact it had in giving birth to new innovative, hugely disruptive technologies in finance, it is worth spending a bit of time on the effect the social networks had on money.

The socialism of money

In the last chapter we saw first-hand the effect that the social networks have had on money with the rise of digital money following the rise of the World Wide Web. In this chapter we have seen the extraordinary rise of the social network. Combine these innovations and we have seen alternative currencies in both cyberspace and the real world.

We have seen the emergence of social payment systems built on PayPal's infrastructure like Facebook Credits and TwittPay.

We have seen the possibilities of moneyless systems like Time Banking allowing people to opt out of the financial system altogether should they wish.

But perhaps the most prolific effects that the social networks have had on the world of money and finance to date come from the free flow of information.

As I write, YouTube is ranked the second largest search engine in the world, behind its parent company Google. I did a few quick searches on YouTube to get an indication of what people are searching for and viewing today.

When I searched the name 'Bitcoin', the first video that comes up is titled "What is Bitcoin?" and has over 700,000 views, followed by a video titled "Bitcoin: The future of currency" and "Bitcoin: The end of state collected money".

Interesting.

When I type the term 'Goldman Sachs', the first thing to notice is that the search engine immediately suggests I should be searching for the term 'Goldman Sachs conspiracy'. Ignoring that suggestion, I simply search 'Goldman Sachs' and the search gives me firstly a video cartoon which describes how graduates who want to work at Goldman Sachs are employed to 'screw-over' the world.

Interesting.

When I typed in the term 'Google Wallet', the first video is two months old and has already had over 60,000 views for an-hour long video entitled 'Google Wallet Product Launch'.

Compare that with my search for the word 'MasterCard', where the first offering is a one month-old video with over 750,000 views describing the scandal of how MasterCard had stopped giving WikiLeaks access to payment facilities.

Interesting.

When I type in the word 'money', after a few music videos from Pink Floyd, I am given the option to watch a cartoon titled "Money As Debt" with close to 1 million views describing the corruption of banking.

Interesting.

When I type in the word 'banking', I am given a four day-old video with over 12,000 views titled 'Dylan Ratigan's Epic Rant on the International Banking Cartel and Political Corruption.'

Interesting.

When I type the words 'social media', the first video I get is entitled 'Social Media Revolution' with close to 3 million views in a year.

Interesting.

When I type in the term 'Social Banking', the first video I am given is an interview that I conducted with Triodos Bank that I uploaded only a few days ago with over 1,000 views from my very own YouTube channel dedicated to banking reform that you can subscribe to at www.YouTube.com/user/bankingreform.

QR 25 Simon Dixon's banking reform YouTube Channel

Interesting.

When I type in the word 'finance' I am given a video titled 'The Descent of Finance'.

What does this tell us? The public is looking for something new, and trust in our current financial system is at an all-time low, while conspiracy theories and scandalous accusations of our current financial system are at an all-time high.

So, aside from the monetary innovation that the social networks made possible, the financial literacy of the world has only been made possible due to the socialism of information through YouTube, spread virally through Facebook, Twitter, LinkedIn and other social networks, and checked for accuracy through crowdsourced websites like Wikipedia.

Don't trust the information? Well, with a few clicks on an iPad or Amazon Kindle, books can immediately be read, or recommended to you through your trusted network, with full reviews and opinions given from a range of readers before you buy.

But there is more, much more ... The social networks gave birth to three more hugely disruptive technologies with the potential and power to transform the world of money and finance forever.

With the social networks came the birth of crowdfunding, person-to-person lending, peer-to-peer equity investing and microfinance platforms.

In the next chapter we look at the rise of crowdfunding and the impact it can have on us all. Later, we explore alternative lending, equity and microfinance opportunities. We also explore alternative finance's potential when it is unleashed as a fair competitor to traditional finance, under our Bank Charter Act reforms, after our adventure in time travel where we rid ourselves of our reliance on banks for the creation of money as debt.

You may not know it, but lack of money is no longer the reason why you may not be achieving the results you want to achieve any more. It is either your lack of knowledge on alternative finance, or your lack of social capital.

Hold on! Before you start Chapter 8, tweet me your thoughts on the #SocialNetworks.

QR 26 Tweet Simon Dixon about #SocialNetworks

1 Shapiro, Eben."THE MEDIA BUSINESS; New Features Are Planned By Prodigy", The New York Times, September 6, 1990 (The French Minitel had one
   million, but was used mainly from passive low-cost ASCII/Teletex terminals).
   Accessed February 4, 2008. "Prodigy has become the second-largest and
   fastest-growing computer-information company since it was introduced in
   1988. It has 465,000 subscribers, compared with more than 600,000 for
   Compuserve Information Services, a unit of H & R Block Inc."

2 "A Student-created Company is the Talk of the Web", Cornell Chronicle.
   Dated April 11, 1996. Retrieved on June 27, 2007. http://www.news.cornell.
   edu/chronicle/96/4.11.96/webgenesis.html

3 "The Story of Bubble Boy", review of Stephan Paternot's book, A Very Public
   Offering: A Rebel's Story of Business, Excess, Success and Reckoning at smart-
   money.com. Dated August 6, 2001. Retrieved on June 27, 2007

4 "TheGlobe.com's IPO One for the Books" at news.com. Dated November 13,
   1998. Retrieved on June 27, 2007

5 "Spinning the globe: The Net Bubble Through the Eyes of Callow Youth ",
   review of Stephan Paternot's book, A Very Public Offering: A Rebel's Story of
   Business, Excess, Success and Reckoning at thestreet.com. Dated September
   1, 2001. Retrieved on June 27, 2007

6 "Compare Online Dating". Retrieved 12 January 2010

7 United Online, May 6 2008 http://investor.untd.com/releasedetail.
   cfm?ReleaseID=328744

8 SixDegrees.comWikipediacontributors http://en.wikipedia.org/w/index.php?
   title=SixDegrees.com&oldid=447494094

9 Plaxo (May 22, 2008). "The Plaxo Directory Is Now Live". Press Release http://
   blog.plaxo.com/2008/05/the_plaxo_direc/

10 RyzeWikipedia contributors //en.wikipedia.org/w/index.php?title=Ryze&oldid
   =451398177

11 Press Release, October 21, 2008. "Friendster is the #1 Social Network for Adults and Youth in Malaysia", Press Release. Retrieved October 27, 2008.

12 Gary Rivlin, October 15, 2006. "Wallflower at the Web Party." New York Times. Retrieved December 4, 2008

13 LinkedIn – About Us

14 Mashable Business, LinkedIn Surpasses 100 Million Users [INFOGRAPHIC http://mashable.com/2011/03/22/linkedin-surpasses-100-million-users-info-graphic/

15 The Facebook Effect, David Kirkpatrick, 2010

16 "100,000,000th Account". MySpace. 2007-02-25. Retrieved 2007-02-21

17 "Orkut.com Site Info". Alexa Internet. Retrieved 2011-10-02

18 Locke, Laura. "The Future of Facebook", Time Magazine, July 17, 2007. Retrieved November 13, 2009

19 Williams, Chris (1 October 2007). "Facebook wins Manx battle for face-book.com". The Register. Retrieved 13 June 2008

20 "Your world, more connected". Twitter. 1 August 2011. Retrieved 1 August 2011

21 Wasserman, Todd (2 August 2011). "Google+ Hits 25 Million Visitors; Users Are Spending More Time There [STUDY]". Mashable. Retrieved 29 August 2011

22 www.thejakartapost.com

23 20+ Mind-blowing social media statistics: One year later http://www.barnes-graham.com/resource-centre/industry-news-and-articles/article-771-2011-3/20-mind-blowing-social-media-statistics-one-year-later

24 Twitter Information, http://techtips.salon.com/twitter-information-2093.html

25 45 Useful Social Media Statistics http://www.evoapp.com/45-tweetable-so-cial-media-stats

26 13 Mind-Bending Social Media Marketing Statistics, http://coppermoon.pos-terous.com/great-stats-13-mind-bending-social-media-mark

27 Facebook, Statistics, https://www.facebook.com/press/info.php?statistics

28 Facebook, Statistics, https://www.facebook.com/press/info.php?statistics

29 Facebook, Statistics, https://www.facebook.com/press/info.php?statistics

30 Internet 2010 in numbers, Pingdom, http://royal.pingdom.com/2011/01/12/internet-2010-in-numbers/

31 LinkedIn - About Us http://press.linkedin.com/about

8 Hugely disruptive technology #4 – crowdfunding

YOU MIGHT LIKE to take a look at the introductory video before we start.

Scan QR Code and watch video!

You Tube

Can't scan? http://bit.ly/qHopiN

QR 27 Introductory video on hugely disruptive technology #4

Hugely disruptive technologies 1–3 – the World Wide Web, digital money and the social networks – gave us all the ability to build social capital and contacts around the world and trade globally, easily.

With the stability of money taken care of via our adventures in time travel, we have also watched the emergence of non-banks. These smaller companies that are not banks, but seem to perform some of the functions of banks, were only made possible on the shoulders of the three technologies discussed in previous chapters.

Before our reforms, non-banks were restricted in size, as we all relied on the banking monopoly for the creation of money, but this time round, there is genuine room for innovation in financial services, as banks and non-banks compete for the trust of customers, thanks to our reforms.

Out of the ability to build social connections comes the ability to benefit both personally and financially from strong online relationships.

Your most treasured asset of the future

The more time and effort that you strategically invest into your social capital using the social networks, the more value you will have, both now and more so, in the future.

Just as a computer (physical capital) or a university education (human capital) can increase productivity (both individual and collective), so do social contacts (social capital).

This has always been the case, but the last three hugely disruptive technologies have opened up what used to be reserved for a few, to everybody with an internet connection.

Figure 40 Building your social capital

In the future, your social capital score will become one of the most treasured and prized assets you own. If you are not actively and strategically building it right now, it is already costing you financially, physically and emotionally – big.

Social capital is a measure of your connections within and between social networks. Your success, however you define it, now and in the future, will correlate to the value of your social capital score. Today and in the future, the cooperation and confidence of your social connections will determine your collective or economic results.

Social capital is the fruit of social relations, and consists of the expected benefits derived from the preferential treatment and cooperation between individuals and groups that are connected.

The power of your 'crowd' of friends and followers will become one of your key indicators of trust, respect and your tool for future prosperity. In times of hardship, if your crowd of friends and followers is strong enough, no problem is too big.

In times when you need advice, if your crowd of friends and followers is strong enough, no information is restricted.

In times when you need services, if your crowd of friends and followers is strong enough, you will never need to work with those you dislike and distrust ever again.

In times when you have been scammed, if your crowd of friends and followers is strong enough, you can collectively prevent it happening to others and the scammer is penalised through a reduction in their social capital score and an increase in yours.

In times of financial hardship, if your crowd of friends and followers is strong enough, finance is never going to be a problem again.

Everybody is going to be held to a higher standard and people will have to treat each other better, or pay. Your social capital will become your measure of success.

This may be exciting or scary, depending on how you have acted in the past, but the change is inevitable, it has already begun and you need to adjust accordingly now.

Tools like Klout, Peer Index and Empire Avenue are some of the first online tools developed to give us a measure and score of your online influence, with more to follow, but in the future, those with real photos and profiles online, those who treat others with respect online, those who support each other online, those who do what they say they are going to do, those who embrace change, are all going to be rewarded physically, financially and emotionally for supporting each other online with a higher social capital score.

If you have been using the social networks, blogs, forums, chat rooms, instant messenger services and other online tools with anonymous profiles, hidden behind fake photos and fake user names as a way to bully, abuse, gossip and tear down others online, your social capital score will be very low.

Even if you have been using them to support and connect with others in a constructive way, if you have been using them under an anonymous user name, your social capital score is useless and it is about to cost you your future.

While many use the social networks as a tool to anonymously abuse others without using their real names, photos and identity, a new hugely disruptive technology comes along to reward those who respect each other online, those who support each other online and those who only act and say things that they would say without a faceless anonymous online identity.

It turns out that your presence, connections and how you treat others online are the very tools that will be your most valuable asset for succeeding in the future. In fact, they shape your entire financial success as we move into the future and beyond.

With the birth of hugely disruptive technology #4 – crowd-funding – people are given the opportunity to raise funds for their ideas, businesses, education and projects, based upon social relationships built online, the viral nature of social networks and their social capital score.

And this is just the beginning. We are about to see a wave of innovation in this field change the rules forever.

The rules of finance are starting to move from begging banks and VCs for money, to building strong connections online and building your social capital score.

Have you been a part of it? Because at the time of writing, it is still in its infancy and you will need to start investing in your social capital score now.

If you have not started to invest in your online personal brand or social capital score yet, you are about to find out why that will become your most prized asset in the future.

Why don't you know that money is not the thing that is stopping you?

I recently did a series of interviews where I asked randomly selected people in different environments five questions:

1   What would you love to create in this lifetime if money were no issue?

2   What has stopped you from creating it so far?

3   To get started this year, how much money would you need?

4   If I told you that you had to raise the funds to get started this year or the world was going to end and you believed me, how would you raise the funds?

5   Have you ever heard of crowdfunding before?

I conducted these interviews by approaching random people at carefully selected locations to compare results.

The first set of interviews were conducted in the heart of the shopping district in the West End of London; the second set of interviews were conducted at the home of London's financial district outside Bank station; the third set of interviews were conducted at a recent summer school that I was invited to participate in with the Institute For Social Banking; the fourth set of interviews were conducted at the home of London's hedge funds and private equity houses in Mayfair; and the final set of interviews were conducted at a conference for entrepreneurs.

For the rest of this chapter, I will call these groups of people the shoppers, the financiers (it turned out that the results in Bank station and Mayfair were very similar so I merged them together after the interviews), the social people and the entrepreneurs.

My goal was to find out how many people actually had goals to create something that they really wanted to create, the things that stop them from creating what they really want and whether money was a contributing factor towards them not creating what is important to them.

I also wanted to compare different people's understanding about raising funds and how many of them knew how to raise funds for their creations through crowdfunding.

The survey results

While I could write a whole book on the results I got, I have to limit it to a few interesting relevant results. What was originally meant to be a quick and simple exercise, actually turned out to give me amazing insights into many different areas, but I stick to the results I originally set out to achieve.

So firstly, every person within every group had a creation that they really wanted to create in this lifetime, when pushed to think about it. The only slight difference was that the entrepreneurs and the social people were able to answer the question with less thought and had a more defined creation in mind already.

Most of the other groups were pushed to think about it, but eventually had a dream creation in mind that they could get excited about. So everybody wants to create something from my interviews.

Most of the social people had a creation around changing a social aspect of the world and most of the entrepreneurs wanted to make a difference through a particular niche area of business helping them to achieve financial freedom. But most wanted to make a difference through some kind of creation important to them.

The reasons for not achieving those creations so far were split into three main categories across all groups. The three main reasons were either that they did not have the money (financial); they did not have the time (physical); or they simply did not believe it was possible (psychological).

Over 90% of every group said that they needed money to get started – responses ranged from buying a guitar, to getting an Apple computer, to hiring staff and getting an office, to technology creation, to raising £500 million through an IPO, and everything in between.

But the interesting facts were in the differences.

The shoppers

The shoppers were split 53% to 47% between not believing it was possible to achieve their lifetime creation dream and not having the money.

62% of the shoppers would turn to friends and family to raise money if they were forced to start this year and 31% would turn to a bank; the remainder had savings.

Over 70% of the shoppers needed less than £10,000 to get started.

Nobody in the shopping centre had ever heard of crowdfunding.

The financiers

The financiers attributed time as the major reason for not creating their lifetime dream, by a majority of over 86%.

All had finance jobs and the time spent in their job demanded everything they had, plus the financial rewards for achievement in their career seemed to cast aside their lifetime creation dreams, which, interestingly, had nothing to do with their jobs in most cases.

For the financiers, the money they needed to start on their creations was a lot larger and they wanted money that could normally only be raised through the capital markets, ranging from £5 million through to £500 million.

In both financial districts, almost all said they would turn to savings and existing investor contacts if they were forced to start this year, but, interestingly, many expressed the view that if they had just a little more time they would raise money through venture capital and a stock market flotation and seemed confident about raising the funds.

Only 12% of those at Bank station had heard about crowdfunding and 6% in Mayfair.

The social people

Over 91% of social people gave financial reasons as the main reason that they have not achieved their lifetime creation dream yet, with time as the small runner-up.

They needed an average of about £750,000 to start.

22% thought that they could turn to a bank for a small amount, but those that wanted larger sums did not think they could get the money this year, no matter what they did.

Interestingly 73% of the social people knew about crowdfunding and said they would consider it a viable option for raising funds in combination with social loans.

The entrepreneurs

Over 62% of the entrepreneurs gave financial reasons as the main reason that they have not achieved their creation, and the minority due to lack of belief.

83% of the entrepreneurs believed they needed less than £100,000 to achieve their goals.

46% thought that they could not raise funds this year, but 33% were actively looking for high net worth business angels, with no success so far.

Less than 11% thought that they could get the money from the bank.

Only 9% of the entrepreneurs knew that they could raise funds for their creations through crowdfunding.

So what does this tell us?

Let's make some sweeping generalisations from the results. I know there are many more variables, but let's just go with it ...

When people are pushed to answer the question, it turns out that everybody wants to create something in the world that means that their life is making a difference. People want to leave a legacy.

Everybody I interviewed wants to do it in a different way, but almost all wanted to make a difference in some way when pushed to think about it. Some think about it, others are trying to achieve it proactively and many have left it as just a dream.

It is clear people need money to start on their creations. Finance is a huge factor that stops people from starting in the first place, as well as time, as they are working to survive, rather than working on what they want to create.

So the time reason seems to merge with finance, as they spend almost all of their time trying to make money.

Different people hold completely different beliefs about what is possible.

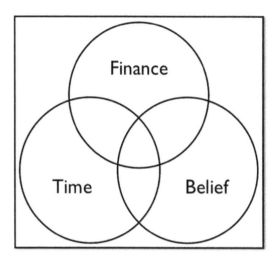

Figure 41 The main forces that stop people from achieving their dream creations from our interviews

Most of those who spend their time shopping, in general, don't believe they will ever achieve their creation and cannot raise the money to start.

Those who work in finance believe they have no issue with raising funds, but are too busy to work on their goals.

Financiers believe they need a lot of money to start on their goals and the task seems too big and risky to give up their financially rewarding jobs.

Entrepreneurs and social people just can't get the money they need. They have a vision, but money stops them.

Very few know how to raise funds to achieve their creations and dreams outside of those who understand the world of money and finance.

The vast majority have no idea that they can use crowdfunding as a way to fund their creations and dreams.

I found the results very interesting, and hope it has made you think about your goals too.

So before we discuss how crowdfunding emerged and why people don't know that money is not the reason why they are not achieving their creations, let's take a look at what crowdfunding is.

So what exactly is crowdfunding anyway?

If you are anything like the people I interviewed for this chapter, my guess is that you probably have an idea for a creation that you have always wanted to get started on, that needs some sort of investment. It could be a book you have always had stuck in your head, a social enterprise you want to start, a film you have always wanted to shoot, a class you have always wanted to attend, a business you want to start up, or whatever.

In fact, right now, write down one thing that you would love to get started on that would require a bit of funding.

In my lifetime I would love to create

....

Go on, if you have not written it down, stop reading and write it down now.

OK, with that in mind, think about how much money you would need to get started and how you would go about raising these funds.

In order to create that, I need .... in funds.

I would most probably raise these funds by

....

So now you have something you want to create, you know roughly how much you need and how you might raise those funds, what is stopping you?

Well, most people I meet just simply don't believe they could raise the funds or they just don't know how to start.

Just so you know, I have never known how to execute my creations before I started, so by a process of elimination, most are stuck on funding.

In the past you either saved up the money to get started, asked friends and family to invest in you, or you turned to financial institutions like the banks.

If your idea is a business and you are looking to fund it through financial institutions, then traditionally, there are two main types of financing for you – debt or equity.

Debt financing tends to be the type of financing you receive from a traditional bank loan and equity financing tends to be financing you receive from venture capital or business angels.

The benefit of debt financing has always been that you will pay down the debt over time without any further obligation. The disadvantage of debt financing has always been that your business will be burdened with some type of regular payment.

On the flip side, with equity financing or venture capital you will be receiving money in exchange for stock in your business or some other form of equity like percentage of income or sales.

The benefit of this type of financing is that, typically, there is no monthly payment. Instead, you are giving up ownership, often permanently.

In the past, raising funds through debt or equity has been a rigorous, costly process that only a few get access to.

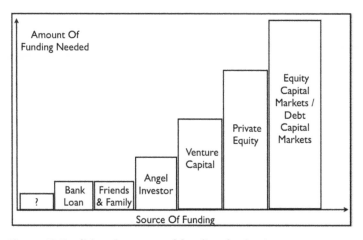

Figure 42 Traditional sources of funding for business

You are either credit worthy and regularly pay off your credit card bills or you can pitch a deal like Donald Trump and are connected to the world of money and finance.

If neither of these is you, then you are left with friends and family or savings to fund your creations.

But hugely disruptive technologies 1–3 gave birth to hugely disruptive technology 4 – crowdfunding, producing an interesting and potentially life-changing alternative.

Most people refer to crowdfunding as the collective pooling of money to fund a project, idea, cause, campaign, business, creation or anything that needs funding to move forward.

These funding needs are most often 'crowdfunded' through a specialist online platform that allows users to pitch their ideas, projects and funding needs to 'the crowd' and spread them through the online social networks, where people can 'pledge' or invest small sums of money to the project until fully funded.

In some cases, like our platform BankToTheFuture.com, investors are collected together into an online community where they update each other on the project with the original pitcher.

With crowdfunding, the online platform is simply facilitating the transaction and putting people together, as opposed to a bank that actually issues the loan with the bank's money.

Well, as we have seen already, the bank does not actually use their own money, they simply create it out of thin air, but you get the point.

This means that people are funding, lending and investing in each other people without the banks, financial markets or VCs, hence often referred to as person-to-person or peer-to-peer transactions, also shortened to P2P.

That being said, everybody I have met and will continue to meet will have a slightly different idea of what crowdfunding means to them, although far too many have never heard of it at all.

For the purpose of this book I think further clarification and definition needs to be made.

Don't worry, I am not going to give you a load of financial jargon and debate the meaning and philosophy behind each definition, but I do need to make some distinctions for the rest of this book to make sense.

I want to make a distinction between person-to-person lending (P2P lending) (or business-to-business lending and other cross-combinations), crowdfunding and person-to-person equity investing (P2P equity investing) (or person/business-to-business investing and other cross-combinations).

I define P2P lending as when a borrower uses an online platform specifically for the purpose of borrowing from multiple lenders, who are investing for a return in the form of interest, where the platform is not acting as the actual lender.

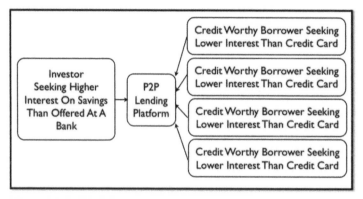

Figure 43 A simple diagram of P2P lending

Borrowers are credit checked and investors' funds are matched with many borrowers in order to offer some protection from default risk. The platform matches lenders and borrowers and provides a community for them to interact as well as administering the payment process.

I define crowdfunding as the process by which a person uses an online platform to raise funds (not to be repaid) for a specific purpose, where multiple funders give money in exchange for rewards and bonuses rather than financial gain.

These rewards could be emotional benefits, like giving to charity or exclusive rewards like meetings with movie directors.

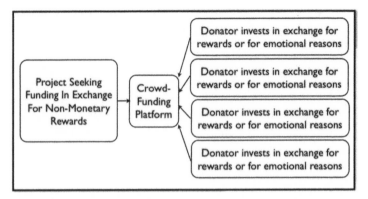

Figure 44 Crowdfunding platforms allow projects to get funding through many donators who invest for emotional reasons and rewards

I define P2P equity investing as the scenario where a business uses an online platform specifically for the purpose of raising funds from multiple investors who invest in exchange for equity, where the platform is not acting as a shareholder in the agreement.

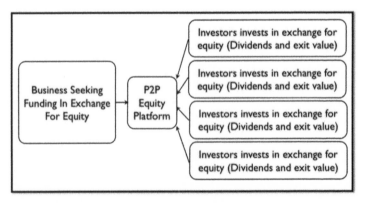

Figure 45 P2P equity platforms allow businesses to offer equity to many investors where investors can start investing with a very small sum of money

If you read further on this topic with other sources, you will not find these standard definitions. Some will refer to all of the above scenarios as simply crowdfunding.

Pim Betist posted a blog on www.crowdsourcing.org where he developed a simple matrix to help classify these different offerings. The matrix consists of two domains: donating vs. investing; and financial/tangible returns vs. emotional/intangible returns, as can be seen in the diagram below.

Financial / Tangible

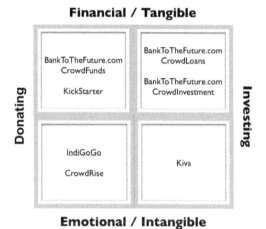

Emotional / Intangible

Figure 46 The crowdfunding quadrant

I have added example online platforms that offer services in each of the quadrants to give you further clarity.

In the top-left quadrant of the diagram (financial/tangible returns and donation based), you find online funding platforms like BankToTheFuture.com's CrowdFund service and KickStarter.

These platforms enable users to donate funds in return for specifically advertised rewards depending on the amount they donate, while people pitch their funding needs and offer the rewards to donors. Perhaps this is best illustrated with an example.

After releasing the book 'Blue like Jazz', the authors wanted to turn the book into a film. Half way through the project they ran out of money before it could hit the big screen. 'Save Blue Like Jazz' supporters crowdfunded US$345,992 to save a movie project that was going to be cancelled[1].

In exchange for contributing funds for the film's production and release, a minimal donation landed you some 'Save Blue Like Jazz' goodies like posters, and script pages as an incentive.

Moving over to the bottom-left quadrant of the diagram (emotional/intangible returns and donation based), you have online platforms like CrowdRise and IndieGoGo. These platforms allow you to donate to projects that you want to see happen on a more emotional than a reward level.

You might remember the time when Facebook was getting a lot of negativity about privacy? A company called Diaspora took advantage of the situation to start working on its privacy-centred social network. Diaspora crowdfunded US$200,641 from 6,479 people[2]. One of those donors was none other than founder and CEO of Facebook himself, Mark Zuckerberg.

This incredible example highlights how people contribute based on emotions. They were not offering any incentive in return for donating, it was purely emotional.

Many charitable causes use such platforms to raise funds for their charities and causes in a similar way.

Now let's take a look at the top-right quadrant of the diagram (financial/tangible returns and investment based). Example online platforms in this quadrant are BankToTheFuture.com's CrowdLoan or BankToTheFuture.com's CrowdInvestment service.

A great example comes from a recent interview I conducted with the founder of the Personal Development Bureau, Rupert Honywood. Rupert wanted to help thousands of people who had lost their jobs after the 2007 financial crisis and wanted to help them find their mission, purpose and passion in life again.

The Personal Development Bureau works with those who are losing their jobs to help them find their true passion and purpose, so that they can choose the most appropriate new career, consider self-employment or starting up a new business.

To get started they needed funding of £50,000 and offered the crowd a 25% stake in the company to CrowdInvestors.

> "In the current economic climate, most banks, despite the hype, are not very supportive of small businesses, so I chose not to waste time speaking to them. I also did not want to grow the business based on having debt so we went for equity funding instead.
>
> It was also very attractive to us to seek investors who were an 'army' of advocates and we did not want any one shareholder to have too much dominance." *Rupert Honywood.*

As part of the CrowdInvesting model, Rupert was able to set the terms of the offer and once people bought at that price, his start-up had a set value in the market.

Most start-ups find it impossible to value their businesses, but now it had a clear, real value based on the vote of the crowd. He also has a team of investors to communicate with as he launched the Bureau and no debt to hold back the business at an early stage.

Rupert had strong social capital and had many connections online, allowing him to work with and win over the crowds.

He went on to share:

> "With crowdfunding it is about engagement and appealing to people's herding instincts. The first few investors you get, however big or small, will be the most difficult to win over and put their hands in their pockets-people don't like being first. Think about how you can be 'social' to engage with people – the technology available today just makes this far easier."

Rupert managed to achieve what so few manage to pull off when searching for a business angel or venture capitalist to get them started.

Finally, in the bottom-right quadrant of the diagram (emotional/intangible returns and investment based), you have online microfinancing platforms like Kiva. Microfinance focuses on small loans in less developed countries which normally suffer from high levels of poverty.

The list of stories in this quadrant are endless, but Lina Elisaia from Samoa provides a classic example of funding in the fourth quadrant.

Lina, a doughnut entrepreneur and grandmother of three, crowdfunded a 1,000 Tala microloan (roughly USD$400). Lina used the microloan to open a doughnut bakery and shop in her front yard[3].

Lina then used her profits to diversify and opened a vegetable stand, while repaying the microloan to her CrowdLoan investors.

So that covers the complete spectrum of what most would put under the crowdfunding umbrella.

For those of you that are new to the crowdfunding concept and are reading such examples for the first time, there is a movement of people and businesses raising funds and investing without banks, financial markets or venture capital – just ordinary people and businesses funding other ordinary people and businesses.

Because of the popularity of the World Wide Web, digital money and social networks has made this movement possible.

People and businesses can raise funds by offering rewards to funders on one extreme. At the other extreme they can raise funds in exchange for monetary rewards in the form of debt or equity that can offer interest returns in excess of depositing money with banks.

For the purpose of this chapter we focus on the rise of crowdfunding, referring to online platforms that offer funding in exchange for non-monetary rewards.

We turn to other debt and equity platforms in the next chapter on hugely disruptive technology #5 – person-to-person lending.

If you are one of those people hearing about this now for the first time, you are discovering the future of funding, borrowing, raising funds and investing, that will be your lifeline if the government does not reform banking soon.

Armed with these definitions, I focus this chapter on the rise of hugely disruptive technology #4 – crowdfunding, and why your social capital score will become your most valuable asset.

The rise of crowdfunding

Crowdfunding has been around for centuries, and was commonly used to fund charities.

However, online crowdfunding has only really been possible in the age of social networking. It has not only made it possible for charities to raise collective pools of funds, but for the whole world to raise funds for whatever is important to them commercial or social.

This innovation has all the potential to compete with traditional banks and financial markets for those seeking funds.

It is still in its infancy as I write, and only really just begun, but with the way technology and finance is moving, I see no reason why crowdfunding, as a means to raising finance, will not be a major financial product in the next five years.

Combine the rise of the World Wide Web, social networking and social digital money with the global financial crisis and the breakdown of traditional funding models and financial markets, and the time is right for crowdfunding.

1997 was a year to truly celebrate the power of the internet and the democratisation of financial services.

But before we look at what happened in 1997, to really appreciate our future, let's step back into our time machine and take a look at what we would have to have done to make it in the music industry at different times throughout history.

I want to be a world famous musician ...

Let's say you are an extremely talented musician. I would like to join you back in time and experience what your typical journey may have looked like.

Let's hop into our time machine and travel back.

Back to the 18th century...

It's the 18th century and you are a hugely talented composer. To have any chance of reaching a wide audience and surviving financially, it turns out that you need to be rubbing shoulders with aristocrats or an influential member of the church. If not, sorry – game over! Or maybe there is a slim chance that you will be invited to be a freemason and join the fraternity.

But to see how one might make it, let's follow the journey of one Wolfgang Amadeus Mozart.

After 20 years of toil and brilliance, Mozart was deep into debt and was reduced to selling possessions for income.

By a stroke of luck and a chance connection, Mozart is summoned to Vienna to work for Archbishop Colloredo. When Mozart realised Colloredo simply wanted him as a mere servant with musical talents, he tried to quit, but was refused.

Due to his past position and talent, he was requested to perform before the Emperor. But, even when Mozart attempted to resign in order to perform for the Emperor, he was refused.

One month later Mozart fortunately was kicked out by the archbishop's steward. Still trying to follow his muse, he decided to settle in Vienna and attempt to succeed without patronage.

Mozart, through sheer determination, established himself as the finest pianoforte player in Vienna and his work as a composer was finally receiving recognition.

Mozart was one of the very few that made it without having the correct pedigree, due to his experience with the archbishop as a servant.

As his reputation grew, he started managing his own business affairs, with space in the theatres scarce, and his work ever more popular, he often booked unconventional venues himself. Mozart finally started to gain substantial returns from his concerts because he did everything on his own.

Once he had fully established himself, he further increased his circle of influence when he became a freemason (the largest and oldest fraternity in the world with influential members throughout history including George Washington, Benjamin Franklin, Sir Winston Churchill and Henry Ford, to mention a few).

But even though Mozart was able to establish himself with the richest and most influential of his time, in the following years, he stopped appearing frequently in concerts, and his income shrank. It was a difficult time for musicians in Vienna because Austria was at war, and the ability of the aristocracy to support music had declined.

So we see first hand, that to make it in the 18th century, success was dependent upon the aristocracy, no matter how talented you were.

Disillusioned with Mozart's story of struggle, let's travel forward in time and try again.

... To the 19th century...

The world has changed since Mozart's time and there is one key innovation that means musicians have a chance to make it without being backed by the aristocracy – printing.

The effect that printing has on musical careers is breakthrough, as musicians are now able to write song sheets and sell them to those who wish to compose, without the influence of the aristocracy.

To see what it was like to be a musician in the 19th century we try to make it ourselves.

We are able to spread our work faster, more efficiently, and to more people than ever before because we learn how to write music rather than create it ourselves.

We start writing our music for amateur performers, knowing that it could be distributed to them at an affordable cost.

However, the cost of printing is still fairly prohibitive and we need to raise funds to take our musical artistry to print.

As we get a bit strapped for cash we try to earn some extra money by teaching others how to read and compose music, as it is a highly sought-after skill in this age.

But then something happens. The aristocracy don't like our new-found magical powers to create music without their say-so and we receive news that the right to print music is only granted by the monarch.

We soon realise that only those with a special dispensation are allowed to print song sheets. Now we are back in the same scenario as we were when we left the 18th century.

It's not just about being talented again, but having the right pedigree.

Moving forward a few years, we overhear a conversation about a musician who managed to raise the funds to travel to New York and publish their music with something called 'Tin Pan Alley'.

It turns out that there is a movement going on in the US music industry and publishers are now dominating song sheet music. After raising funds from teaching, we plan a two-month long journey and eventually arrive in Manhattan armed with our song sheets.

As we step off the train and head to Manhattan, we start to feel the energy, with a steady stream of songwriters, Broadway performers and musicians coming and going. We now realise that we have simply been in the wrong place all along. So in this time, geography determines your success.

Our music can now finally get recognised as we have arrived in the right place – New York. We are surrounded by the right people who can further our career and better still, they are not aristocrats.

We very quickly show our song sheets to a major music publisher who makes us an offer. As a talented unknown with no previous hits, all rights to our songs are purchased outright for a flat fee, including rights to put someone else's name on the music as the composer.

Desperate for the money, we agree and get busy writing our next hits.

After several successful sales, we are hired to be on the staff at one of the music houses. The problem is, that no matter how hard we try, we cannot get past writing music.

To sing music in the 19th century, you had to be beautiful and tick all the boxes of what people like to see in a singer, as well as be able to sing.

Disillusioned and fed up with writing, we step back into our time machine and travel forward in time again.

... To the 20th century ...

Now it's the 20th century and we try for a third time to make the most of our musical talent.

This time, we start to notice some serious changes in the music industry. We read in a local newspaper that Thomas Edison had created this new technology called a phonograph that enabled sound to be played by anyone with the device. At the same time, another disruptive technology has been invented that allowed for the recording of sound.

These two technologies combined to create radio communications that changed the way music was heard forever.

We start to believe that this century will be the time we finally make music and sing to the world. Thanks to the radio we are now able to spread our music without needing people to see our beauty, or lack of beauty.

We hang out at the opera houses to meet people in the industry and find ourselves speaking to record label producers. One in particular tells us stories of all sorts of strange music becoming popular nationwide, in all sorts of shapes and sizes. He tells us the story of a band that made it on a worldwide scale and was touring the world.

Soon we start to realise that the trick to making our music dreams a reality, was to get noticed by somebody at the 'Big 6' production companies – EMI, CBS (bought later by Sony), BMG (bought later by Sony), Polygram (bought later by Universal Music Group), WEA or MCA (later Universal Music Group).

This world was very different, yet it reminded us of previous attempts to make it, where we were unable to be a part of the aristocracy.

We continually get gigs on radio, but struggle to get an opportunity to sing in front of any of the key people at any of the Big 6, because we still don't look 'right'.

Just when we were about to lose hope, we start to meet others that were doing it without the Big 6. All around us, we notice little radio station studios popping up. One day we knock on the door of a local radio station that played music similar to ours. We are given the opportunity to sing on the radio live to a small but devoted audience and start to build more fans.

We are happy to have been given the opportunity to sing, but after several years struggling and very few having heard of our music, we travel forward to another time to see if there is another way to reach more people.

... To the 21st century ...

The world looks completely different the fourth time around.

It is 1998 and we decide to get together with friends, excited after persuading all our parents to invest a few thousand in kitting out our sound-proof garden shed with recording equipment that produces sound to a greater quality than equipment that the Big 6 used to invest millions in previously.

After a recording session, we end up with a completed album and burn our music using our own little CD factory in the bedroom. We print our own CDs with our colour printer and PC and make a couple of hundred CDs. We fund it by selling CDs from the back of the room when we get gigs.

One day we get a Friendster message from an ex-employee at Tower Records who lost his job when they went bust. We were connected through a mutual friend and we had accepted him into our social network.

He contacts us and asked if we can arrange a phone conference call. On the call, he explains to us that revenues from the record industry have been hit big time and that he cannot find a job any more. He is looking to partner with talented musicians to distribute music with all the contacts and knowledge he developed from his years in the industry.

As many in the music industry have been laid off from the big record labels, there are a lot of experienced distributers in the marketplace that cannot find work and are building their own freelance careers.

The next week we agree to pay him a fee from our 'back of the room' CD sales and he puts us in touch with ex-record distribution employees, record producers, people with studios, recording engineers and musicians all wondering what happened to their careers too.

Inspired by the possibilities of building connections online we decide to create our very own website. As we start building our site, the television is running in the background and we overhear news about an entrepreneur called Sean Parker whose company, Napster, was being sued by the music industry for contributing to illegal file sharing.

Napster was another hugely disruptive technology that pioneered peer-to-peer file sharing, mainly focused on sharing audio MP3 files. We get curious and register our details with Napster only to find that somebody has taken our CD and is sharing it for free without our permission.

Enraged, we cheer on as the music industry sues Napster and it is taken down. But, a few months later we start to notice that many more people were visiting our website after sharing our music on Napster.

We decide to turn our website into a blog that we created using a free open-source blogging software called WordPress.

This now allows our fans to directly communicate with us and we get input from our fans and followers on the next album we decide to create. As we start to attract more fans to our blog we begin to build a database of fans and with their input, we record our second album.

It is now 2003 and funds are still tight. So instead of going to the cost of printing our CDs and trying to find people to buy them, we get a Skype message from a fan one day telling us about a place where we can upload MP3 files of our songs to sell and go into partnership with Apple which holds millions of credit card details for people to buy our music with a couple of clicks.

Intrigued, we call him on Skype for free and have a video conference. On the video conference he explains how he saw our music on MySpace and wanted to download it onto his iPod, but could not find it. He gives us a demonstration how iTunes works.

After partnering with Apple through iTunes, revenue starts to come in and we decide it is time to expand our distribution beyond Apple.

We sign a deal with Amazon and eBay to distribute our CDs by simply signing up for an account, followed by a two-minute deal with one of the largest distribution media companies in the world by accepting the terms and conditions on the YouTube signup form for free.

We now have a major outlet to stream live videos of our gigs, and three distribution contracts with three major public companies, so we decide it is time to invest in some high quality video production equipment and build our brand.

We estimate that our total cost to create our first video for streaming, to distribute it to a potential audience of millions, and to have a fully designed brand will only cost us a tiny amount.

After a few calculations, we decide to expand and all we need is a video camera, a Macbook Pro with software to edit music and video, and we could easily do everything ourselves.

We login to BankToTheFuture.com and, rather than getting a rejection from our bank, we upload a sample of our music and use the camera on our phone to record our pitch explaining what we will do with the money.

We offer funders once-in-a-lifetime rewards for backing the project financially, including signed copies of a CD, a behind-the-scenes look at the recording studio and consulting on how to create their own music launch.

We share our BankToTheFuture.com pitch on Linkedin, Facebook, Twitter, Google+ and share it on our WordPress blog, all for free.

One month later we receive all the funds we need to launch our music video to a potential audience of millions, with full creative and artistic control, marketing to a global audience that love our style of music and get to keep all the money minus Apple's, eBay's and Amazon's commission on sales.

We also begin to pre-sell tickets to our next gig to our Facebook fans and community of funders at BankToTheFuture.com. With the pre-sold tickets, we hire a venue that was offered to us for cheap on GroupOn.com, allowing us to keep all ticket sales from the gig.

This time, rather than being invited to perform and selling CDs at the back to an audience where we never knew how many were going to turn up, we film the gig with a packed audience and upload the recording to YouTube.

We embed the YouTube video onto our blog and guide people to it through our MySpace page, the forums and communities interested in our type of music, Facebook, Twitter and the other hundreds of social networks where our fans hang out.

Enjoying our freedom, we read stories of lawsuits, lay-offs and crisis at the large record labels and feel lucky to be in charge of our own destiny.

We get more and more requests on Linkedin to join our network from record labels, as they see how many views our YouTube video has received and read all the comments underneath the videos from raving fans.

One day we get offered the possibility of a '360 deal' through a contact on LinkedIn, where the music company agrees to provide financial support for us, including direct advances as well as funds for marketing, promotion and touring, in exchange for a percentage of our income, including sales of recorded music and live performances.

We sign a contract and celebrate as we realise that we have just signed the very same deal that Robbie Williams signed with EMI, and we did it all on our own.

To give back to the fans that treated us so well, we start to consult other aspiring artists on how to make it in the music industry in the 21st century through our blog.

We give the rewards to all our funders at BankToTheFuture. com who offered us support all the way through, and engage with them in the online community as we grow our fan base and success together.

Finally we have made it, thanks to the technology of the 21st century – the World Wide Web, social networks, digital money and crowdfunding.

Are you starting to see how social capital and crowdfunding has changed the game?

There is nothing that we just saw, that you cannot do too in your area of passion and talent. All you have to do is decide how you want to live your life.

So what changed the game in 1997?

In 1997 a band called Marillion scheduled a tour of Europe to promote its new album release. When band member Mark Kelly posted on the internet that they are unable to tour the United States due to funding issues with their record label, an event took place that marked a new beginning in the history of finance.

If you ask the average banker how a rock band changed the game of financing forever, they would look at you puzzled, and if you then nudged them along with a clue by mentioning the word crowdfunding, my guess and interview results suggest that they would still be puzzled. But bankers have never been famous for their innovation (more famous for them being the last to react).

Fans of the band worldwide joined forces to raise over US$60,000 online to support them in touring the United States[4]. This was the first of many fan supported tours and recordings based purely on the demands of the fans who were so passionate about seeing their favourite band play live that they took on the large music corporation and funded the tour themselves, despite the lack of support from the record publishing company.

This worldwide support and funding was all made possible owing to the internet and the tools that made this possible sparked an internet-led crowdfunding revolution.

Crowdfunding is now marking its place in history as the future way to fund, borrow, raise funds and invest without the need for banks, the financial markets, corporate sponsors or venture capitalists. It is the purest form of the crowd dictating what they want.

Marillion was able to step outside of the traditional music industry business model and fund its own path with its fans.

Years later and this approach for funding has been innovated to the point where it is now used widely by music industry artists to bypass music publishing companies and go direct to their fans, who are now seen as much as investors as listeners.

But still many have not heard of this route to market for their talents.

Inspired by the success of crowdfunding for musicians, a movement in the film industry was catalysed by two French entrepreneurs – Guillaume Colboc and Benjamin Pommeraud.

They successfully launched an online campaign to crowdfund the entire creation of the film 'Demain la Veille' (Waiting for Yesterday). Within three weeks of launching, the online campaign had raised US$50,000 that allowed them to start shooting the film[5].

Shortly after the success of the French film makers, Franny Armstrong launched a campaign to fund a documentary on climate change called 'The Age Of Stupid' which raised more than £900,000 to cover both the production and promotion of the film[6].

Today crowdfunding is being used as a funding mechanism for creative work, journalism, education, music, independent film making, publishing, start-up business fundraising and a host of other fields.

Those who understand its power, who are building their social capital score and are actively using it to fulfil their goals and ambitions, look at traditional financing methods as both archaic and unnecessary.

Aspiring fashion designers can bring their latest clothes designs to market on Catwalk Genius; musicians launching and recording their latest albums can crowdfund on RocketHub and IndieGoGo; journalists are finding topics to report on and crowdfunding unreported news at Spot.us; start-up businesses in the US are being crowdfunded through ProFounder; WealthForge describes themselves as a platform where investment banking meets crowdfunding; GrowVC help start-ups raise seed funding through crowdfunding; PRIMARQ is bringing crowdfunding to the property and real estate markets; social enterprises are being crowdfunded through 33needs; ArtistShare has been enabling fans to finance artist projects in exchange for access to the artist's creative work; two ex-Sony/BMG Europe executives started Sellaband, allowing fans to invest US$10 each in a band, until the goal of US$50,000 is reached – the band then gets to record an album with professional producers and studios; SliceThePie created a marketplace for the trading, promoting, financing, and finding of new bands; creative projects are getting crowdfunded all the time through KickStarter; and the list goes on and on.

In the future every niche industry will be crowdfunded, and you will see the crowdfunding industry grow and become the future acquisition targets for banks.

When I founded BankToTheFuture.com, I sought to create a platform where people with ideas and dreams of all shapes and sizes could meet people with money and combine crowdfunding with other alternative financing products.

My goal was to give people a place where they could build and 'cash in' on their social capital score.

I wanted to create a platform that would allow those who had been using the social networks, or wish to use the social networks from now on, to its full potential, to support others in a place where they could raise funds for their creations and get support from fans and followers using their social capital scores as collateral.

While many great niche crowdfunding platforms exist, I simply could not find one that had the community properties of the social networks we have grown dependent upon today for organising our communication and connections, the ability to borrow and invest for a return, the huge benefits of being able to raise money for your projects through offering rewards and also providing a genuine place to get social and credit ratings and identification checks of the people you intend to fund.

So I created it.

But every great business is built on the shoulders of giants and credit has to be given to those who contributed to the four hugely disruptive technologies leading to the latest innovation that is BankToTheFuture.com.

A new world of possibilities

I hope you can start to imagine how these hugely disruptive technologies have all the potential to completely transform the way we live our lives, as it did for us in our musical time travel adventure.

But what happens when the innovation behind hugely disruptive technologies one through four meets traditional financial products offered by venture capitalists and banks? What happens when financial services opens up to the developing countries?

What happens when this can all be done from anywhere in the world with an internet connection from our mobile smart phone?

Too late. It already has.

Person-to-person lending has taken the lessons of crowdfunding and combined it with debt and equity products.

Online microfinance platforms have taken the lessons of person-to-person lending and combined it with microfinance to open up financial services to the developing countries.

The mobile smart phone has made it possible for people to transfer money to the vast non-banked and access our hugely disruptive technologies from anywhere in the world with an internet connection.

Where is this all going?

The possibilities are endless, and the only thing that seems to be holding all this back from true progress – banks have the licence to create money through debt. Put an end to the unsustainable debt trap and you will see these hugely disruptive technologies unleashed to their full potential.

And we have only just begun.

With crowdfunding came the birth of a new innovation in the loan market, that we discuss in the next chapter – the rise of hugely disruptive technology #5, person-to-person lending.

Hold on! Before you start Chapter 9, tweet me your thoughts on #Crowdfunding.

QR 28 Tweet Simon Dixon about #Crowdfunding

1   Save Blue Like Jazz http://www.savebluelikejazz.com/2010/09/26/our-story/

2   Crowdsourcing.org   http://www.crowdsourcing.org/document/20-kickstart-er-projects-that-raised-hundreds-of-thousands-of-dollars-16-diaspora/5339

3   Samoan Donut War: A Microfinance Success Story, 23 March 2010, http://fel-lowsblog.kiva.org/2010/03/23/samoan-donut-war-a-microfinance-success-story/

4   The biography of Marillion, "NEWS - Press Room - Anoraknophobia". maril-lion.com. Retrieved 2011-08-19. http://www.marillion.com/press/anorak.htm

5   Mashable Business http://mashable.com/2011/01/17/kickstarter-crowd-fund-ing-infographic/

6   "Money". Spanner Films. 2009-11-11. Retrieved 2010-01-10 http://www.spannerfilms.net/new_money_page

9 Hugely disruptive technology #5 – person-to-person lending

BEFORE WE BEGIN, let's take a look at the introductory video below.

Scan QR Code and watch video!

Can't scan? http://bit.ly/pJjLc6

QR 29 Introductory video on hugely disruptive technology #5

Thanks to the rise of crowdfunding (hugely disruptive technology #4), for the first time in history, it is possible for all with an internet connection to raise funds based on the strength of their social capital and the power of their pitch.

Thanks to the World Wide Web (hugely disruptive technology #1) you can pitch for digital funds (hugely disruptive technology #2) through your social network of funders and contacts (hugely disruptive technology #3).

It is my forecast that crowdfunding will become a major source of finance in the economy of freedom, once we reform banking and eliminate the debt trap.

People just like you will be raising funds to start their own entrepreneurial ventures, as the free economy gradually replaces employment with contractors and entrepreneurs in the economy of freedom.

Shortly after crowdfunding started, another innovation emerged, this time in the loan market, that was only made possible thanks to hugely disruptive technologies 1–4.

Person-to-person (P2P) lending rose to offer an alternative to borrowing from banks and loan sharks. P2P lending is a loan which occurs through an online platform directly between individuals or 'peers' without a traditional financial institution or banks, and it has only just begun.

With the rise of the World Wide Web, digital money, the social networks and crowdfunding, the possibilities opened up for people to become their own mini-banks and venture capitalists with small amounts of money.

By offering ordinary people's money to credit worthy borrowers direct through an online platform, where money can be spread across hundreds of pre-screened borrowers, it seems to me that the future of borrowing and investing money will not actually come from banks.

Banks will increasingly find it difficult to compete with the lower interest rates offered to borrowers and superior interest rates offered to lenders who use P2P lending platforms, as more become aware of its advantages.

The P2P lending industry experienced massive success when the banks were being bailed out by governments after the 2007 financial crisis, but wait until these platforms are developed further to offer secured mortgages and larger loans with reserve funds in case of repayment defaults, as they have started to do already.

But isn't this just another way of fuelling the debt trap?

It is easy to mistakenly believe that debt is a bad thing when you hear about the consequences the debt trap has on the world as described in Chapter 2.

The ability to borrow money is something that can serve or destroy, but one thing is for certain, economies that have been built on financial systems that allow for the flow of debt have outperformed economies where borrowing is less accessible.

While the debt was unsustainable, it provides a model for the development that can happen when you make debt sustainable.

It is important to consider the ethical arguments put forward by Islamic bankers, who forbid the charging of interest, and the sustainable arguments put forward by social movements. It is clear that economic growth is not the only factor to be considered when debating the value of debt.

It is my belief that interest-bearing loans in isolation are not the cause of the problem, and therefore abolishing them is not the solution we all seek.

Sustainability can still be achieved and can coexist alongside debt when you tackle the root of the problem.

By understanding these issues, the possibility of a truly social loan market exists, and by social I mean loans that make a positive social impact on the world, as well as social in the sense that the loans are formed through real people and social networks.

While almost all economies have been built on debt traps that are near their end, we have learnt from history that there are certain flaws in the market for loans that lead to unsustainability and eventual disaster.

The good news is that history has taught us these lessons already. Without the flow of debt, the economy of freedom brought about by hugely disruptive technologies would not exist today and many of the great entrepreneurs behind the stories in this book would never have got past the idea stage.

The amazing situation that we find ourselves in today is that we have enough historical lessons to solve the debt trap once and for all without the end of society as we know it, and we have enough historical data to understand the types of lending that can become destructive, as well as having enough financial innovation to have a sustainable loan market.

P2P lending is an innovation that can solve many of the flaws that we have seen from our history of debt.

The story of the rise of P2P lending perfectly highlights many of the flaws in the traditional loan markets and how we can learn from history to live in the economy of freedom where debt flows for productive and sustainable use.

In fact, the story of the rise of P2P lending takes us from the founding of banks developed as an alternative to lenders, through to bankrupt governments indebted by the innovation of debt markets, through to the rise of loan sharks and housing bubbles created for political reasons.

To appreciate the true impact that P2P lending can have on your future, it is first necessary to understand what history has taught us about debt.

Before we account the rise of P2P lending, it is worth outlining four of the vital lessons of debt that will help us in understanding our past failures from the history of debt.

Debt lesson 1: There is good debt and there is bad debt

Without borrowing and lending, the history of our world as we know it would not have got off the ground. There is no question that the financial revolution preceded the industrial revolution and that the rise of each of the hugely disruptive technologies leading to our economy of freedom, was all built by the ability of entrepreneurs to borrow money.

It is wrong to think of lenders of money as leeches, sucking the lifeblood out of unfortunate debtors. Credit and debt are among the essential building blocks of economic development, as vital as the World Wide Web to social networks and the economy of freedom.

Despite what many think, poverty is often caused by a lack of financial institutions, as we will see with the rise of miicrofinance platforms in Chapter 10 and the rise of m-payments that we will see in Chapter 11.

It is for this reason that I do not believe that debt is always a bad thing. It must, however, be spent in the right way to be productive. In the right hands, debt changes the world; in the wrong hands it causes nothing but a lifetime of indebtedness for the borrower.

If you go to a bank today to borrow money to do something productive like start a business or make the world a better place to live in, you will more than likely not leave with a penny more than when you entered, and will quickly be shown the door.

If you enter the same bank and request a loan to buy a car (as long as it is for pleasure and not business).and as long as you have been buying TVs and shoes on your credit card and paying a bit of your debt off each month, you will more than likely leave with money in your bank account with monthly interest payments to follow.

Why? Because when you lend to those who spend on nice shiny objects, history has proven that they are more likely to continue paying interest to the lender without ever repaying the actual loan, choosing to take on more debt instead, secured by their monthly salary.

Lending for something productive is too risky for banks now.

Figure 47 Banks tend to favour personal expenditure lending over business productive lending

This has led to a world where borrowing to simply buy nice shiny objects has become normal and encouraged.

So our main lending system encourages borrowers to take on debt to buy nice shiny objects and money rarely reaches entrepreneurs to do something productive – the exact opposite of what makes the ingredients of good debt.

Even the original intention of bankruptcy has gone against its origins. The American culture of 'land of opportunity' was founded on laws to encourage entrepreneurship and the creation of new business. The law of bankruptcy was originally passed with the intention to give entrepreneurs a break when their plans go wrong.

If their businesses failed, they could call it quits and start over. Their reputation might have suffered, but they have a second chance to rebuild without the burden of being forced to pay for their unsuccessful venture forever.

Bankruptcy laws allowed the natural-born risk takers to learn through trial and error until they finally figure out how to make their millions. Today's bankrupt might be tomorrow's successful entrepreneur.

Many of America's most successful entrepreneurs failed in their early ventures. These entrepreneurs eventually became rich because they were given a chance to try, to fail and to start over.

But today the people that are given access to debt are not business people going bust. Today, 98% of bankruptcy filings are classified as non-business. The principal driver of bankruptcy turns out not to be entrepreneurship, but indebtedness.

Our current financial system does not serve people who take on debt to start businesses, create value or do something productive.

So the first lesson in the history of debt – there are two types of debt: debt which leads to value creation, and debt which leads to further indebtedness.

If debt is made available for those who are seeking to add value with it, then debt becomes an essential tool for economic prosperity.

If debt is used as a tool to simply drive consumption of nice shiny objects, as it is today, then the result is nothing more than the redistribution of money from the borrower to the lender and the entrepreneur who is selling the goods, with no creation of further value for the borrower.

This creates a false economy based on indebtedness and massive redistribution of wealth.

Breaking the second lesson can only lead to new and dangerous ways to lend more money in a world where prosperity can only happen if ever increasing numbers of people, companies and governments go deeper into debt.

Debt lesson 2: The process of creating money should never be mixed with the process of lending for profit

This was the original intention of our adventure in time travel and the Bank Charter Act of 1844.

The history of debt has shown us that when you give banks the ability to create money as debt, you can end up in the ridiculous scenario where the economy has more debt than money and the guaranteed financial crisis that follows bankruptcies, always leaves the government deeper in debt.

When you have a business model that combines profit-making by offering loans, with supplying the main form of payment for goods and services, both under one roof, you play the crazy game we play today, characterised by two rules:

1 In order to have more money in the economy, you have to have more debt.

2 In order to reduce debt when everybody is maxed out, you have to have less money.

As we know, politicians have been scratching their head over this one for decades. Most political parties have been encouraging the mass creation of money through debt to stimulate the economy.

When people cannot afford to repay the debt and we have a recession, it is followed by policies to encourage banks to lend more and conflicting messages to encourage people to save.

Make up your mind – do you want the world to be enslaved by debt or the world to be in a depression?

Hmmmm... no wonder politicians can't get it right – which would you prefer?

Well, debt seems like the easier option, so debt it is until we cannot borrow any more – then what?

It is simply the second lesson of debt that has been violated for decades and is still violated to this day.

But what really makes the government go deeper and deeper into debt is that they are under pressure to end poverty, feed the poor, protect the planet, give homes to all, pay for education, health, etc, etc.

The reality is these issues can never be tackled sustainably by asking a stretched government to go deeper into debt to solve these problems. The reason they have to go into debt is because they have allowed the combination of profit-making loans and money creation to occur under one roof, giving the billions earned from money creation to the banks instead.

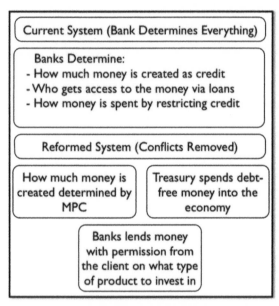

Figure 48 How our reforms separate the conflicts of interest in determining how much money to create and how it is spent.

But to get any closer to tackling the world's major issues, debt needs to be seen as more than simply a vehicle for profit.

Debt lesson 3: Debt has a triple bottom line

The phrase 'triple bottom line' was coined by John Elkington in his 1998 book 'Cannibals with Forks: the Triple Bottom Line of 21st Century Business'.

The triple bottom line (abbreviated as 'TBL' or '3BL', also known as 'people, planet, profit' or 'the three pillars') describes the values and criteria for measuring societal success: economic, ecological and social.

In our current banking system debt is almost always only made available based on the interest that can be charged and the borrower's ability to repay, without any consideration of ecological and social impact.

When debt is allocated based on profit alone, it will be used to finance things that will lead to the eventual destruction of our economy, ecology and society.

In practical terms, triple bottom line accounting means expanding the traditional lending framework to take into account ecological and social performance as well as financial performance.

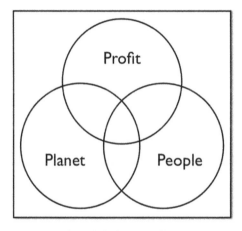

Figure 49 The triple bottom line

Debt lesson 4: Borrowers and lenders must have a relationship

The history of debt has shown that when there is no knowledge of who is borrowing from whom and who is lending to whom, the incentives to repay the loan break down.

Also, as we saw with the 2007 financial crisis, when you lend money and sell the risk and loan on, you are more likely to lend recklessly. This is all because the relationship between borrower and lender has broken down.

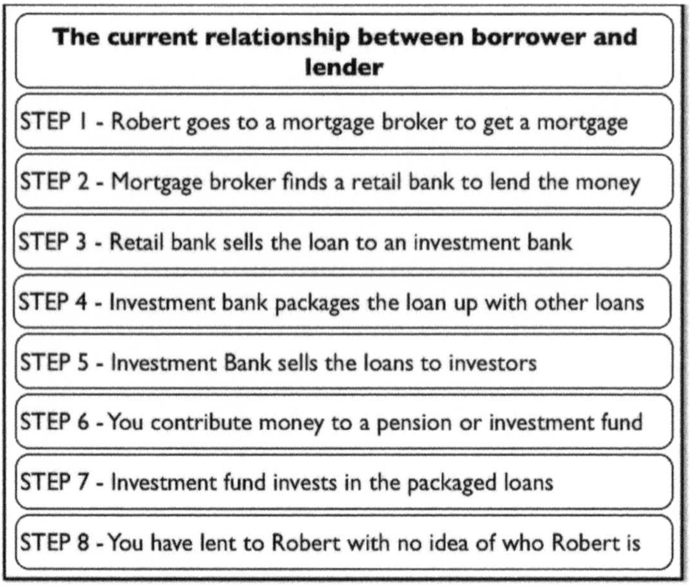

The current relationship between borrower and lender
STEP 1 - Robert goes to a mortgage broker to get a mortgage
STEP 2 - Mortgage broker finds a retail bank to lend the money
STEP 3 - Retail bank sells the loan to an investment bank
STEP 4 - Investment bank packages the loan up with other loans
STEP 5 - Investment Bank sells the loans to investors
STEP 6 - You contribute money to a pension or investment fund
STEP 7 - Investment fund invests in the packaged loans
STEP 8 - You have lent to Robert with no idea of who Robert is

Figure 50 How the process of securitisation of loans takes away the relationship between borrower and lender

As humans we feel more of an obligation to repay when we have some relationship with our lender. This could be a relationship with a bank manager or ideally the person lending the money to you, but with no relationship, history has shown time and time again that the foundations of what makes debt work well for both parties break down.

Couple this with the ability to easily declare yourself bankrupt when you can no longer afford to repay and you have an economy of mass indebtedness.

After all, when you declare bankruptcy, it is just the bank that suffers, and they are not real people that you know ... and besides, it was never their money they lent out – they created it, right?

The history of debt has shown that the only sustainable use of debt is when it is allocated with consideration to all four factors. So these four lessons would suggest that its productive use would be to lend mainly to the productive economy based on people, planet and profit.

The perfect TBL business would not use child labour and would monitor all contracted companies for child labour exploitation; it would pay fair salaries to its workers; it would maintain a safe work environment and tolerable working hours; it would not otherwise exploit a community or its labour force; it would not produce harmful or destructive products such as weapons, toxic chemicals or batteries containing dangerous heavy metals, and it would be sustainable by producing a profit both internally and for society.

The 4 Lessons Of Debt

LESSON I - There is good debt & there is bad debt

LESSON 2 - The process of creating money should never be mixed with the process of lending for profit

LESSON 3 - Debt has a triple bottom line

LESSON 4 - Borrowers & lenders must have a relationship

Figure 51 The four lessons of debt

Ever been asked any of those questions when applying for a loan?

The perfect debt

So to recap, an ideal system for the productive use of debt would allocate the majority of its loans to the productive economy, rather than speculation and personal indebtedness; would not get involved in money creation, instead only lending out money created debt-free, independent of banks and government; and would access lendability based on a TBL analysis where both the lender and borrower have some kind of accountability and relationship with each other.

So this makes up our framework for sustainability in the debt market.

So how are we doing?

Banks are our main source of debt and violate all four lessons, hence why we live in unsustainability. Fortunately, thanks to hugely disruptive technology #5, it is now possible to follow all four lessons in the debt market.

In fact ... surprise, surprise ... these were the four founding principles used in founding BankToTheFuture.com. Social banks passed lessons 1 – good debt; 3 – TBL; and 4 – relationship, they failed in lesson 2 – money creation.

The major P2P lending platforms that we will discuss in this chapter pass lesson 2 – money creation, but most fail in either lesson 1– good debt, 3 – TBL, and 4 – relationship.

The only lending institutions that I could see that was passing all four lessons were in the microfinance sector (discussed in the next chapter).

That is where we positioned ourselves at BankToTheFuture. com. We provided a platform for those focused on adding some form of value to human development to pitch for funds, funded by real people who wanted a return on their investment. We refused to engage in money creation, we only accepted loans that met our criteria for people, planet and profit and we insisted on everybody registering with their real name and photo while displaying all their social capital details for all to connect with them and sustain a relationship throughout the transaction using online communities.

So today we have all the tools for the perfect debt system, the only thing holding us back is that we rely on banks for the creation of money.

No other institution is able to grow big enough to make a major sustainable change, but thanks to our adventure in time travel, we created the perfect environment for non-banks to compete with banks in offering a sustainable alternative; but the question we now answer is, how did we get here?

The rise of P2P lending

The story of P2P lending has evolved from the evolution of lending through the ages.

I break down the evolution of lending into seven phases: lending from benches; lending from banks; lending from nothing; lending through capital markets; lending through securities; lending through sharks; and lending through social networks.

But it all began with the publication of one book in 1202. A now famous mathematician named Fibonacci published a book titled Liber Abaci, 'The Book of Calculation', showing the practical importance of the new numerical system by applying it to commercial book-keeping, conversion of weights and measures and most importantly to this chapter, the calculation of interest and money-changing[1].

This book was the first application of mathematics to making money and most importantly – lending money.

Lending from benches

While the history of lending can be traced a lot further back, lending as we know it today can really be attributed to medieval and early Renaissance Italy, namely Florence and Venice.

Jewish lenders provided commercial credit from a building known as the Banco Rosso, sitting outside on benches in the ghetto outside the city of Venice. Benches were used as desks or exchange counters by bankers, who used to make their transactions atop desks covered by green tablecloths.

Merchants had to travel to the Jewish ghetto to borrow money as lending money at interest was a sin amongst Christians.

Jews were not supposed to lend at interest, but a work around can be found in the Old Testament book of Deuteronomy:

> "Unto a stranger thou mayest lend upon usury; but unto thy brother thou shalt not lend upon usury."

In other words, Jews could lend to Christians at interest, but not to fellow Jews at interest.

In 1516 the Venetian authorities designated a special area in the city for the Jewish community as it had become apparent to the government that they might prove to be a useful source of money and financial services, since they could be taxed as well as borrowed from.

So the bench certainly met lesson 1 – good debt, as loans were made to merchants only; lesson 2 – money creation, as all loans were made from their own money; and lesson 4 – relationship, as they were dealing person-to-person with their borrowers. However, they violated lesson 3 – TBL, as profit was there only motive for lending. Three out of four is not bad though, right?

Lending from banks

When borrowing from the Jewish community became an essential source of finance for merchants, the bank was born.

The Bardi and Peruzzi families dominated banking in 14th century Florence, establishing branches in many other parts of Europe, but were wiped out in the 1340s as a result of defaults from two of their clients, King Edward III of England and King Robert of Naples.

But the most famous Italian bank was the Medici bank, set up by Giovanni Medici in 1397. The Medici family successfully made the transition from financial success to status and power. They achieved this by making their bank bigger than any previous financial institution.

By lending huge and varied, it allowed them to spread their risk across many lenders, minimising the risk of somebody defaulting on the repayment of their loans.

The early Medici bank demonstrated the sustainability of not violating lesson 1 – good debt, and lesson 2 – money creation. They were simply making depositors' money available to merchants in exchange for interest. The sheer size and scale, however, meant that the person-to-person relationship enjoyed by the Jews was not feasible with all customers and they had to violate lesson 4 – relationship.

Two out of four lessons from the first mega bank was a whole lot more sustainable than what came next.

Lending from nothing

When banks started to violate lesson 2, the lessons from the Medici bank were not spread to the next generation of bankers when the Italian banking model was exported to Northern Europe, notably to the Dutch, the English and the Swedes.

It was in Amsterdam, London and Stockholm that three innovations contrary to lesson 2 were born.

The 17th century saw the foundation of the Amsterdam Exchange Bank. The bank allowed merchants to set up accounts denominated in standardised currencies to combat the problem of trading in the 14 different currencies that were being traded at the time.

This innovation laid the foundation for modern monetary transfers as we know them today, allowing later for the rise of hugely disruptive technology #2 – digital money.

The bank did, however, maintain equal levels of deposits and reserves of precious metals and coins, thus preventing it from violating lesson 2 on money creation.

It was in Stockholm in 1656 that a bank called Riksbank, the central bank of Sweden, took the systems built in Amsterdam and became the first to make loans above its level of deposits, pioneering the business model of money creation by banks.

Then came the Bank of England in 1694, designed to assist the government with war finance, completely violating all four lessons.

These three banks were the founding fathers to the debt trap described in Chapter 2, namely interbank transactions, fractional reserve banking and central banking monopolies on the issuance of notes.

With the final scrapping of the usury laws in 1833 in England, money creation led to a lending boom the like of which the world had never seen.

Lending from capital markets

After the creation of credit by banks, the birth of the bond was the second revolution in the history of lending.

With its origins in war fundraising, its loans would obviously violate lesson 1 and lesson 3. As the money to buy the bonds can be created by banks, it also indirectly violates lesson 2, but money is not created when bombs are bought, directly violating lesson 2, and completely removes any type of relationship between borrower and lender, violating lesson 4.

Governments and large corporations issue bonds as a way of borrowing money from a large number of investors and institutions other than just a bank.

Sticking to my promise, I have no intention of going through the complications of how the bond market works; all you need to know is that it allowed governments to borrow easily and in vast quantities, allowing any investor to receive interest payments from the government loan with the ability to sell the loan on if they needed the money back.

The important part is that this innovation gave the government the ability to easily borrow from the world.

The ability to finance war through a market for government bonds was also an innovation from the Italian Renaissance. For much of the 14th and 15th centuries, Florence, Pisa and Siena were at war with each other and needed vast sums of money to continue battle.

Wealthy citizens of Florence were effectively obliged to lend money to their own city government. In return for these forced loans, they received interest. Essentially, Florence turned its citizens into its biggest investors and gave them the option to sell their loans to other citizens.

From that moment on, the system of funding war through bonds spread far and wide. War generated some of the wealthiest families in the world, like the Rothschilds.

The history of the bond market and war is beyond the scope of this chapter, but it is worth noting the importance of the bond market to the outcome of many historical wars. The Rothschilds actually decided the outcome of the Napoleonic Wars by putting their financial weight behind Britain and they helped to decide the outcome of the American Civil War by choosing to sit on the sidelines.

But now, thanks to the bond market, when governments step in to inject a lifeline into the debt trap, rather than borrowing from banks as they did in the past, they simply create some bonds.

When you hear or read about a country's national debt, it consists of thousands of outstanding pieces of these IOU papers called bonds.

The method of issuing these IOUs and administering the national debt is quite simple. In order to obtain money to cover its annual spending shortfall, an appropriate number of government bonds are drawn up by the Treasury. These are then sold – in fact, they are auctioned off in what is called the money markets to the highest bidder.

These bonds are bought by investors because they promise to repay a larger sum of money at some future date. As the government promises to repay this higher amount of money, the government obtains the money to meet the payments by selling more bonds, promising even more money in the future.

The government draws up enough new bonds to cover the repayments due on the old bonds, then uses the money to pay off the interest owed.

Now this might seem a quite sufficiently barmy arrangement, but it should be remembered that the money held by pension funds and insurance companies, or whoever buys the government bonds, is money that had to be borrowed into existence in the first place.

In other words, by this bizarre process, governments borrow money which has already been borrowed into existence, and they thus create a second massive institutional debt in respect to money which already has a debt behind it.

This is why the addition of the national debt to the total of private debt places a country and its people in an absurd position of owing far more on paper than the amount of money that exists in the economy.

So just in case you missed it – to obtain the additional revenue our economy needs, and upon which the economy is completely reliant, the government sells IOUs which increase in value with time.

When the time comes for them to be cashed, the government sells even more IOUs and uses this money to pay off the old ones – remember the Ponzi scheme?

This provides the government with a small amount of money on the condition that they repay a much larger sum in ten or 20 years' time. The government then proceeds to flood the market with these meaningless promises to pay, which are almost always redeemed by the issue of yet more promises.

The government draws on money already created as a debt, and relied upon for future payments on insurance claims and the pensions of the elderly.

Welcome to the bond market.

But remember, this only happens because the money used to buy bonds has violated lesson 2 – money creation.

With the rise of lending from nothing and lending through bonds, the world's governments are the world's largest borrowers. In some cases governments have actually borrowed more than the total value of goods and services produced within the country itself, known as Gross Domestic Product (GDP).

In 2011 Spain was running a national debt equivalent to 60% of its GDP, the UK 76%, France 82%, Germany 83%, USA 92%, Portugal 93%, Ireland 97%, Italy 119%, Iceland 126% and Greece 142%[2].

Doh! Think this was an accident? It is simply a symptom of violating the four lessons of debt.

Lending through securities

Following the birth of bonds, governments have used their ability to accrue massive debt to stimulate a whole new form of money creation.

By encouraging the world to own property and by partnering with banks and central banks to balloon debt through mortgages, lending institutions successfully created enough money to burden both the government and society with indebtedness beyond return.

Many today believe that the philosophy, promoted by politicians, of encouraging everybody to own a house is a philosophy all should adopt.

In Neil Ferguson's book 'The Ascent of Money', he tells how property booms fuelled by mortgages were exported around the world, modelled from a series of governmental policies in the US.

Before the 1930s, little more than two-fifths of American households were owner-occupiers. The few people who did borrow money to buy their own houses in the 1920s found themselves in deep difficulties when the Great Depression struck.

In 1932 and 1933 there were over half a million foreclosures. By mid 1933, over a thousand mortgages were being foreclosed every day.

President Roosevelt's answer was his New Deal, designed to stimulate home ownership and the mass creation of money through debt.

First, a Home Owner's Loan Corporation was founded to re-finance mortgages for borrowers to longer terms of repayment.

Next, a Federal Home Loan Bank Board was set up in 1932 to encourage and oversee local mortgage lenders.

Third, a Federal deposit insurance was introduced, effectively meaning that if borrowers defaulted on their mortgages, the government would simply compensate the customers who had money in the bank.

Fourthly, The Federal Housing Administration provided federally backed insurance for mortgage lenders to encourage large, long, fully authorised and low-interest loans.

Finally, in 1938, a new Federal National Mortgage Association (Fannie Mae) was authorised to issue bonds and use the proceeds to buy mortgages from mortgage lenders, effectively providing a place for mortgage lenders to sell their mortgages on, which were in turn purchased by investors in exchange for a monthly interest payment.

This essentially turned ordinary investors into mortgage lenders, without knowing who they were lending to.

From the 1930s onwards, the US government was effectively guaranteeing the mortgage market and encouraging a lending boom through the banks favourite vehicle for creating money – mortgages.

As a result, mortgage debt soared, along with so-called 'home ownership' after the Second World War.

Everybody finally had the chance to 'own' their very own house, but it is worth pointing out, buying a house through a mortgage essentially means a bank creates money out of thin air, and gives you the ability to stay in 'your' house, secured by your income, but the bank holds the title deeds to 'your' house until you repay the loan that they created, plus the interest outlined in your terms and conditions. If you fail to repay, you will soon find out who the house really belongs to. If you want to go into this type of transaction, fine, but you should know how it really works.

Government incentives to borrow and buy a house encouraged more and more to take on huge mortgage loans in order to 'own' their very own home.

This form of debt became the dominant methodology for creating money in both the US and UK, and created an almighty boom and bust in the housing market that changed the face of the lending market forever.

Leading up to the 2007 financial crisis, the home ownership philosophy was spreading fast, with house price booms not only in Australia, Canada, Ireland UK and US, but also in China, France, India, Italy, Russia, South Korea and Spain.

But it was after the US housing crash caused by a Savings & Loan crisis in the US in the 1980s and 1990s, that a new form of lending through securities was born.

Bond traders at investment bank Salomon Brothers came up with an idea to capitalise on the housing crash. The idea was to bundle thousands of mortgages together to back a new bundled product that could be sold as alternatives to traditional bonds – in effect, to convert bundles of mortgages into bonds. Thus in June 1983 mortgage-backed securities (MBS) were born.

Remember, the US government had passed policy to guarantee these mortgages and hence these securities could be sold similar to 'safe' government bonds.

Between 1980 and 2007 the volume of such MBS grew from US$200 million to US$4 trillion. By 2007 56% of the home mortgage market was securitised through such products[3].

The original bankers knew both the depositors and the debtors when agreeing a loan. By contrast, in the securitised market, the interest you were paying on your mortgage is going to someone who has no idea you exist.

The full implications of this transition would become apparent 20 years later when many lost their home during the 2007 global financial crisis.

> "We want everybody in America to own their own home." *George W. Bush speech, October 2002*

George Bush challenged lenders to lend and create enough mortgage backed money to create 5.5 million new home owners. Fannie Mae came under pressure from the government to support the sub-prime market, essentially those who cannot afford to repay their mortgages.

The model worked well as long as interest rates were kept low, as long as people kept their jobs and gave most of their money to mortgage lenders, and as long as house prices kept rising.

The problem was that the lender did not worry that these conditions could not continue; after all, they were simply selling the loan on through the magic of securitisation. It was not their money at risk, nor that of the the investment banks. The securities were hence sold as safe as government bonds.

As we all know now, the borrowers could no longer afford to repay their mortgages and the securities turned out to be weapons of mass destruction resulting in huge bank bailouts and a global financial crisis that sent countries and governments bankrupt.

The securitised lending market was inevitably going to crash as it violated lesson 1 – good debt (the money was used for speculation on house prices); lesson 2 – money creation (all the money lent to home buyers was created out of thin air by banks); lesson 3 – (there was no consideration of people and planet, simply profit); and lesson 4 – relationship (we eventually saw that not even with the collective effort of bankers, central bankers, economists and politicians could anybody figure out who was lending to whom.) All four lessons of debt were violated.

And what has been the government's response? Get people in more debt and patch up the system so banks can make more loans that violate all four lessons of debt.

Another doh!

Lending through sharks

If the bank won't lend to you, you are not big enough to issue a bond, or you don't want to buy a house, you always have the option of borrowing from a shark.

A 'loan shark' is the term for a person or body that offers unsecured loans at often illegally high interest rates to individuals, often enforcing repayment by blackmail or threats of violence.

In late 19th century America, legal interest rates made small loans unprofitable, and small-time lending was frowned upon by society, as a borrower of small loans was seen as an irresponsible person who could not manage a budget. Banks and other major financial institutions thus stayed away from small-time lending.

There were, however, plenty of small lenders offering loans at profitable, but illegally high interest rates. They presented themselves as legitimate and operated openly out of offices. They only sought customers whom they felt were good risks: a steady and respectable job (a regular income and a reputation to protect), married (unlikely to flee town), and legitimate motives for borrowing. Gamblers, criminals and other disreputable, unreliable types were avoided.

They made the borrower fill out and sign seemingly legitimate contracts. Though these contracts were not legally enforceable, they at least were proof of the loan, which the lender could use to blackmail a defaulter.

Alternatively, the lender often resorted to public shaming, such as complaining to the borrower's employer, who disdained indebted employees and often fired them, or shouting demands outside the borrower's home. Whether out of gullibility or a desire to protect their reputation, the borrower usually succumbed and paid up.

Consumer protections and capped interest rates were introduced on loans in the US, as well as banning additional charges such as late fees to attempt to regulate the market.

Small loans started becoming more socially acceptable, and banks and other larger institutions started offering them as well.

In the 1920s and 1930s, American prosecutors began to notice the emergence of a new breed of illegal lender that used violence to enforce debts.

The new small lender laws had made it almost impossible to intimidate customers with a veneer of legality, and many customers were less vulnerable to shaming because they were either self-employed or already disreputable. Thus, violence was an important tool.

Those who could not get a legal loan at 36% or 42% a year could secure a cash advance from a mobster at the going rate of 10% or 20% a week for small loans[4]. Since the mob loans were not usually secured with legal instruments, debtors pledged their bodies as collateral.

Payday loan companies more recently emerged offering small, short-term loans that are intended to cover a borrower's expenses until his or her next payday.

Licensed payday loan businesses are often described as loan sharks by their critics due to high interest rates that trap debtors, stopping short of illegal lending and violent collection practices.

Today's payday loan is a close cousin of the early 20th century salary loan, the product to which the name 'shark' was originally applied, but they are now legalised in many countries.

By 2011, payday loans in the UK were rapidly growing, with four times as many people using such loans in 2009 compared to 2006. In 2009, 1.2 million people took out 4.1 million loans, with total lending amounting to £1.2 billion[5].

There are no restrictions on the interest rates payday loan companies can charge in the UK, although they are required by law to state the effective Annual Percentage Rate (APR).

Payday lending is legal and regulated in 37 states of the US. In 13 states it is either illegal or not feasible, given state law[6].

The payday and shark models have also gone digital.

Wonga launched in the UK in 2007 providing short-term finance to consumers as an alternative to personal loans or credit cards.

Wonga became one of the UK's most successful technology start-ups, attracting investment from backers including Balderton Capital, one of the backers of LoveFilm, Greylock Partners, one of the original investors in LinkedIn, and Meritech Capital Partners, one of Facebook's backers. In 2011, Wonga hit the headlines because of the large APR interest terms it is forced to advertise, as high as 4214 per cent[7].

It is easy to condemn loan sharks as immoral and criminal, yet it is also important to look at the other side. They are simply stepping in where no other mainstream financial institution would extend credit.

The people that borrow are very likely to default on their debt and they are taking a huge risk, after all; unlike a bank, it is their actual money they are lending, so only high interest rates can compensate for the high level of defaults.

Sites like Wonga only intend to lend for up to 30 days, so the APR is never meant to be paid; they are charging for short-term borrowing.

So let's do an impartial analysis based on our four lessons of debt, sharks and payday lenders meet more of our lessons of debt than banks as they do not violate lesson 2 – money creation, and also does not violate lesson 4 – relationship, but most however, fall short by violating lesson 1 – good debt, as most short-term loans are not put to productive use and lesson 3 – TBL, I am not sure threatening with violence is good for people, planet and societal profit.

So that only leaves us with one more option to meet all four lessons of debt.

Lending through social networks

Could social networks provide the answer to our lack of success in finding a lending method that meets all four lessons?

The social networks made it possible for us all to build social capital from the strength of our interactions with others online, and it is my belief that our sustainable future of lending will come from the hugely disruptive technologies covered so far in this book.

I also believe that after banking reform, other lending institutions will model their practices from the innovation in this area of lending.

There is no reason why the capital market, like the bond and stock market, cannot learn from lessons 1–3. However, only person-to-person social networks can simultaneously meet the relationship lesson and still provide the size and scale to meet the huge demand for loans.

Let's look at each of the four lessons individually.

1. If a social network could provide a marketplace for borrowers and lenders to pitch their financial needs or be automatically matched to investors filtered by a criteria for what constitutes a productive loan (for example education, business etc.) compared to just a 'consumptive' loan (for example car, shoes, new kitchen etc.), then it would pass debt lesson 1 – good debt.

2. If it was illegal for that social network to create money because it does not use a banking licence to create money as debt out of thin air, then it would pass lesson 2 – money creation.

3. If that social network only accepted loan requests that met standards for the sustainability of people, planet and profit, then it would meet lesson 3 –TBL.

4. If that social network provided effective tools for lenders and borrowers to maintain a relationship with each other throughout the contract, as well as making sure members use their real names, photos, social media profiles, complete

identification checks, complete traditional credit checks done by banks and provide a feedback mechanism for investors measured through a social capital score, then they would meet lesson 4 – relationship.

And thanks to the hugely disruptive technologies this can be done on a large scale while maintaining millions of micro relationships between lenders and borrowers.

And all this is possible on a global scale, if only a sustainable monetary system existed. Oh yeah ... we fixed that in our adventure in time travel.

P2P lending came as a by-product of the five hugely disruptive technologies discussed so far.

In February 2005, Zopa, the first person-to-person lending company launched in the UK, allowing borrowers and lenders to be matched together without banks. It provided an online money exchange service, allowing people who have money to lend to those who wish to borrow, instead of using savings accounts and loan applications that violate all four lessons of debt.

One year later in February 2006, Prosper, the first P2P lending firm in the US, was launched, followed shortly after by Lending Club and in September 2010, P2P Financial launched in Canada.

In 2005, there were a total of $118 million in current loans via P2P lending[8].

Lending Club was the first P2P lender to register its offerings as securities with the Securities and Exchange Commission (SEC), completing its SEC registration in October 2008.

As of July 2011 Lending Club had originated a total of over US$313 million in 30,868 loans and declined US$3.3 billion in loan applications[9]. In June 2011, Lending Club originated a record US$20 million in loans[10].

Reasons for P2P borrowing have ranged from education, mortgage loans, business funding, vet bills, weddings; the most popular loan is debt consolidation.

The P2P lending market was further boosted by the 2007 global financial crisis when P2P lending platforms promised to provide credit at the time when banks and other traditional financial institutions were having difficulties.

While most of these platforms violate lesson 1 – good debt, and lesson 4 – relationship, as they allow users to register with anonymous usernames and no photo, I saw the potential to meet all four lessons of debt and provide a social network where people could actively build their social capital integrated with the major social networks like Facebook, LinkedIn, Twitter and Google+.

In 2011 we launched BankToTheFuture.com as the first social network in the world that allowed users to fund, borrow, raise funds and invest while simultaneously meeting all four lessons of debt, to create a sustainable alternative to other lending institutions.

The vision is to provide a place where users can crowdfund, borrow and raise funds in exchange for equity through the power of their social capital score combined with traditional credit and identity checking, providing a sustainable marketplace while we transition from the debt trap of 'free'dom to the economy of freedom.

Our vision for the years ahead is to become a full reserve bank that does not engage in the creation of money as debt, where depositors are the legal owners of their money and all investments are made P2P by our customers' separate investment accounts, making it the only sustainable financial institution in the world that provides a working model of sustainable banking reform as outlined in this book.

I would love for you to create your profile, connect with me and build your social capital for the future at www.BankToTheFuture.com

Scan QR Code & join Simon Dixon on BankᴛᴏᴛʜᴇFuture.com

Can't scan?   www.BankToTheFuture.com/SimonDixon

QR 30 Connect with Simon Dixon on BankToTheFuture.com

Today, crowdfunding and P2P lending have combined to create a hybrid model, allowing business owners to raise funds in exchange for equity, offering an alternative to angel investment, venture capital and private equity. At BankToTheFuture.com we call this our CrowdInvestment service.

The possibilities are now limitless. The models of crowdfunding and P2P lending in the future will provide a sustainable alternative to every financial product you can think of.

What happens when P2P insurance products are launched to protect borrowers against default? Who is going to launch the first institutional P2P managed fund?

Could this evolve into a social stock exchange or a social bond market? Or how about The London CrowdFunding Exchange or the New York P2P Lending Exchange?

Who knows?

As long as this innovation all happens with all of our four lessons of debt in mind, without the institutions that engage in money creation, we can have the best of both worlds – the innovation from finance over the centuries and the lessons of sustainability outlined in this chapter.

If this is what comes out of the current economic situation, then it will be worth the temporary pain it causes while we transition to the economy of freedom.

The future of finance

When our banking system is reformed, probably following the inevitable collapse of our traditional banking system or the bankruptcy of governments, we have the opportunity to choose sustainability once and for all.

It is also my belief that traditional credit scoring will slowly be replaced by social capital scoring. If you want to fund, borrow, raise funds or invest in the future, then you will need to start investing in the strength of your social capital score now.

With the rise of P2P lending, we have all the tools we need to move to a future of sustainable finance. And it has only just begun.

Finance has just started to reach developing countries, too.

The two big innovations that follow – microfinance combined with mobile payments – can meet all our rules for sustainability.

So how exactly did women in developing countries become a better investment than men in the developed world?

Hold on! Before you start Chapter 10, tweet me your thoughts on #P2PLending.

QR 31 Tweet Simon Dixon about #P2PLending

---

1   Sigler, Laurence E. (trans.) (2002), Fibonacci's Liber Abaci, Springer-Verlag,

2   No More National Debt, Bill Still, 2011

3   The Ascent of Money, Neil Ferguson, 2008

4   John Seidl, "Upon the Hip"– A Study of the Criminal Loan-Shark Industry, unpublished Ph.D. dissertation (Cambridge, MA: Harvard University, 1968)

5   Marie Burton, Consumer Focus,Keeping the plates spinning: Perceptions of payday loans in Great Britain http://www.consumerfocus.org.uk/assets/1/files/2010/02/Keeping-the-plates-spinning.PDF

6   Payday lenders hope to return in Georgia, 3/18/07". Retrieved 2010-10-03 http://www.pliwatch.org/news_article_070318C.html

7   www.wonga.com

8   Amy Hoak Bypassing the bank: How to use peer-to-peer lending sites to borrow money Market Watch, Jan. 28, 2008

9   [Lending Club]. (07-20-2011) https://www.lendingclub.com/info/statistics.action Retrieved (1-22-2011)

10 [Lending Club]. (07-20-2011) https://www.lendingclub.com/info/statistics.action Retrieved (1-22-2011)

10 Hugely disruptive technology #6 – microfinance platforms

YOU MIGHT LIKE to take a look at the introductory video before we start.

QR 32 Introductory video on hugely disruptive technology #6

NOTE: If you are manually typing the above URL, the first 'l' in the URL is a lower case 'L' and the second 'l' is also a lower case 'L', not a capital 'i'

As we travel forward in time we watch the spread of sustainable financial services across the world.

Due to our reforms, banks legally have to disclose what they intend to use our different investment accounts for and can no longer engage in money creation.

Thanks to the World Wide Web, digital money and the social networks, information and finance is able to flow.

Due to the democratisation of media through the social networks, more are made aware of investment accounts that are not investing with a TBL in mind. While this does not stop funds going to socially unsustainable individuals and companies, the investment accounts reflect the investment appetite of society.

But what is truly remarkable is what emerges when microfinance institutions observe the rise of crowdfunding and P2P lending and start to adapt their models digitally, allowing microfinance to meet all four lessons of debt sustainability outlined in Chapter 8.

With the birth of online microfinance platforms comes real development. This movement spreads virally through the social networks.

The story of how finance reached developing countries through microfinance is one that defied conventional wisdom.

Thanks to our new Bank Charter Act, the funding made available through microfinance grows to record highs, allowing investors to make a real difference and still have a decent return on their investment.

Investing micro amounts in entrepreneurs in developing countries turns out to be a real win/win scenario that leads to a massive increase in worldwide wealth, and the best part is, the funds are not about to be wiped out during the banking crash ahead, thanks to our adventure in time travel.

Before we travel through the timeline observing the rise of microfinance platforms, I want to explain an injustice inflicted on the developing world.

Warning! This may make you feel as sick as I did when I first traced the flow of finance in developing countries before our reforms. But here is the tragic reality of our world before reform.

A completely illegitimate debt for developing countries

Our debt trap actually spreads its disease much further than just the developed economies.

It is important to understand a few more things about money and debt to understand why the developing world is where it is today. The flow of money is brilliantly accounted in Michael Rowbotham's book 'The Grip of Death' and I summarise below.

There are two things you need to know about international finance:

Firstly, as we already know, the vast majority of money can only be created if somebody borrows it from a bank.

Secondly, when countries trade with each other and goods are exported from one country to another, foreign money is brought back into the economy that exported the goods, but the debt behind that money remains overseas, in the country that bought the goods.

Therefore, through exporting, money that had been borrowed into existence in one country is brought into another economy, free of debt.

You with me? Great.

The money can easily be turned into domestic currency via the foreign exchange market. All you need to know is that when goods are imported, money created in the domestic economy goes abroad, but the debt associated with that money remains at home.

If a country exports more than it imports, there is a net gain of additional debt-free money for the exporting country. This influx of money provides a boost for the exporter's economy.

However, if a country imports more than it exports, there is a net outflow of money, but the debt associated with the creation of the lost money remains. That country's entire economy is therefore threatened.

The result being, any country that exports more than it imports is healthy, enjoying an influx of money without having any additional debt. The funny thing is, in reality the country is effectively losing real wealth with an outflow of real goods.

Despite the fact that such countries are losing in real terms, in a world run on a debt trap, countries are gaining some debt-free money.

The result is, that everybody fights to be an exporter. You can imagine what impact this has on the possibility of peace!

But anyway, in order to thrive, the world must fight to be a net exporter, resulting in exchanging actual goods that an economy can use for some debt-free money.

A nation's economic goals, should they become successful, are counter-productive to the needs of its citizens.

Only a few nations such as the US and UK can run an economy importing more than they export, as for now everybody accepts our currencies and we can always borrow more in our own currency. As long as people still believe in our currencies, borrowing through bonds continues, but that all changes once people lose faith, as we saw with the US credit rating downgrade in 2011.

The result is that developing countries export all their goods, while starvation remains a problem. Have you ever wondered why a resource-rich developing country would export its food while its citizens are starving? Well, now you know why. But this is just the beginning.

Figure 52 How bank credit creation can lead to forced exports around the world

In order to enhance world development, the World Bank and the IMF were founded in 1944. The World Bank was intended to aid post-war reconstruction, especially in the poorer countries, by providing loans. The purpose of the IMF was to provide an international reserve of money – a sort of financial pool upon which all member countries could call, whether rich or poor, should they hit temporary difficulties.

In the 50 or more years since their formation, these two institutions have largely replaced direct country-to-country lending, and have advanced loans mounting to billions of dollars to developing nations.

However wealthy a country may appear to be, almost all nations are in a debt trap and trade from a position of insolvency. As a result, the wealthy nations unwilling to accept debtor nation's goods, and have been turning to developing countries as a continued outlet for their own goods.

Wealthy countries are willing to lend money to developing nations only with the knowledge that such loans would benefit the wealthy countries. They want to find markets for their own exports, and hence improve their own financial position.

Loans are often made on the condition that purchases are made in wealthy nations. For example, 'tied aid' is a condition on loans that ensures the lending country obtains a market for their exports by issuing loans on the condition that the money is spent with certain nations, equivalent to the value of the loan they advance.

Once this money is spent on imports, the money already advanced to them as loans is absorbed back into the wealthy countries of the world, leaving the developing nation with an unpayable debt.

Where did the money for these loans actually come from?

The World Bank raises money by drawing up bonds, and selling these to commercial banks on the money markets of the world. The money raised is then loaned to nations who require money for development.

The IMF presents itself as a financial pool; an international reserve of money built up with contributions (known as quotas) from subscribing nations. However, its entire function and status radically changed when, in 1979, the IMF created Special Drawing Rights (SDRs). These SDRs were created and intended to serve as an additional international currency.

Although these SDRs are 'credited' to each nation's account with the IMF, if a nation borrows these SDRs, it must repay them or their equivalent (initially 1 SDR equalled 1 US Dollar), or pay interest on the SDR loan.

Now, it is abundantly clear from this that the IMF and the World Bank are not just lending money; they are involved in creating it. Although SDRs are described as amounts 'credited' to a nation, no money or credit of any kind is put into the nation's account. SDRs are actually a credit facility, just like a bank overdraft – if they are borrowed, they must be repaid.

Thus the IMF has itself created, and now lends, vast sums of a new currency, defined in dollar terms and fully convertible with all national currencies. Thus, the IMF is creating and issuing money as a debt, under an identical system to that of a conventional bank – its reserves being the original pool of quota funds.

Money creation is also involved in the loans advanced by the World Bank through the selling of bonds. The World Bank does not itself create the money, but draws up bonds and sells them to commercial banks which, in purchasing these bonds, create money for the purpose. When a bank makes any form of purchase it does so against the deposits it holds at the time, but does not reduce those deposits; hence additional money is directly created.

To appreciate the consequences of the IMF and the World Bank, the detail of money creation, and the path of the supply of international debt money, Michael Rowbotham traces the flow of money as summarised below.

The World Bank draws up bonds to raise the money for its loans. These are bought by the commercial banking sector, and purchased against the deposits held by those banks at the time.

An amount of number-money, usually denominated in dollars, is then paid to the World Bank by the commercial bank.

None of the individuals or institutions with deposits in the bank buying the bonds has their deposit reduced, or affected in any way.

Thus the loan is a creation of additional number-money.

This new bank credit is then advanced by the World Bank to a borrowing nation, and the debt recorded against the borrowing nation. When paid into the bank accounts in the borrowing nation, it becomes clear that the total of global bank deposits has increased. Total global debt has also increased.

When nations borrow using SDRs, the IMF creates and issues a sum of additional money in the form of an international currency, fully convertible into other currencies. Thus the total of global monetary deposits has risen, along with the equivalent debt.

These loans are always associated with a need to purchase foreign goods, so the money received by the borrowing nation will then be spent abroad, generally in more wealthy nations.

It may well be that the money will be used to make purchases back in the country whose banking sector bought the World Bank bonds, returning as export revenues to the wealthy nation whose banking sector created it. This loan money will register as an increase in the total deposits of that nation, confirming beyond dispute that money has been created.

Since these loans are advanced in dollars or pounds, rather than the debtor nation's currency, the money advanced thus instantly becomes part of the money stock of the wealthy nation where it is spent. Meanwhile, the debt remains registered to the developing country.

In summary, by loans being advanced to a developing country, the wealthy nation has found a market for its goods, its economy is boosted, and its money stock increased, whilst the burden of debt has been assumed by another country, crippling their economies and leading to mass poverty.

There is a singular difference between national debt and international debt, a national debt is run up at will, and under the control of the national government. International debt, and the rate of its increase, places an entire nation under the financial control of institutions outside its borders.

This entire process has made a financial playground and economic disaster area out of the developing nations. These debts have been used to buy out private and public companies, pension funds, life assurance firms and many other forms of developing countries' equity. Many developing countries have privatisation schemes in place, and many more are planning them. Thus, the cream of a developing nation's domestic industry is passing into foreign control.

Third world poverty will continue to increase until we learn the lessons of debt. So let's take a look at how the IMF and the World Bank score in our debt sustainability test.

The loans seem to go for productive use rather than for nice shiny objects; however, the benefit ends up in the wrong country, so for me that is a violation of lesson 1 – good debt. We have shown that they engage in money creation, violating lesson 2 – money creation. They are certainly not considering people, planet and profit of the country that is borrowing, thus violating lesson 3 – TBL. Finally, the relationship between borrower and lender is completely broken down when lending to an entire foreign country, thus violating lesson 4 – relationship.

So there we have it, third world debt explained. That is how we get money out of developing countries. But some people are putting money back in, right?

So what exactly is microfinance?

Microfinance refers to the provision of financial services to low-income clients, who traditionally lack access to banking. Broadly, it is a movement whose object is a world in which as many poor and near-poor households as possible have permanent access to an appropriate range of high quality financial services, including not just credit but also savings, insurance, and fund transfers. Microfinance includes microcredit, the provision of credit services to poor clients.

Inspired, we step back into our time machine to watch the birth of microfinance.

To 1864 ... the birth of microfinance

Friedrich Wilhelm Raiffeisen was the Mayor of Flammersfeld in Germany who, when he observed the suffering of farmers, who were often in the grip of loan sharks, founded the first co-operative lending bank (in effect the first rural credit union) in 1864.

Credit unions are co-operative financial institutions that are owned and controlled by their members. Many credit unions exist with the mission of furthering community development on a local level.

Raiffeisen believed that there is a connection between poverty and dependency. In order to fight poverty one should fight dependency first. Based on this idea he came up with the 'three S' formula: self-help, self-governance and self-responsibility.

When put into practice, he believed that people could achieve independence from charity, politics and loan sharks.

Motivated by watching the misery of the poor of his local population, he founded the first rural central bank at Neuwied, the 'Rheinische Landwirtschaftliche Genossenschaftsbank' (Rhenish Agricultural Cooperative Bank). The vision was to bring the kinds of opportunities and risk-management tools that financial services can provide to poor people.

After Raiffeisen's death in 1888, credit unions spread across Italy, France, the Netherlands, UK and Austria, and elsewhere. In 1934, US Congress passed the Federal Credit Union Act, which permitted credit unions to be organised anywhere in the United States.

The idea that financial institutions could serve a community without money creation and simultaneously meet all four lessons of debt was later spread across developing countries throughout the 1970s with the birth of microcredit and microfinance.

Grameen Bank

The origins of microcredit in its current form can be linked to several organisations founded in Bangladesh, most notably, the Grameen Bank. The Grameen Bank, which is generally considered the first modern microcredit institution, was founded in 1976 by Muhammad Yunus.

Yunus began the project in a small town called Jobra, using his own money to deliver small loans at low-interest rates to the rural poor.

During visits to the poorest households in the village, Yunus discovered that very small loans could make a disproportionate difference to a poor person. At the time, Jobra women, who made bamboo furniture, had to take out loans to buy bamboo. Yunus understood the first lesson of debt – good debt – and used the money to help start-up entrepreneurs and existing micro businesses.

His first loan, consisting of US$27 from his own pocket, was made to 42 women in the village, who made a net profit of BDT0.50 (US$0.02) each on the loan[1].

Dr. Akhtar Hameed Khan, founder of the Pakistan Academy for Rural Development, is credited alongside Yunus for pioneering this idea.

From his experience at Jobra, Yunus, an admirer of Dr. Hameed, realised that the creation of an institution was needed to lend to those who had nothing.

While traditional banks were not interested in making tiny loans at reasonable interest rates to the poor due to high repayment risks, Yunus believed that given the chance, the poor will repay the borrowed money and that microcredit could be a viable business model.

After being laughed out of the building by several banks, Yunus finally succeeded in securing a loan from the government Janata Bank to lend to the poor in Jobra in 1976. The bank never engaged in money creation, choosing instead to heed lesson two – money creation, and simply lent money that it borrowed from other banks for its projects.

By 1982, the bank had 28,000 members. On 1 October 1983 it operated as a full-fledged bank and was renamed the Grameen Bank ('Village Bank') to make loans to poor Bangladeshis[2]. The loans met the criteria of the third lesson – TBL.

Yunus and his colleagues encountered everything from violent radical leftists to the conservative clergy who told women that they would be denied a Muslim burial if they borrowed money from the Grameen Bank, but Yunus still continued with his vision.

As of July 2007, Grameen Bank had issued US$6.38 billion to 7.4 million borrowers[3] and by the end of 2008, $USD 7.6 billion.

To ensure repayment, the bank uses a system of 'solidarity groups'. These small informal groups apply together for loans and its members act as co-guarantors of repayment and support one another's efforts at economic self-advancement. These groups highlighted the power and importance of lesson four – relationship, to the Grameen Bank.

Over time, the Grameen initiative has grown into a multi-faceted group of profitable and non-profit ventures, including major projects like Grameen Trust and Grameen Fund, which runs equity projects like Grameen Software Limited, Grameen CyberNet Limited, and Grameen Knitwear Limited, as well as Grameen Telecom, which has a stake in GrameenPhone, the biggest private sector phone company in Bangladesh.

GrameenPhone's Village Phone (Polli Phone) project has brought mobile phone ownership to 260,000 rural poor in over 50,000 villages since the beginning of the project in March 1997, laying the foundation for m-payments, to finally serve the previously non-banked[4].

The success of the Grameen model of microfinancing has inspired similar efforts in a hundred countries throughout the developing world and even in industrialised nations, including the United States.

Many, but not all, microcredit projects also retain their emphasis on lending specifically to women. More than 94% of Grameen loans have gone to women, who suffer disproportionately from poverty and who are more likely than men to devote their earnings to their families[5].

Grameen Bank was followed by organisations such as BRAC in 1972 and ASA in 1978.

Microcredit reached Latin America with the establishment of PRODEM in Bolivia in 1986; a bank that later transformed into the for-profit BancoSol.

Microcredit quickly became a popular tool for economic development, with hundreds of institutions emerging throughout the third world.

Muhammad Yunus was awarded the Nobel Peace Prize in 2006 for his work providing microcredit services to the poor.

Microfinance marches on

It was when microfinance met the previous hugely disruptive technologies outlined in the book - the World Wide Web, digital money, the social networks, crowdfunding and P2P lending, that the scale and impact became truly remarkable.

Kiva Microfunds (commonly known by its domain name, Kiva.org) allows people to lend money using the World Wide Web to microfinance institutions in developing countries around the world.

Kiva was founded in October 2005 by Matt Flannery and Jessica Jackley. Inspired by a 2003 lecture given by Muhammad Yunus at Stanford Business School, Jessica began working as a consultant for the non-profit Village Enterprise Fund, which worked to help start small businesses in East Africa.

While in Africa, Matt and Jessica spent time interviewing entrepreneurs about the problems they faced in starting ventures and found that lack of access to start-up capital was a common theme. After returning from Africa, they began developing their plan for a microfinance project that would grow into online microfinance platform – Kiva.

Kiva itself does not charge any interest; the loans made by Kiva members are passed interest-free to independent field partners. Field partners then post profiles of qualified local entrepreneurs on the website, Kiva.org.

Lenders browse and choose an entrepreneur they wish to fund and Kiva aggregates the loan capital from individual lenders, transferring it to the appropriate field partners to disburse to the entrepreneur chosen by the lender.

As the entrepreneurs repay their loans, the field partners pass the funds back to Kiva. As the loan is repaid, the Kiva lenders can withdraw their money or re-lend it to another entrepreneur.

Lenders' funds are transferred to Kiva through PayPal.

Field partners charge interest to their borrowers, while Kiva keeps track of how much interest is charged and will not work with those charging unfair interest rates.

As of August 2011, Kiva had distributed over US$233 million in loans from over 600,000 lenders[6].

But here is the bit that shocks us all, especially bankers; its current repayment rate is 98.79% – less than a 2% default on their loans[7].

After Kiva's success, MYC4 was founded in 2006 by Mads Kjær, chairman and former CEO of the Kjær Group and Honorary Danish Consul to Ethiopia, and Tim Vang. Since the company's creation, 18,730 investors from 112 countries have invested more than €14 million in 7,163 businesses in seven African countries[8].

United Prosperity followed, but unlike most microcredit or P2P lending organisations, it was founded not to directly lend to the micro-entrepreneur, but instead to provide a guarantee to a local bank, which lends to the micro-entrepreneur. Typically the local bank will lend about twice the amount provided by the micro-lender's guarantee, thus providing larger loans than traditional micro-credit.

In 2007 microfinance hit China when Wokai was founded to fund entrepreneurs in rural China.

In 2009 Energy in Common (EIC) was founded to enable microloans specifically and only for renewable energy technologies. EIC was founded by Hugh Whalan and Scott Tudman in 2009. It has the very ambitious goal of delivering renewable energy to 15 million people in the next five years, while fighting poverty by empowering developing world entrepreneurs through microloans.

Since microfinance went digital, it has been growing rapidly, with US$25 billion currently at work in microfinance loans[9].

While microfinance also has its challenges – you hear stories of microloans charged as high as 80 to 125% interest – what microfinance proved is that women with no security are actually a better credit risk than men with security. The exact opposite of conventional banking wisdom.

It is estimated that the industry needs US$250 billion to get capital to all the poor people who need it. So how might that be achieved?

Enter the smart phone

With the rise of the final hugely disruptive technology – the mobile smart phone, I see no reason why this target cannot be achieved.

But there is one problem. While all this capital is reaching the developing world microfinance platforms, it is leaving faster through Third World debt.

Because both the World Bank and the IMF violate the second lesson of debt, the developing nations are permanently crippled with interest payments and debt beyond repayment. So while entrepreneurs in developing countries work hard to repay their microloans made possible through hugely disruptive technology #6, the country is burdened with debt that results in a redistribution of money from the developing countries to our so-called wealthy nations that are now wrestling with bankruptcy too.

But, thanks to our Bank Charter Act of 1844, perhaps the central banks of the world, the IMF and the World Bank will follow as we demand to put an end to money creation and move to sustainable banking.

Maybe the IMF and the World Bank might be forced to write off the debt, or at least the countries could be given the opportunity to pay it down as they start to benefit from the ability to create their own money supply, rather than giving the profits to their banks.

The story of the rise of the microfinance platform shows to us all that remarkable things can happen, finance can reach the vast unbanked and there is a chance to make a dent in world poverty through financial services.

One thing is for sure, thanks to the mobile smart phone, money can now reach those who need it most, and we can all do everything anywhere with an internet connection with a small device that fits in our pocket.

The glue that fits everything together, that provides freedom for many, that will become the device that helps us run our lives in the economy of freedom is hugely disruptive technology #7 – the mobile smart phone ...

Hold on! Before you start Chapter 11, tweet me your thoughts on #Microfinance.

QR 33 Tweet Simon Dixon about #Microfinance

---

1   First loan he gave was $27 from own pocket, The Daily Star, 2006-10-14, Front page, Retrieved: 22 August 2007
2   Muhammad Yunus: The triumph of idealism, New Age Special, The New Age, 1 January 2007; Retrieved: 11 September 2007
3   "GB at a glance", Muhammad Yunus, Grameen Info; Retrieved: 9 September 2007
4   "Village Phone". About Grameenphone. Grameenphone. 2006. Retrieved 22 August 2007
5   Yunus, Muhammad. Transcript of broadcast interview with Negus, George. World in Focus: Interview with Prof. Muhammad Yunus. Foreign Correspondent; ABC online. 25 March 1997. Retrieved on 22 August 2007

6 "KIVA Stats". Kiva.org. Retrieved August 12, 2011
7 "KIVA Stats". Kiva.org. Retrieved August 12, 2011
8 "Countries". myc4.com. Retrieved 2011-10-10
9 The Township Project South Africa - Microcredit http://www.thetownships-project.org/southafrica/microcredit.php

11 Hugely disruptive technology #7 – the mobile smart phone

YOU MIGHT WANT to take a look at the introductory video before we begin this topic.

Scan QR Code and watch video!

Can't scan? http://bit.ly/nO3CfA

QR 34 Introductory video on hugely disruptive technology #7

NOTE: If you are manually typing the above URL, the 'O' in the URL is a capital 'o' rather than a zero

As we reach the end of Part 2 of the book and our adventure in time travel, we look at the final piece in our puzzle. There is a commonality with each of the hugely disruptive technologies discussed so far.

All these hugely disruptive technologies can now serve us in the economy of freedom on the move through a small device in our pocket.

Your mobile smart phone will touch every part of your life – it will be your wallet, your identity, your car keys, house keys, communication, remote control, social life ... everything.

All of the technologies to run these aspects of your life from your mobile smart phone already exist as I write this book, but they will become a lot more intelligent in just a few years. In fact this chapter will become completely out of date fast.

> "For the past few years, we've thought of smart phones as a way to access the internet while on the go. The next few years will be about thinking of the phone as a networked sensor. We carry our phones everywhere and they often know where we are, where we're going and where we've been. They have the potential to know where we're headed, who we're travelling with and what we may find interesting around the corner." *Dennis Crowley, co-founder of Foursquare*

Everybody and everything is now connected. Information is no longer a barrier to anybody with a connection to the World Wide Web and a mobile smart phone.

The smart phone is the key linking technology

We can pull out our mobile smart phone and connect to hugely disruptive technology #1– the World Wide Web – but rather than simply accessing the web from your smart phone, the smart phone is no longer a device that answers your questions, it is a device that tells you what you need to know before you know it.

We are shifting from search to discovery. Shortly, your mobile smart phone will pull up all the information you need to know based upon the exact location you happen to be in and offer you all the best deals for the exact type of things that you like to do in that area. It will tell you how to get there and where you would enjoy going next. It will plan your day for you.

When hugely disruptive technology #2 – digital money – fully integrates with the mobile smart phone, it will be your wallet, your device that gets you the best prices, your device to pay for all your bills, your device to transfer money anywhere in the world; in fact it will know what and how you should be buying before you know it.

Shortly, it will biometrically identify you and send your money to whoever, wherever you want, instantly. It will tell you when it needs to be paid and whether you can afford it. It will even manage your savings and investments for you.

When hugely disruptive technology #3 – the social networks – really integrate with your smart phone, it will be your primary source for building your social capital. In fact, it will be the only feasible way to keep in touch and stay connected with your Facebook friends, your Google+ circles, your LinkedIn connections, your Twitter followers, your BankToTheFuture investors and investments, and the data and information that will give you your competitive advantage in a world where the information and speed at which you process that information will be your success.

Shortly, it will tell you exactly who you should be connecting with based upon your current location and goals you are looking to achieve.

It will identify your staff, your joint venture partners, your friends, your potential dates, future wife or husband and connect you without you having to search the social networks at all.

When hugely disruptive technology #4 – crowdfunding – truly integrates with your mobile smart phone, you will use it to record video pitches instantly, edit the pitch quickly and easily, add music that you compose and spread virally for your next crowdfunded project as your main source of funding.

If your social capital is strong enough, you can raise the money in hours as opportunity presents itself in the moment.

Shortly, it will match you up with the exact type of people that would look to fund something like your project and connect you with the entire team to make it become a reality, as well as provide you with all the training you need, all delivered from your mobile smart phone.

When hugely disruptive technology #5 – P2P lending – truly integrates with your smart phone, you will use it to check the rate of your P2P loans, to find equity investments, to perform activities that used to be done through an investment bank, a private equity house or a retail bank.

It will not be long until you hit a button on your mobile smart phone and instantly you have a video conference with the person behind the investment proposal that your phone recommends to you. It will make better recommendations to you than any financial advisor or wealth manager, because it will know more about you than any human can possibly know.

When hugely disruptive technology #6 – microfinance platforms – truly integrates with the mobile smart phone, your mobile smart phone will take the change that you used to carry in your pocket as coins and collect it together according to your phone's understanding about how much you are able to allocate to investments based on the countries and types of entrepreneurs that interest you the most.

It will reward you automatically with vouchers for your favourite food or discounts on your favourite movies with every microloan you make.

In fact, it will provide you with a bigger discount on the exact type of products you like most, even more than the amount you invested, ensuring money reaches entrepreneurs in developing countries.

It will also allocate a percentage of your savings each month to microloans, crowdloans, crowdfunds, and the like, and give you a budget for fun stuff, managing your whole portfolio for you.

Your investments will allow you to make a difference in developing countries so that they can eventually get their very own smart phones and work towards living in the economy of freedom, without charity contributions.

Thanks to hugely disruptive technology #7 – the mobile smart phone, you can truly live your life in an economy of freedom, on your terms, and you can trust in the chosen device in your pocket to manage most of the tasks that used to eat away at your day.

Welcome to your future, and guess what?

Some people are still using their mobile phones just to make phone calls!

The rise of the mobile smart phone

All the scenarios above have derived their power from three key innovations that drive the true power of the mobile smartphone – namely applications, location check-ins and artificial intelligence.

If you do not know what a mobile smart phone is then I doubt you would have read this far, but in a nutshell it's a mobile phone combined with a portable media player, a camera, a video camera, touchscreen capabilities, a web browser, GPS navigation, wi-fi and mobile broadband and a mobile operating system like Apple's iOS, Google Android or Blackberry OS.

While this is all impressive, its true power to revolutionise our lives comes from three innovations built on top of the smart phone.

Crowdsourcing the collective intelligence of the world ...

In July 2008, Apple introduced its second generation iPhone and released with it the App Store, adding the capability for the iPhone to deliver applications directly over a wi-fi without requiring a PC for installation.

When Apple released the App store, the days of developers having to work in employment ended as thousands crowdfunded their start-up capital to develop apps to a marketplace of millions, across millions of mobile smart phones.

In effect Apple opened up the collective intelligence of the world to crowdsource innovation from global entrepreneurs who set out to solve every problem anybody could possibly have using their phone.

The App Store has been a huge success for Apple, going from over 500 applications at launch to 65,000 applications and over 1.5 billion downloads in its first year.

The App Store hit 3 billion application downloads in early January 2010, 10 billion downloads by January 2011 and 15 billion downloads, of over 425,000 applications, in early July 2011[1].

Rather than having to wait for a company to innovate, the world now innovates and we benefit from the world's collective innovation at a faster rate than any company could produce.

This business model of crowdsourcing the world's collective innovation was such a huge success that, following on from the success of Apple's App Store, other smart phone manufacturers quickly launched application stores. Google launched the Android Market in October 2008, RIM launched its app store BlackBerry App World in April 2009, Microsoft launched an app store for Windows Mobile called Windows Marketplace For Mobile in October 2009, Amazon launched its Amazon App Store for the Google Android operating system in March 2011, and many others followed Apple's lead.

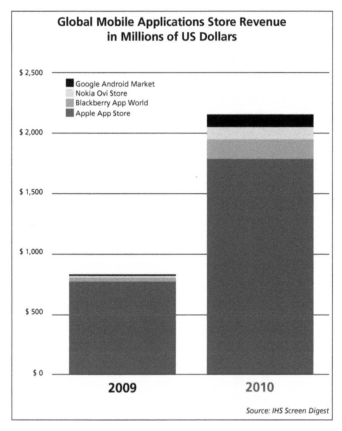

Figure 53 Global mobile applications store revenue chart, Wikipedia

This allowed every mobile smart phone to be powered by the collective innovation of thousands of developers around the world.

The power of the mobile smartphone would have taken decades without the innovation of the App Store. This is one of the main reasons why you will be able to do everything from your mobile smart phone, and if you can't do it now, you can either crowdfund your own developer to build it, or check next week – it will probably be launched in your App Store.

But there also emerged a new breed of apps that knew exactly where you were ...

I've got my eye on you ...

GPS receivers are part of almost every smart phone today. They can be used to determine your location and direct relevant location-specific advertising straight to your device.

But that is just the beginning of what it can be used for; your smart phone can access social networks, individuals, cities, neighbourhoods, landmarks, and actions that are relevant to your past, current, and future location.

Based on this information it can recommend social events in a city; you can request the nearest business or service, such as an ATM or restaurant; navigate to any address; locate people on a map displayed on your smart phone; receive alerts, such as notification of a sale in your favourite store as you drive past it or warning of a traffic jam; get real-time questions and answers revolving around restaurants, services, and other venues; find taxis, service people, rental equipment, doctors, packages and trains; buddy lists, common profile matching (dating); automatic airport check-in; mobile coupons or discounts to mobile subscribers who are near to advertising restaurants, cafes, movie theatres – the list goes on and on.

By giving developers permission to use your location by clicking a button on your favourite location-based app on your smart phone, you are able to literally be guided to the most interesting locations and venues.

I hear you say ... as if we need any more advertising, right?

And besides, who actually gives permission to their mobile smart phone to track their every move? Well, according to a ComScore report released in May 2011, nearly one in five smart phone users are tapping into check-in services and volunteering their location.

In 2011, a total of 16.7 million mobile subscribers are using location-based services on their phones[2] – there has to be some reason. The reason is because we can now choose our advertising based upon our interests.

It is when location-based apps are combined with the third innovation, artificial intelligence, that it starts to make a real difference.

I know you better than you know yourself ...

Artificial intelligence (AI) is the intelligence of machines. John McCarthy, who coined the term in 1956, defines it as "the science and engineering of making intelligent machines."

There is a reason why Amazon seems to know what book you should be buying. There is a reason why Facebook seems to know what advert you should be looking at. It is because they are investing heavily in AI.

Artificial intelligence is the topic of much debate today. Martin Ford, author of 'The Lights in the Tunnel: Automation, Accelerating Technology and the Economy of the Future', argues that specialised AI applications, robotics and other forms of automation will ultimately result in significant unemployment as machines begin to match and exceed the capability of workers to perform most routine and repetitive jobs.

Ray Kurzwell used Moore's Law (which describes the relentless exponential improvement in digital technology) to calculate that desktop computers will have the same processing power as humans brains by the year 2029.

He also predicts that by 2045 artificial intelligence will reach a point where it is able to improve itself at a rate that far exceeds anything conceivable in the past, a scenario that science fiction writer Vernor Vinge named the "singularity".

Robot designer Hans Moravec, cyberneticist Kevin Warwick and inventor Ray Kurzwell have predicted that humans and machines will merge in the future, more capable and powerful than either. Edward Fredkin argues that "artificial intelligence is the next stage in evolution."

It is interesting to speculate and nobody really knows, but AI is attracting billions in venture capital from Silicon Valley and has the attention of all the largest technology companies worldwide.

It is thanks to developments in AI, combined with the apps you buy and the location data you allow your smart phone to use, that your smart phone will eventually become the best personal assistant you have ever hired and shortly will quite literally guide your life.

Use of AI will make your mobile smart phone your ultimate personal secretary, which can receive emails and messages, understand what they are about, and change the individual's personal schedule according to the message.

The working lifestyle will change, with the majority of people working from home rather than commuting. This may be beneficial to the environment as it involves less transportation.

The possibilities are also endless in the developing world, thanks to mobile money.

Vodafone – Kenya's largest bank?

Mobile banking became a huge convenience for us all in developed countries, but in developing countries, it helped build the countries.

Mobile Network Operators like Vodafone, out of nowhere, became the largest banks in Kenya, almost by accident, by allowing their customers to pay cash onto their phone accounts and use it for transactions through M-PESA.

This opened up an alternative person-to-person m-payment system in developing countries run by mobile operating networks.

Access to financial services is crucial to economic growth and poverty reduction. In the past, mainstream financial institutions avoided developing economies, in the belief that low-income countries do not save and are bad borrowers.

As we saw in Chapter 10, the microfinance revolution eliminated that myth when it proved that, not only do poor households save when they have access to finance, but they also have high repayment rates with low default rates.

But microfinance aside, one of the largest sources of income in developing countries is mobile remittances.

The rise of mobile payments gave developing countries the opportunity to build their future and make easier payments. Nearly 2 billion people worldwide have little or no access to traditional financial services.

I briefly mentioned Kenya in Chapter 6. In 2007 over 70% of Kenyan households did not have bank accounts. Today, millions of Kenyans make payments and store their funds for short periods without bank accounts at low risk and cost.

Vodafone's M-PESA attracted 22% of Kenya's 35 million people to use mobile payments in a two-year period[3]. The system now allows Kenyans working in the UK to deposit sterling or Euros in the UK with a remittance agent, and have the family collect the money in Kenyan shillings back in their home country using their mobile phone.

M-payments has changed the game forever in the developing world, and the biggest threat to banks came from the telephone operators, as well as making everybody's life easier in the developed world.

The glue of hugely disruptive technologies

The mobile smart phone is the final disruptive technology in a series of hugely disruptive technological innovation. One thing is for sure; there will be seven more to talk about in my next book.

If you believe the artificial intelligence philosophers, then our biggest threat comes when robots are intelligent enough to develop more intelligent robots at a faster rate than us. Then what?

OK, back to the present. It is clear to see that we live in a time like no other and that we have some choices to make.

While the World Wide Web catalysed the innovation behind digital money, the social networks, crowdfunding, P2P lending and microfinance platforms, the glue that held it together came from the mobile smart phone and the ability to crowdsource the world's intelligence and collective innovation through open source technology and the development of apps.

But as we know, it is all built on a debt trap that was inevitably and predictably guaranteed to crash before our Bank Charter Act reforms.

So in Part 3, attention turns to the choices ahead – to reform banking or not to reform banking?

Hold on! Before you start Part 3, tweet me your thoughts on #SmartPhones.

QR 35 Tweet Simon Dixon about #SmartPhones

---

1   Apple Special Event, June 6, 2011". Apple. June 6, 2011
2   Andrew Ward (2011-07-21). "Apple overtakes Nokia in smartphone volumes". FT.com
3   Bank 2.0, Brett King, 2010

Part 03

THE ROAD AHEAD

12 To reform or not to reform?

BEFORE CONTINUING our discussion, take a look at the introductory video below.

QR 36 Introductory video on the final chapter – to reform or not to reform?

We have reached the end of our adventure in time travel and we have successfully reformed banking through the Bank Charter Act.

We are now faced with a decision. Do we destroy the time machine in an attempt to prevent bankers going back in time and reverting to the original Bank Charter Act, or do we destroy the time machine in an attempt to prevent such reforms?

After some quiet contemplation we figure it does not matter. While collapsing our banking system as a means to reach reform is drastic and destructive, we figure that banking reform is inevitable whether we leave the banking system to collapse or whether we stick to our time travel reforms.

We have tinkered enough with time and don't want to interfere any more.

Without reforms, the path to future reform would look something like this

As governmental debt spirals out of control, one of the leading credit rating agencies will downgrade a major country as it did in the US in 2011, with others to follow as the percentage of debt to GDP spirals out of control.

As people, companies and governments are unable to take on any more debt as the poor are maxed out and the rich don't need to, the central banks will step in with further quantitative easing to restimulate economies.

In an attempt to get the banks lending and in response to public outrage, conflicting regulations will be implemented, such as Basel III requiring banks to hold more money on reserve at the very same time as trying to get more people into debt.

The free economy, driving deflation and quantitative easing, driving inflation, will battle it out, meaning that the monetary policy committee and the government will have fewer concerns about inflation and continue to create money as debt through the central bank.

So essentially, as nobody else can take on the debt, the central bank steps in.

The net result of the regulations is more unemployment without any increase in stability. As quantitative easing gives a false sense of calm, investors start leveraging up and buying property on debt again as they think it is relatively cheap, but increasing unemployment causes more and more to default, leading to a return to the conditions of 2008, when AIG and Lehman Brothers collapsed.

This time around government is unable to bail out as fewer are willing to lend to them owing to their credit rating downgrades and governments are insolvent.

An emergency meeting is called as traditional economists get booed out of the room and politicians start listening to our 'crazy' reforms.

We put to them our three commandments and our four lessons of debt:

1. Thou shalt make the banks ask depositors' permission before they lend.

2. Thou shalt make the banks disclose to the depositors how they use their money.

3. Thou shalt give the licence to create money to a democratic power.

The four lessons of debt:

Lesson 1 – There is good debt and there is bad debt.

Lesson 2 – The process of creating money should never be mixed with the process of lending for profit.

Lesson 3 – Debt has a triple bottom line.

Lesson 4 – Borrowers and lenders must have a relationship.

So how would we move from banks that can create money to banks that cannot create money?

In-depth analysis on making the shift from banks that create money to banks that do not create money can be found in publications drafted by Positive Money. But without violating my 'no-jargon' promise, here is a very simple explanation. And it does not need to be more complicated, really.

Every bank has a number on its balance sheet that represents the total amount of money that customers can withdraw from their account at any one time.

This is the total of every customer balance (your balance that you see when you login to your online banking, plus everybody else's).

Imagine every customer of that particular bank logging into their online banking and somebody going to everybody's house and asking them their balance.

This total is the total amount of demand deposits for that particular bank. This figure can be calculated for every bank or by simply looking at their company accounts. This money is then converted into digital money held with the central bank.

The central bank will go through a regulatory restructuring as it must be an independent nationalised central bank, like the Bank of England, which has a newly appointed monetary policy committee that answers to parliament and reports all meetings for us all.

Converting this money into real money is essentially as simple as inputting a few numbers into a computer. This money is now taken off the bank's balance sheet.

Your current account money is now secure even if the bank fails, without any guarantee from taxpayers' money. It is held with the central bank and banks are free to boom or bust without this money being at risk. There is no requirement for the central bank or government to offer any insurance or bailout funds.

This amount of money now forms a debt from each bank to the central bank and shows as a liability on the bank's balance sheet. This is important, because if you remove a liability from the bank's balance sheet, it will show a massive profit on that year's accounts and the share price will rocket.

As people gradually start to repay their debts and assets mature, the bank gradually pays off the debt they owe to the central bank. In effect, the banks are repaying the money they created and that made them 'too big to fail'.

Banks now pitch like crazy to get you to sign on the dotted line to move money from your risk-free current account that pays no interest to your investment account, where they are able to claim the money from the central bank and invest it in loans or however they told you they would use it in that particular investment account, as both the bank and yourself share the risk.

You are given full disclosure of how the banks are going to invest the money for all investment accounts and many products are developed.

Banks and non-banks compete with each other for your money, or you simply engage in crowdfunds, crowdloans or crowdinvestments, using your social capital as collateral and tool for investment analysis.

This is the simplest and easiest way to make the shift and I am sure detailed analysis will follow.

The central bank gifts money to the Treasury debt-free as it sees fit, based on inflation/deflation goals and the Treasury injects the new debt-free money into the economy.

This money can be used to pay down the national debt, reduce taxes and increase expenditure on public services, preventing the bankruptcy of our governments.

The economy functions how most people think it should and further reforms can be made as the economy sees fit.

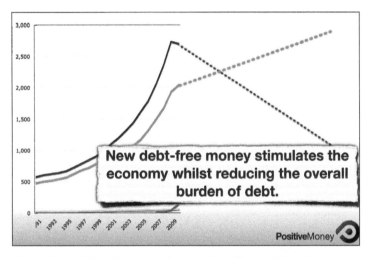

Figure 54 Positive Money estimates the effects of banking reform on economic growth and debt

We have a fully transparent money creation system that removes the billions in subsidy the banks used to receive for having the ability to create our nation's money supply.

We are met with a series of objections from the politicians, mainly fearing that the banks will flee the country.

As banking reform applies to a particular currency, there is no flight from banks to other countries. If they want to be involved in that particular currency, then they have to play by these rules, or leave it to new banks and non-banks to compete for the business.

I gave a presentation on this process when I was invited to the 2011 Occupy London Stock Exchange protests. The video is just over an hour long and you can watch it here:

QR 37 Simon Dixon's presentation for the Occupy London Stock Exchange protestors

So either way we get banking reform

I would much rather stick to our time travel reforms, but if the government and banks need to go bankrupt in order to be persuaded, perhaps we do not want to interfere in this vital lesson.

But we are delighted to see that our reforms remain and we do not need to go through such value destruction as outlined above.

Other countries that are not operating such a system, one by one will suffer a banking collapse and look to the reformed countries on how to drive sustainability.

Organisations like the IMF and the World Bank will have to stop engaging in money creation and decisions will be made to the legitimacy of their debtors' loans, as they go through a similar transition as our country does.

Perhaps developing world debt will be simply written off in a way that does not cause a collapse of the financial markets.

There are many ways of doing this, but I think you get the point without me boring you with excessive legal and financial jargon.

Job well done ...

We have successfully made the transition from the debt trap of 'free'dom to the economy of freedom and can now watch the birth of the next seven hugely disruptive technologies without the debt trap collapse.

Money now reflects the values of society. Banking finally becomes stable.

The World Wide Web becomes more artificially intelligent and reaches those who previously did not have access. It is accessed more and more frequently from mobile smart phones.

Money goes social, it goes mobile and who knows, maybe it goes invisible?

Society can choose to opt out of the financial system, choosing to live moneyless in the free economy through time banking or choose a combination of virtual currency and central bank debt-free stable currency.

The free economy drives unemployment into the ground and as people adjust when technology evolves; people start to live their lives on their terms, choosing their passion as their tool for income, either trading time or money as their assets. We enter an entrepreneur- and innovator-led economy.

Social capital self-regulates behaviour online; those who support and invest in their social capital are rewarded. Social capital becomes the most important investment every individual can make.

Based on their social capital, funds are made available through the crowd, as crowdfunding becomes a major player, competing with banks and venture capital as a primary source of finance for every innovation you can think of.

Crowdloans and crowdinvestments compete with private equity houses and banks.

Crowdfunding exchanges, crowd insurance products, crowd managed funds and many other financial innovations are crowd-sourced through the collective intelligence and innovation of people behind the economy of freedom.

Money reaches developing countries through mobile payments and micro-entrepreneurs are funded through microloans.

The spread of internet infrastructure and the adoption of mobile smart phones allows the speed of information and the speed at which information can be processed to move us from a world of increasing abundance.

Welcome to the economy of freedom.

Now it would be ridiculous to believe that we will live in Utopia and the world's problems will disappear ... people will still break laws, politicians will still engage in corruption, countries will still wage war (but it will be harder for them to raise the funds), money will still go to socially harmful companies, there will still be financial scams, hackers will become a major problem and who knows ... robots could become more intelligent than humans.

Life is full of challenges and without them no innovation would occur.

But one thing is for sure: under an economy with access to finance and a stable monetary system, a lot of the inherent flaws that allow for many of the world's tragedies will be reduced.

Your mission, if you choose to accept it ...

Finance is behind many of our world's problems and my mission to reform banking continues.

Here is my plan. To drive reform, I see three areas that need to be tackled.

Education

Firstly, politicians do not act unless they have the support of voters.

There are two ways voters will force reform: either the government goes bankrupt during the next crash when it can no longer raise funds on the bond market to bail out the banks and we riot; or the central banks create debt money en masse through quantitative easing, driving the value of the country's currency worthless, and then enough people demand banking reform.

My contribution to this field is through education, as I own the world's leading training company for students seeking careers in banking and finance. An integral part of our training programs with students and graduates is to educate them on the need for banking reform and how to be a more social banker, combined with training in how to effect big change and develop a mind-set that will allow them to achieve right to the top. Through BankTalkShow.com, and with this book, I hope to drive this change forward.

I also have blogs, videos and social networks dedicated to banking reform where people can learn more as our world shifts.

You can subscribe to my banking reform YouTube channel by clicking the link below and hitting the big yellow 'subscribe' button:

QR 38 Simon Dixon's banking reform YouTube Channel

You can watch presentations, videos and stay up-to-date with the latest in banking reform by leaving your name and email on my blog here:

QR 39 Simon Dixon's banking reform blog

You can join my Facebook page dedicated to keeping you up-to-date on the latest in banking reform by hitting the 'Like' button here:

QR 40 Like Banking Reform on Facebook

Politics

Banking reform can only happen with political support. The banks are not going to self-regulate and give away their licence to create money, so as well as education, political support is required.

In the UK I support non-profit Positive Money and Prosperity UK; in the US there are others making good progress like the American Monetary Institute.

I recently presented at a Positive Money conference in London where two members of parliament from both the Conservative and Labour parties were also presenting. Without mentioning names, one of the MPs told me that he believes that only four members of parliament in the UK had a correct understanding of how money is created! This has to change.

I spend my time campaigning in the UK as it is my home country and the birth place of most of the problems.

Movements for reform need to happen in every country. If you have a movement or plans for one in your country, the best place for us all to meet is through my banking reform Facebook page mentioned earlier.

A portion of my time is dedicated to giving commentary in the press, television, radio and of course social media, to make politicians aware of how they can fix their debt problems and banking headaches.

Business

If the public does not demand it, then politicians will not act until collapse occurs. If politicians do not act, there is an alternative.

Create the alternative system. So my final activity and my labour of love is to grow and build our online social network where people can fund, borrow, raise funds and invest at BankToTheFuture.com.

While a banking reformer, my core passion is business and as an entrepreneur I channel all that energy into creating a working model of banking reform.

Don't get me wrong, this is a 'for-profit' business – I don't want to mislead you – but it has a social mission.

Maybe by the time you read this book it will already be done, but I would like to create the world's first full reserve social bank, built upon a foundation of social capital.

Other alternatives and innovation will come from the world of business.

As we have seen with the movement in social enterprises, profit is a great motivator and can be sustainable when driven by a triple bottom line. I am far from a Marxist.

While I provided all the start-up capital for my business out of my own pocket without banks and private equity, I think it will be interesting to see how far we could get by using crowdfunds, crowdloans and crowdinvestments to fund all development.

One thing is for sure – we will stay on the edge of technological innovation as more and more hugely disruptive technologies evolve and we will adjust as we move from the debt trap of 'freedom to the economy of freedom.

I would love for you to create your profile, claim your social capital score and connect with me on BankToTheFuture.com right here:

QR 41 Connect with Simon Dixon on BankToTheFuture.com

I have huge visions, but on its own the alternative cannot drive reform, for even if everybody in the world took their money out of a money-creating bank and moved it to ours, as we refuse to engage in money creation, there would be a massive decrease in the country's money supply, so banking reform is still essential.

But I believe through education, through creating a next generation of social bankers, through campaigning politicians, through the collapse of the old system, through an alternative non-banking revolution, through entrepreneurs and through your support, that banking reform is not a question of 'if', but a question of 'when'.

The old system will self-destruct and banking reform is inevitable, predictable and guaranteed. It is just a question of how much we are willing to endure before we take action.

One thing is for sure, we humans are resilient and technology means we live in a world of abundance where there is always a way.

As long as you stay on top of the information curve and as long as you develop yourself to adjust to change and actively learn how to process information faster than others, you will be fine whatever happens.

As long as you start investing in your social capital and your networks are strong, you will be stronger and a source of leadership and support for others that are not so resilient to change in the economy of freedom ahead.

I know that there is plenty in this book you will disagree with. I know that some will love what I say and many will hate it. And that is OK; as long as we are respectful to each other, we can engage in productive debate.

I am open to other solutions and will continue to learn from everybody's perspectives.

A closing request

I would like to be a part of your social capital, increase your network and keep you up-to-date with the latest in change. So I have collected all the places we can connect in one place.

If Mark Zuckerberg will allow me to accept more than 5,000 please join me as my friend on Facebook, or otherwise subscribe:

Scan QR Code & join Simon Dixon on Facebook!

Can't scan? facebook.com/SimonDixonBankingReformer

QR 42 Add Simon Dixon as a friend on Facebook

If I am not allowed to accept any more friends, then join me on my Banking Reform Facebook page:

QR 43 Like Banking Reform on Facebook

Connect with my professional network on LinkedIn:

QR 44 Connect with Simon Dixon on LinkedIn

Stay up-to-date each day by following my tweets:

QR 45 Follow Simon Dixon on Twitter

Share your thoughts as I interview experts and update you on the latest by subscribing to my YouTube Channel:

QR 46 Simon Dixon's banking reform YouTube Channel

And finally ... connect with me and start to actively build your social capital by claiming your free training and reserving your profile on BankToTheFuture.com:

QR 47 Connect with Simon Dixon on BankToTheFuture.com

I look forward to hearing your comments and being a part of your social capital. Here is my final closing video:

QR 48 Watch Simon Dixon's closing video

And of course a final tweet! Tweet me your thoughts on #BankToTheFuture.

QR 49 Tweet Simon Dixon about #BankToTheFuture